June 1

ROOSEVELT
AND HIS AMERICA

BY BERNARD FAŸ

FRANKLIN: The Apostle of Modern Times

SINCE VICTOR HUGO: French Literature of To-day

THE TWO FRANKLINS: Fathers of American Democracy

ROOSEVELT AND HIS AMERICA

Roosevelt

AND HIS AMERICA

BY BERNARD FAŸ

1934

LITTLE, BROWN,

AND COMPANY · BOSTON

Copyright, 1933,
By Little, Brown, and Company

———

Published November, 1933
Reprinted January, 1934

PREFACE

THE world seems to be enjoying an era of bad feeling. Europe misunderstands the United States, not so much because it knows nothing of America, but because it has a too dry and intellectual knowledge of America and has ceased seeing it as a living unit. It has heard so much about "American standardization", "American prosperity", "American methods", that it has forgotten America itself. For most Europeans America is a big factory, where everybody is busily engaged in following the rules elaborated by a few famous engineers, such as Messrs. Ford, Edison and Hoover, and by Owen D. Young. America appears as the incarnation and summing up of the industrial civilization of to-day, and as such it is condemned and denounced. Nobody seems to remember that America is a nation which has already gone through several stages and kinds of civilizations and whose real greatness has been to forge ahead and develop from generation to generation constantly new forms of social life and human culture.

My first aim and hope in writing this book was to remind Europeans that America is a force, not a formula.

It would have been easier to praise America, but it would have led nowhere.

I should have enjoyed writing an "Apology for the United States", or a "Eulogium of the new World."

But it would have been useless. I might have put asleep a few people; I should not have reached their minds or their hearts.

But President Roosevelt gave an opportunity to study American energy and initiative and its freedom from all formulas and methods. During the eventful months of 1933 the President and the people of the United States have proved that they were able to discard the past entirely — everything, even the most valuable and cherished tradition — to keep life and activity in the country, to keep the nation alive, working and going ahead.

In contrast with eight years of blind prosperity these eight months of lucid sacrifice are one of the most enlightening sights that the modern world has seen, and one of the most hopeful.

To make it understandable to the European reader, I had to begin by taking his point of view, which may sometimes surprise the American reader; and to give an accurate picture, I had to be somewhat outspoken and crude. Politicians all over the world have the habit of clothing their acts and methods with such elegant words and philosophic formulas that, when they are translated into precise English, the whole thing looks surprising. This is particularly true of the years 1920–1930, during which the whole world lived in a fool's paradise and fed itself upon the most childish optimism. A study of France, of England, of Germany, and of practically each of the great countries of the world would show very much the same kind of things going on there as in America during that period. As a matter of fact, the whole world was then imitating America, and following her as closely as possible. That is why in these pages I have not tried to praise or to blame America. I do not feel that anybody has a right to do it, but I thought that for the sake of the world and of America it was better to speak plainly.

The United States is a great nation, probably the strongest nation of to-day, and their influence on the evolution of the century cannot but be dominating. Their actions and decisions will have fateful results throughout the world and for the ages. Even though they are not anxious to assert this world-leadership and to exploit this imperial supremacy, they will sooner or later have to recognize this situation. This book, which is less a picture of what happened in the United States than a picture of the United States as they acted and as the world saw them while they were acting, may help to bring and prepare this hour. I should be very glad if it did.

A nation is not great because it has never made a mistake or experienced any failure, but because of the continuity of its life and of the energy of its reactions at critical hours.

That is why I have thought it useful to study the year 1933; and the period that led to it, the great American crisis, and the great American revival.

BERNARD FAŸ

CONTENTS

PART ONE

IN SEARCH OF AMERICA

IN SEARCH OF AMERICA

AMERICA is always a new subject, for she is always a new country. From the outset she was dubbed the New World, and the New World she has remained; it became a habit with her and one which has been a constant source of amazement and irritation to the Old World.

America changes so rapidly! With every new President she assumes a new aspect, just as an amiable woman changes her hat and her expression to please each new lover. We have witnessed the imperial and industrial America of Theodore Roosevelt, the idealistic and democratic America of Woodrow Wilson, the bourgeois, banking America of Calvin Coolidge, the technical, depressed America of Herbert Hoover. Now Franklin Roosevelt, with a smile, introduces us to a new America, an emancipated, liberal, slightly fantastic America — an America which likes young people's company and despises elderly bankers. Let us hurry to make her acquaintance while she is still young and attractive.

This book must not be blamed for being hurried; life passes hurriedly in America, and, if the image is to be faithful, it must conform to the rhythm of its model.

It must be forgiven if it is sometimes gay or flippant; whatever people may say, gayety is no more foolish than sorrow, nor yet more deceitful, and our modern life, though it is by no means satisfying, at any rate affords us a picturesque spectacle, of which it is well to take advantage. The spectators pay so high a price that they have every right to enjoy the spectacle.

Let us take a look at Roosevelt's America and, in order that we may better relish her youthful charm, let us devote a few words to her ancestors, all those colonial, puritan, romantic, traditional Americas, from whom she is sprung and whose blood courses in her veins.

Let us set out in search of her in this age which gave her to us and will very soon take her away from us again.

CHAPTER I

THE DISCOVERERS

"ONE fine day, by mistake, Christopher Columbus, who was looking for India, discovered America. He did not do it on purpose; the idea never even entered his head. It was a mistake, and he was punished for it; for, as we know, he came to a bad end. He inaugurated very sadly that series of discoverers of America, which is even now not yet concluded. Since 1493 the people of Europe have never ceased to discover America and to make mistakes and to be punished for them."

The above remarks were uttered in a melancholy tone by an Italian, who added immediately:

"Columbus was seeking gold for the Catholic King and converts for the Pope. He discovered brick-red savages who went about entirely naked and could not learn anything, not even to clothe themselves or to live in the company of white men. They died, bequeathing to their discoverers a useless and pernicious weed, tobacco, and diseases which decency forbids us to name.

"It was we who discovered America, and in return they despise our religion, refuse our wines, and reject and insult our race. It was not Mr. Roosevelt, but Mr. Smith who should have been elected President of the United States, and he was not elected because he is a

Catholic. In 1933, the fact of being Catholic and Italian is a serious handicap in the United States. The common people have given the name 'dagos' to immigrants from the Mediterranean, and Congress, the faithful servant of its electors, voted laws designed to reduce to a minimum the entrance of Italians into the United States. This is called the defense of the Nordic races, and it is a part of American civilization. In a little town in Illinois, I heard a lecturer describe Christopher Columbus as a citizen of Norway.

"Our discovery has not been of any use to us; nor, apparently, has it been of much use to America, where the Indians died after having been corrupted and persecuted by the whites, and where the whites seem to have gained from their victory only a surfeit of wealth, which is choking them at this moment.

"It is time Mr. Roosevelt civilized them."

"You are right," said an Englishman. "We too discovered America, and we took a great deal of trouble to discover her thoroughly, to populate her, and to furnish her with our language, our institutions, our laws, our religion and our race. We spent a lot of money on it, not to speak of time, trouble and genius. From 1600 onwards our greatest men toiled to discover America.

"When the toil was ended, the Americans, who didn't want to pay their share of the money we had spent in the course of our war with the French, turned their guns on us and drove us out. And ever since they have persecuted us with a conceited and callous rivalry. Any one would think our civilization belonged to them, for they do what they like with it. Any one would think our laws and our religions were their property, for they appropriate them all and — incidentally — spoil them all. They have made English a nigger language and our literature into a ridiculous piece of machinery — simplified, noisy and, apparently, destined first and foremost for advertisement purposes. The pure flame of Protestant idealism which we handed on to them they have transformed into a combination of Y.M.C.A., W.C.T.U., prohibition and football games.

"We discovered them; we taught them the little they know, we gave them such traditions and decencies as they possess, and, by way of return, they began by laughing at us on the plea that we were behind the times and knew nothing about modern methods of finance and industry; and now they are angry with us because they say we are better business men than themselves and that we prevent them from selling their products in South America.

"Our discovery was mere waste of time and a source of endless annoyance. It is quite time Mr. Roosevelt, if he knows how, should give his people some notion of their duties and their proper rôle."

A Frenchman, who was just passing, took up the story:

"We are just as much to blame as you, and we have been just as much punished. It may have been you Italians and you English who discovered America, but it was we who discovered the United States. Up to the reign of our King Louis XVI, they were merely English colonists, utterly despised by their mother country and utterly ignored by the rest of Europe.

"Just as our Jesuits and travelers brought the redskins of the savannas into fashion, so our philosophers and diplomats, our journalists and our Freemasons brought the American insurgents into fashion. We launched them, we made them, we paid for their revolution with our gold and our blood, our enthusiasm and our faith. We championed them in the face of the indifference of Europe and the hostility of England. Then, when our revolution came and we in our turn had to fight England, they did not stir a finger.

"Later, to be sure, they sent us some of their goods. America was the ideal of our liberals; but, as every one knows, our liberals never made a success of anything. Not long ago our capitalists were preaching to us an American gospel: 'Imitate,' they said, 'this great nation, which has succeeded in adopting and adapting the machine, which does everything on a big scale and whose modernism has made such marvelous strides.' We were told to profit by America's example, and so the Loewensteins and Kreugers flourished in our midst, so the Oustrics prospered, until the day on which, throughout the world, the workmen began to hurl execrations against the machine, because it robbed them of work, while the merchants reviled it for flooding the markets, and the financiers were ruined because it had tricked them into extravagant sales and purchases. Monsieur de Tocqueville discovered America and spread among our political theoreticians all sorts of optimistic and mistaken ideas; our captains of industry discovered the America of Ford and Rockefeller, and we should all have been taken in, if Monsieur Siegfried had not in his turn discovered that America was on the verge of bankruptcy, and if Monsieur Duhamel had not discovered the slaughterhouses in Chicago, which opened his eyes. He saw clearly that a people which had such big slaughterhouses could not have any true civilization, and he proclaimed this fact with so much eloquence that he convinced our public. In that way, we were put on our guard. But all these discoveries have left an unpleasant recollection, and they cost us too dear. In spite of the Great War, in which Allies and Americans fought side by side, America is very far away: we are separated from her by over 3000 miles of ocean and two hundred sixty milliards of debts.

"Let us hope that Mr. Roosevelt, since he looks so pleasant and has such a nice smile, will find some means of making his people more human. It is quite time."

"That's all very fine," interposed a German, who happened to have joined the group; "but what would you say if you were in our place? I think that you discoverers are very foolish to complain, since you have only been punished for your sins; but we sober, honest Germans, — what had we done? Not one of us discovered America, or even took the trouble to look for her, as long as he could help it; but when you other Europeans began to fight in our country and to devote yourselves to great struggles for freedom and democracy, we had to leave Europe; and we set to work to discover America on our own account. We took over there our wives, our children, our ploughs, our oxen, our trades, our beer, our sauerkraut and our churches. We were the first to cultivate the soil properly and to teach the people the arts of sausage-making, music and pious convulsions. Our discovery was not as picturesque as that of Christopher Columbus or as noisy as that of the English, or as elegant and philosophic as that of the French, but it did the Americans a very good turn. But for us, what would have happened to their agriculture, which we developed in the eighteenth century; their universities, which we revived after 1840; and their industry, which we helped on in all sorts of ways?

"And yet, we have been the most despised and hated of all the European nations. America made war on us and crushed us at the critical moment; since then she has treated us very haughtily. No matter what we do, she always tries to patronize us, despite our ten centuries of civilization and glory!

"Mr. Roosevelt had better instill a little wisdom into America, but he will find he has his work cut out for him."

Even the Russian has to put in a word. As a rule, the Russian says very little about America, but in 1933 he is full of spleen and he exclaims:

"Those wretched Americans! You have all discovered them, but the spirit of America I alone have discovered. It is the very soul of capitalism. The French think themselves *bourgeois* but they are peasants; the English fancy themselves *bourgeois* but they are sailors; the Germans want to be *bourgeois* but they are clerks. Only the Americans, who think themselves Americans, are really *bourgeois* and capitalists. Every American is and desires to be a *bourgeois* and a capitalist. He instinctively hates socialism; his mind is closed against all coöperation and progress; he is puritanical, conceited and individualistic. He is my worst enemy. Roosevelt cannot alter that fact."

The European newspapers repeat every day statements of this nature; and the old "concert of Europe", which our ancestors liked to prate about in the days when diplomacy still had some prestige, only survives in this concert of abuse of America.

The conservatives accuse America of having disseminated and having been the stronghold of republican and democratic ideas. The radicals reproach her with being the citadel of capitalism and of *bourgeois* individualism. The artists declare that she has no sense of beauty and prefers negro music to Wagner, a railway station to St. Peter's, Rome, and an electric sign to Mona Lisa's smile. The industrialists cannot forgive America for having upset their business, and the bankers, her last defenders, cannot recover from the shock caused them by the collapse of the dollar.

Their common irritation and their unanimous discontent would pass all bounds if they were not kept in suspense by the expectation of the morrow. Whatever antipathy they may feel for America, she excites their curiosity, and Mr. Roosevelt, with his smiling eyes, with the handkerchief which he flutters before his face while he is speaking, with that sinuous tact which marks his every action, surprises and disconcerts them more than any other living celebrity.

Without any very good grace, then, they will turn towards the American who is about to speak, and they will listen to him in the hope of finding out whether they ought to buy dollars or sell them short.

CHAPTER II

THE INVENTORS

AMERICA, EUROPE'S NIGHTMARE

IT may truly be said that we rediscover in America all the elements of Europe. America has been peopled with all the heretics and nonconformists of Europe. And this was perhaps the greatest service that Europe rendered her. If France had not expelled first her Huguenots, then her monarchists, then her Bonapartists, then her nuns and her monks, there would be hardly any French in the United States. If England had not driven out her dissenters, her royalists and her Catholics in the seventeenth century, and, later on, her republicans and millions of Irish; if Germany, by her wars and her revolutions, had not rendered life impossible for her farmers, her intellectuals and her professors, there would be hardly any Americans, and there would be no United States.

America is crammed with all the exiles from Europe. Every war, every revolution, every European catastrophe has brought her thousands of refugees; everything that was thrown away by the Old World was picked up by the New. The criminals whom England let out of her prisons and deported to America formed the aristocracy of a new country; the Jews who were ejected by Central Europe became the potentates of world finance; America did not give Europe the gold of which she went in search, but with the mud which Europe sent her, she has made gold.

America irritates Europe the more, because Europe finds in America all her own faults and crimes, all her own bad habits and most of her vices, but she finds them clothed with a magnificence and grandeur which they did not possess in their original home. America has served as a sort of magnifying and distorting mirror for Europe.

Even now, what most troubles the French, English, Germans and Italians in the United States is little else than the incarnation of their own desires and aims.

Modern America is a dream of eighteenth-century Europe, which was realized by the twentieth century and the United States in a sort of tremendous game.

This material civilization, based on recognition of facts, aimed at well-being, supported on optimism, and, above all, inured to the discipline of useful work, faithfully embodies the ideal of the philosophic, Franco-English eighteenth century. France and England, and all the intellectuals of Europe, preached these doctrines from 1730 to 1800; but in Europe, the more people preach, the more they distrust the consequences of their preaching. In America, the land is rich and reckless; every word is a fruitful seed and every theory develops into an institution. The Constitution of the United States in 1933 is still what it was made by the leading minds of 1788, who conformed to the taste of the time and fashioned an ideal constitution on the English pattern, with three quite distinct powers, an elected President, two legislative bodies, a sovereign people, and the majority of the officers, from the Senate to the lowest local officials, subject to election. It is a wholesale application of all those English principles which were venerated by the Whigs of Great Britain in those days, and were expounded so brilliantly by Monsieur de Montesquieu. This Constitution, which so irritates us and whose strange workings have cost Europe so dear, since it has nullified the Treaty of Versailles and turned the League of Nations into an illegitimate offspring of President Wilson, is merely one of Europe's presents to America.

That passion for work and action, which makes men forget rest, leisure and amusements, and replaces even love of enjoyment by love of the game: all this is the discipline extolled by the French eighteenth-century philosophers. The most witty of their number, Monsieur de Voltaire, in the most delightful of his works, after having passed in review the world's institutions and the ideas of its citizens, concluded that nothing had any value or meaning save work.

"Let us cultivate our garden," said Candide, and he wanted people to stop devoting themselves to dreams, philosophy, thought, or even love. "Let us cultivate," said Candide.

"Let us work," replied all the eighteenth century in chorus. "Work alone has any meaning. Let us be philanthropic. Let us have everywhere more work, more activity, more production; that alone is of lasting value. Let us henceforth judge men not according to vain distinctions of blood, race, inner virtue or private and egoistic philosophy, but according to their gift for success and creation."

The eighteenth century preached that man ought to pay less attention to being and more to doing. For spiritual and inward virtue, it substituted beneficent and social virtue, and, for the moral act accomplished in the sight of God, the useful action accomplished in the sight of men. It tore the monks from their cells, the scientists from their laboratories, and the men of the world from their salons, and transformed them into politicians, industrialists and journalists.

In Europe the old order resisted. The old indolence, the old wisdom, the old leisureliness prevented the eighteenth century from realizing its programme; and its prestige was thus saved. In America, the new land, on the contrary, an eager and docile, sincere and energetic population hastened to act as it thought, and to build up the ideal world of which it had been told.

We see this to-day. In America, activity reigns supreme; work is her discipline and success her goal. Everything has been sacrificed in order to encourage and exalt labor; the machine enables man to multiply indefinitely the effectiveness of every movement. Politicians, priests, judges, professors, writers, women and children — all conform to the rule; every one hurries, every one acts. It is the apotheosis of useful work. *And it is a catastrophe!*

In 1933, two centuries after philosophic Europe began her preaching, America, her docile pupil, looks like a country which has been devastated by a cyclone; many factories are empty and silent; millions of unemployed tramp the roads; the poor clamor for work which cannot be given them; the rich go on working, and every article they turn out adds to the confusion of a world which has no idea what to do with all this merchandise that nobody wants; the millionaires tremble amid dollars which have lost their value, and the farmers pray Heaven not to complete their ruin by sending them a good harvest.

America has gone bankrupt, people say. But the America gone bankrupt is the America the European eighteenth century invented and shaped. She began like a dream; she is ending in a nightmare.

She believed what philosophic Europe told her: "Nothing matters save work and material creation." And now she is crushed by this work, which she can neither stop nor use, and by products which she can neither disgorge nor assimilate. She is perishing of feverish indigestion.

One America is dead!

But America is not dead. America is not a mere article imported from Europe. The bankruptcy of a method is not the bankruptcy of a people, of a race, of a continent.

The America of Roosevelt is very much alive.

It is not the America of the discoverers, the America received from Europe; it is the America of the inventors, the America who has made herself anew in a new world, and who is still lively in spite of all her troubles.

She has her past, she has her native character, she has her own personality, and if Franklin Roosevelt succeeded at the outset in impressing the nation, and, under the most difficult circumstances, in winning the confidence and enthusiasm of the masses, this was due to the harmony which existed between his personality and that of his country.

This portrait of Roosevelt will also be a review of America's inventors.

GEORGE WASHINGTON, ROOSEVELT AND
ANGLO-SAXON LOGIC

Franklin Roosevelt is an Anglo-Saxon. In spite of his Dutch name and his French blood, he comes of a race in which the Anglo-Saxon strain predominates, and the American people elected him because he is an Anglo-Saxon.

In 1928, Herbert Hoover had defeated Alfred E. Smith, who was the better man, because Mr. Smith was not an Anglo-Saxon, and the American masses can trust only an Anglo-Saxon.

A traveler who was staying in Hollywood at the time of these elections had the following little conversation with the Chinese servant who attended him.

"I suppose you will be voting for Mr. Hoover, sir," said the Chinese very politely.

"No," replied the European, "I shall not vote, for I am not an American citizen; I am only a tourist."

"Neither shall I," said the Chinese. "I shall not vote because I was not born in the United States. But," he added, after a little pause and a little sigh, "my son will vote, because he was born in the United States. My son will vote for Mr. Hoover."

And as the Chinese uttered these words with an air of pride, the stranger thought it only polite to ask him: "Why will your son vote for Mr. Hoover?"

"Because Mr. Hoover is an Anglo-Saxon."

Such was the explanation given by the Chinese, and he gave no other, because to him it seemed sufficient.

The Anglo-Saxon hegemony is recognized by the country; it is recognized by every element in the

country, however undisciplined, and by every corporation, however refractory. Even Congress, which usually
protests and shouts against everything, agreed without
a murmur to favor the Anglo-Saxon race at the expense
of all the rest, when it came to discussing the laws of
immigration. There was hardly any debate; it was an
established fact: America is an Anglo-Saxon country.
Canada has some consideration for the Canadians who
speak French and want to preserve their language, their
customs and their French civilization; the French
Canadians who come to settle in the United States must
submit to Anglo-Saxon discipline; and most rigorous of
all in compelling them to use the Anglo-Saxon tongue
are certain Irish priests and prelates who yet make no
bones about setting St. Patrick above St. Peter and
preach against the English as zealously as they preach
against the devil. In order to appear good Anglo-Saxons,
the Italians, who in Europe are so proud of their name,
their race and their country, do not hesitate to shave
themselves, clothe themselves, and conduct themselves
like Anglo-Saxons, and thousands of them — Calabrians,
Sicilians, Piedmontese and Romans alike — have entered
the Methodist Church, hoping thereby to become more
like the Anglo-Saxons.

Ever since the foundation of the United States, all
the Presidents have been Anglo-Saxons and, by tacit
agreement, the country promotes Anglo-Saxons to the
most important offices. Nothing will prevent the Jews
from making money or the French from being fashionable, the Italians from selling pictures and directing
orchestras, or the Germans and Scandinavians from
populating the country, but none of these races or groups

will ever be allowed to stand on an equal footing with
the Anglo-Saxons in the United States.

From 1630 onwards this was so in North America.

From 1776 onwards it has been so in the United States.
And it was George Washington who founded this tradition.

Who would venture to assert that the Anglo-Saxons
are the most intelligent race in the world? No one has
ever maintained such a thing, and those who have
thought it have refrained from giving any explanation.

The superiority of the Anglo-Saxons over the other
white races seems rather to be based on the fact that
they are one of the least gifted and least intelligent races.
Their skins are white and their minds are white — that
is to say, blank; their hair is fair, rather like tow, and
their brains are of the same texture. This is not a bad
thing in a race; it produces fewer noteworthy individuals, but those it does produce have more chance of
making themselves known and are not swamped by the
vain hubbub of noisy absurdities and brilliant nonsense
which encumber the Latin countries. In nations,
stupidity, provided it is not pretentious or learned, is a
sort of ballast which insures social stability and replaces
popular wisdom. Where countless minor leaders dispute
the palm, it is difficult for a great leader to win speedy
and unquestioned supremacy. Where men are conscious
of their personal mediocrity and native sluggishness, an
impression is produced more easily, more swiftly and
more effectively, without being distorted or debased.
It would be fairly plausible to assert that the supremacy
of the Anglo-Saxon race must have sprung from the
consciousness of his own weakness inherent in each of

its individual members, whilst one cause of the defeats suffered by Italy in the sixteenth century and France in the eighteenth was undoubtedly the disastrous rivalry which developed between all the shrewd, gifted and vigorous minds which lumbered up the nation and dragged it first this way and then that.

France lost her colonies in the eighteenth century because she peopled them with individuals and not with a race. America remained English,. for the Anglo-Saxon colonists established themselves as a group, stuck together, did not venture too far from one another, did not invent anything very remarkable, and detested everything that was not themselves. The French were interested in and had a liking for the Indians; the Anglo-Saxons despised, detested and exterminated them. This was not very intelligent, for the savages were extremely picturesque, but it was rather sensible, for there was nothing to be gained from the savages. In the end, the two million Anglo-Saxons had no great difficulty in driving from the New World the sixty thousand French who were settled there and occupied four fifths of the continent. (Certainly one could cite other reasons, and in plenty, but why trouble, since this reason is sufficient and is the most important?)

Thus, in 1763, by law of war, the continent of America became Anglo-Saxon.

Ten years later America narrowly escaped ceasing to be Anglo-Saxon. The colonies fought against England; they sought allies everywhere; they invoked heaven and earth and they heaped curses on England. They appealed loudly to France, who had the sense and tact to come

to their aid. After ten years of struggle America was
free, and free to make what she liked of herself. Then
her people hesitated. Some were attracted by France;
others wanted a German king; some, prompted by
their piety and their love of the Bible, claimed that
America ought to adopt Hebrew as its national language.
And, without going quite so far, Franklin wanted the
United States to be a free and separate nation, and to
sever all ties with England.

It was George Washington who preserved Anglo-
Saxon prestige and supremacy in the United States.

The eighteenth century produced any number of men
more brilliant, more intelligent, more eloquent and more
seductive than George Washington. After all, he was not
particularly handsome; he was a bad speaker; his writ-
ings were pompous and not very brilliant; he lacked
charm, wit and culture. In this elegant century, he had
no elegance.

Seen from one side, travelers tell us he had the air of a
god; seen from the other, that of a nanny goat.

He had no idea how to make himself agreeable to
ladies, and he ended by marrying a plump widow who
had a fortune but little grace, amiability or genius. He
made hardly any friends in the army or in politics, for,
though he was always surrounded by admirers, he does
not appear to have been on a footing of real intimacy
with any one of them. And even those who, like La
Fayette and Hamilton, were in closest touch with him
remained strangers in his private life.

He was a man of wealth who was always crushed
and harassed by debts; he was a general who never
managed to win a pitched battle and whose finest ex-

ploit was achieved in a siege, when he had with him a French fleet and a French army outnumbering his own. As a captain, he was not a success; as a colonel, his services were not much appreciated; and it was said in the eighteenth century that, of all the great generals of the age, he alone obtained a great result without great battles.

Washington was the apotheosis of silence and good sense.

The century was overflowing with ideas; he had none. America abounded in eloquent legislators only waiting to apply their theories. As Washington had no theories, the legislators cheerfully selected him to give the casting vote. Throughout this long and lamentable war, in which he had no opportunity of winning great battles, Washington did at least have the opportunity of showing that he was more patient, more orderly, more punctual, more polite, more persevering, more energetic and more courageous than any one else.

Every morning he made his appearance in an immaculate uniform.

Every day he wrote, politely and at length, to the Continental Congress, although this body had fallen into the greatest disrepute and no independent spirit would have paid any attention to it.

Hour after hour, he busied himself with the details of the military organization. And whilst the strategists and legislators of the country filled the newspapers with their programme, George Washington contented himself with filling, as best he could, the empty stomachs of his soldiers; with covering, as best he could, their shivering limbs; and with soothing their tempers, which

were not improving. Mrs. Washington knitted socks
for them and he himself went to buy them pants.

Thus did he win this war; which was a war of "wear-
ing down", to borrow an expression current in 1917;
and thus too did he win the prestige of a civic hero, a
citizen general.

In the disorder which ensued, the people naturally
looked to him to command and reorganize the country.
They knew him to have a practical and methodical
mind, they believed him to be devoid of theories, and
so they hoped that he would be a useful and not too
tiresome leader. In 1789, when the United States
emerged from the anarchy which had followed the war,
to Washington was allotted the overwhelming task of
governing this republic and impressing a character upon
its administration. He accepted it, though he guessed
what worries it would entail, what affronts he would
have to stomach and what difficulties he would be forced
to surmount. In the end he succeeded; he managed to
prevent his country from declaring war on England and
quarreling with her irremediably; he did not allow
democratic principles to be established in America, and
he checked the movement which was carrying the
country towards another leveling revolution. His chief
work was the organization of the government; he was
the first President of the United States, and for eight
years he chose all the high functionaries — the ambassadors, the judges and the generals. He organized the
machinery of the State and selected the administrative
staff. He did it in the style of a worthy English gentleman concerned for the good management of his farm
and his domains. When he departed, he left everything

in good order and good condition; and he even had the supreme and perfect wisdom to die at the very moment when his political adversaries were about to come into power. Thus he made it easy for them to forgive and appreciate him and to carry on his work.

Since that time the memory of Washington has been venerated in the United States; his birthday is a holiday which takes precedence of all others save Christmas, and his legend, which has been piously handed down, is used to educate the children in the schools. Despite the crisis, Congress has just voted the necessary funds for a complete edition of his works, and even if it means printing forty volumes, it is safe to assert that the text of every note ever penned by Washington will be presented to the American people. In 1933, Washington is still America's greatest hero.

He is the typical Anglo-Saxon hero and he possesses all the qualities which the American prizes most in everyday life.

The Anglo-Saxon is a devotee of simplification; he has no liking for complicated theories or subtle formulas, and this is very convenient in a country comprising countless different races, come from the four corners of the globe, who could not be converted to a common ideal if it were formulated too precisely. The vagueness of the Anglo-Saxon formula allows of tacit understandings as well as of misunderstandings, which make it possible for the Negro from Guinea, the Japanese disembarked from Osaka, the Spaniard from Mexico and the Norwegian from the confines of Lapland to live side by side. Provided that they stammer a few very brief phrases in the same way, accept a few very simple social formulas and submit to a strict and rudimentary discipline, no one objects to them, and they themselves are quite content. Anglo-Saxon tolerance is perhaps only clumsiness and lack of insight; it is, none the less, very suitable to a hastily populated country where all the world's adventurers rub shoulders with one another.

With its logical and simplified grammar, its exact but concise vocabulary, and its easy syntax, the English language is, moreover, admirably adapted to the conversations of a mixed people; and such insurmountable difficulties as the phonetics might present have been eliminated by the employment of a more logical and sonorous pronunciation. It is said that the Negroes of Georgia get on very comfortably without knowing or employing more than two hundred English words. They neither know more nor ask for more, but this does not prevent them from drinking and eating, marrying and having children, talking and even voting, when the whites allow them to do so. With their two hundred English words they are as good electors as Shakespeare himself would be, if he came back to this earth, and they are quite aware of the fact. They are very proud of their Anglo-Saxon civilization. Do not try to talk to them of Africa; they would knock you down.

Even the tinge of hypocrisy which permeates Anglo-Saxon civilization has been of service in the New World. What is hypocrisy, in fact, if not the habit of demanding from human beings an outward discipline, without bothering very much about their thoughts, their feelings and their actions? The Anglo-Saxon spirit and America demand from the individual an external conformity, but they do not go into details, and a parliamentarian who has voted for prohibition will feel no compunction about drinking heavily himself; just as a statesman who preaches equality and democracy will not scruple to have his four or five domestics. . . . This is true of great and small alike, and it is just as well, for sincerity and cynicism are luxuries of the old countries, of stable and homogeneous nations, in which the differences are not unduly great and the divergences do not entail the risk of conflicts.

In America it would be useless to try to force an Italian, an Armenian, a Chinese, a Malayan and a Filipino — all of them citizens — to see eye to eye with an Anglo-Saxon concerning the prohibition of alcohol, the notion of the deity and the concept of liberty. It is therefore well, on all these points, to stick to formulas and gestures which enable each community to lead its own life, without forcing the individual to do anything too greatly at variance with his deeper instincts.

Anglo-Saxon civilization has become the everyday discipline of the United States, because it is the most rudimentary and superficial of all the European civilizations. As a result of having been trailed across all the oceans of the globe with English sailors and of invading all the ports of the universe with English traders, Anglo-Saxon civilization has been reduced to a very simple and easy code. It comprises hardly any opinions about the universe; it has no very clear philosophic trend; it does not develop the individual in any particular direction; but it does at least confer upon him forthwith a certain prestige, and it obliges him to show a certain regard for the community. It is as stiff as a ready-made garment. But it chafes an Irishman little more than a Hottentot. It is, in fact, the least common denominator of all the races assembled on the continent of America.

It is not for love of Shakespeare, Byron or Bernard Shaw that the Calabrian of New York prefers his English to any other tongue, and his Anglo-Saxon customs to those of any other race with which he mixes. But he feels instinctively that it is less tiresome to adopt this Anglo-Saxon veneer than to model himself on the Irish or Germans. All the other races and civilizations in the world conjure up in addition a rich and complex idea; they have a strong flavor and a clear significance. The Anglo-Saxon civilization is hardly more than a social framework, and this is the source of its success.

Anglo-Saxon civilization would not have established or maintained itself in the United States if it had not been rudimentary and vague.

Washington would not have been accepted as commander in chief and first President of the United States, if the people had distrusted his intelligence.

And Mr. Roosevelt's brilliant success in 1932 was due to his Anglo-Saxon quality, the quality of one born to rule.

Like Washington in 1776 and 1789, he created an atmosphere of unanimity by inspiring in all that wholehearted confidence which results from absence of fear. "Mr. Roosevelt," people said, "is a good Anglo-Saxon; he has never in his life done anything very striking; he is not believed to be very intelligent; his character is not thought to be remarkably energetic; he is not known to be endowed with any exceptional superiority, but he is an honest man, who has suffered and who has had plenty of experience of life; he is a man whose mediocrity is in no sense odious or vulgar, and who will not bear his subordinates a grudge for being cleverer than himself. He is just what we want. He will carry on the line of the Washingtons."

The newspapers murmured it, the lecture halls rang with it, the clubs repeated it, and the party workers echoed it far and near. And the upshot was twenty-five million votes for Franklin Delano Roosevelt, descendant of a good Dutch-Anglo-Saxon family and legitimate heir of the men who invented the United States.

Roosevelt, Jefferson and Space in America

However, he profited by these advantages with great tact, and in his speeches he made no mention of his great ancestors; he referred politely, but not very often, to Washington, and he allowed a legend to grow up around him without refining upon or spoiling it.

On the other hand, he referred very often to his other great ancestor, Thomas Jefferson, who was the third President of the United States, but who yields to Washington alone in respect of the rôle which he played in the national life of the country.

Thomas Jefferson was a tall, red-haired and ungainly youth, who did not speak very well in public, who did not express himself very fluently in conversation and who wrote letters which were both too long and too dull. However, he was a man of no little wit and very great learning, who belonged by birth to an aristocratic set, and possessed a considerable fortune, vast debts, an inexhaustible philanthropy and an endless supply of brilliant, vague and — for the most part, as it now seems, — mistaken ideas. He achieved world renown at a very early age, for he had the honor of drafting the Declaration of Independence of the United States, and he was hailed by the philosophers of the universe as the most dazzling luminary of the political world.

Was not this Declaration the first official text to proclaim in set terms the right of the peoples to shape their own destiny and all the other democratic doctrines?

Thomas Jefferson was a convinced and eloquent democrat. After having assisted the revolution in his own country — America — he went to France, as Minister of the United States, and assisted the revolution there. At his house the French revolutionary leaders foregathered to discuss the question of a constitution and of a declaration of rights. He blessed and cherished the young French Revolution at its first stage, when it was still idealistic and chary of spilling blood. Nevertheless, Mr. Jefferson, though he resented blows aimed at himself, was never afraid of the blood shed by the masses. He looked upon it as one of the inalienable rights of a democracy and as proof of a true zeal for liberty.

This doctrine, and certain others which he proclaimed without undue restraint between 1788 and 1799, won for him in America the reputation of a great democrat and the position of leader of the party hostile to Washington. In 1800, a few months after the death of Washington, Jefferson was elected President of the United States and opened a new era. After the conservative and aristocratic republicans of the Washington type, the American people raised to power the

Republican-Democratic Party, which plumed itself on its French conception of equality, on not fearing liberty and on being imbued with the purest spirit of fraternity. In 1800, then, Mr. Jefferson was swept into power by what we should call to-day a "wave of radicalism."

The American historians sometimes call this election a revolution and make great capital of the fact that a number of governmental traditions trace their origin to Jefferson rather than to Washington. The latter surrounded himself with a certain pageantry, whilst Jefferson reduced the life of the President of the United States to a free-and-easy affability and substituted for the style and the "cant" of the English gentleman farmer, whom Washington instinctively imitated, the manners and the hypocrisy of the Anglo-Saxon gentry. The people had the satisfaction of feeling more at ease in his company, and they highly approved of this familiar vulgarity.

But this did not really solve the problem. Mr. Jefferson had been elected amid cries of "*Vive la France!*" His partisans donned the Liberty cap and danced the *carmagnole;* they favored a war with England and governmental reforms which would have weakened the central power for the benefit of popular clubs and committees, somewhat similar to the Soviets of a later date. All these ideas and projects had not been displeasing to Mr. Jefferson, so long as he was a candidate for the Presidency, but now that he had to govern, he did not seem to find them very practical.

However, he had been elected by the Francophile radicals, the urban masses and the democratic philosophers and clubs. He had to satisfy somehow all these supporters.

He gave them a continent.

He did not want to fling them human heads to feed on, since he was not bloodthirsty by nature, but only by philosophy; he did not want to fling them the government — though they would have liked nothing better — for since he was in power, he was anxious that the State should be strong, unyielding and centralized. He could not offer them the posts and offices which they desired, for, before retiring, his predecessors had filled all the available offices with very robust and docile individuals, who were prepared to swallow every sort of affront and were never obliged to retire for reasons of health. Mr. Jefferson regretted this, but he did not want to incur the enmity of his functionaries, even to please his partisans, and so he made very few dismissals. However, he had to satisfy somehow or other the appetites of the radicals who had elected him.

In the eighteenth century, as in our own time, radicalism contained an element of political idealism, as well as some odious passions, just as conservatism contains an element of practical wisdom and also a tincture of egotism. The American radicals aspired to emancipate the whole world, and they also wanted to acquire power, offices, money and prestige. They were prepared to give their lives for liberty and also determined to exploit this liberty for purposes of self-enrichment as soon as it was at their disposal.

Every country has its own way of satisfying its radicals: in England, they are given sermons of the Methodist type and a low customs tariff; in France, they are given pacifism and licenses to sell tobacco; in Russia, they are given the lives of a few million citizens; in America, Mr. Jefferson gave them the Mississippi Valley.

The radical elements of America were the poor in the towns and the needy farmers in the West. The big merchants and property-owners in the East had no complaint to make; they were the bulwarks of the established order and of the Government. But the small folk who carried on small trades in the towns and the small farmers who drudged on small farms grumbled and moaned. They had come to America in the belief that they were coming to a land of ease and plenty, and instead they found themselves, as in Europe, the slaves of acquired rights, social prejudices and organized groups. They threatened to smash up everything.

Mr. Jefferson gave them Louisiana. To tell the truth, it was Bonaparte who gave it to them, for Bonaparte had just recovered it from Spain in the hope of converting it into a vast French colony or empire in the New World; but, as he himself was engaged in building up his empire in the Old World, and was encountering some difficulties in the process, and since his fleet was nothing like sufficient for his needs, he finally found himself saddled with this large, empty and troublesome colony, for which he could not find a use. After some haggling and bitter words, he made it over to Mr. Jefferson, who paid him sixty million francs. It was thus that the continent of America became the domain of the United States, which had until then been a coastal power. Before Bonaparte's time, the United States resembled Portugal; henceforward they were a continent, like Russia.

This purchase was not strictly legal. Mr. Jefferson, democrat as he was, had ventured a throw such as Alexander himself had never risked, and, of all civil or military conquerors, Mr. Jefferson proved himself both the boldest and the luckiest. To tell the truth, it is doubtful whether the Constitution of the United States warranted him in thus taking a whole world for his country; it is even probable that the transaction was irregular, but Mr. Jefferson needed the territory and he took it. He was right, for he thereby gained what he wanted for his radicals.

The wars of the republic and of the empire assuaged the ardor of the French revolutionaries but did not leave them a very pleasant recollection and did not yield very lasting results. Mr. Jefferson was luckier. He offered an enormous, unpopulated country to his farmers, who were hungry for land, and opened a vast territory to his embittered and discontented small citizens, who longed for solitude and opportunity. Henceforward all the adventurous spirits of the United States repaired to these immense savannas, which offered a field for man's audacity, whither all could betake themselves without too greatly jeopardizing life or fortune, and where they had a chance of gaining wealth and position. The shifting frontier of the West served them as a substitute for political dissertations, socialistic diatribes and protestations of social equality. There was always in the United States a place where sincere and restless individuals could find equality, fraternity and adventure. By this stupendous and brilliant conjuring trick, Jefferson had transformed the United States, which had until then resembled a tightly closed boiler in which a liquid was seething, into an open vessel, whence the steam was escaping as fast as the water was heated.

Now that it could expand in the West, American radicalism became scattered and vanished from sight. Before, it had been a concentrated and organized social force; it now became a personal state of mind; it even inclined to individualism and became every day more widely removed from socialism. Whilst the radicals of Europe gradually inclined towards Communism, under the influence of the big towns where they lived crowded together, and of the factories where they suffered side by side, the radicals of America, now scattered over the plains and among the mountains, became cowboys and ended as movie heroes, defenders of the oppressed, of the widow and of the weak, and as riders of savage steeds and mad steers.

The demand of radicalism in America was not, as in Europe, for social rights but for space. As long as there was space in which to advance, to find solitude and to work off one's bad temper, there was no radical movement in America corresponding to those which divided Europe. There were conflicts of interest, disputes between the different regions, rivalries between the professions, big centers and groups, but there was no class war, there was no proletarian crusade, there was no anticlericalism.

The most clear-sighted of the Americans realized that their people needed space, and that the taste for a wandering life which served the masses as a substitute for anger must be satisfied always and at any price. Unfortunately, in the West, these wanderers had finally, before the end of the nineteenth century, reached the sea, an insuperable barrier beyond which lay overpopulated countries. To the north lay Canada, a friendly and well-governed country, which some day, perhaps, they might be able to absorb but which it would have been madness to try to conquer. To the south the States abutted on Mexico, a booty by no means to be despised, but which it was difficult to assimilate because of the savage and warlike customs of the inhabitants, the tropical climate and the enormous distances to be traversed. Theodore Roosevelt saw all these difficulties and he tried to direct the thoughts of the Americans towards world supremacy and to make them a great imperial people. He dispatched his fleet across the seas; he meddled with everything that happened in any part of the globe, and he prepared the advent of a new generation of Americans, capable of making their way about the world.

Destiny did not allow him to succeed; he was not in power sufficiently long; the War came too soon and he himself disappeared too early. He failed. The American did not develop the habit of leaving his native land, as the Englishman does, in order to settle down on the great highways of the world and live there in his own fashion amid the hurly-burly of nations. The American traveler or emigrant neither transplants nor adapts himself; he always dreams of his own country and he preserves its customs wherever he goes.

A century later, therefore, radicalism was reborn in the United States. In the towns, the unemployed, who at first numbered a few hundred thousands, then three million, then six, and finally twelve millions, began to grumble and protest; but they were poor devils and it was not very difficult to crush them. The same could not be said of the farmers. The latter had, from 1914 to 1919, enjoyed years of brilliant prosperity, during which it fell to their lot to feed the whole of the United States and part of Europe. Then suddenly, from 1920 onwards, the lean years began, and they succeeded one another without interruption or any change save a gradual and persistent increase of the difficulties and distress. In the preceding decades the farmers had been wont, when things were going badly, to take their carts, their horses, their cattle, their implements and their wives, and advance towards the West in search of virgin land, more fertile and less exhausted. In this way they had exploited, one after the other, all the regions which extend from the Mississippi to Canada, and they had extracted from these new lands magnificent harvests.

In 1930 there were no more new lands; there was nothing left in front; and behind there were immense stretches of fields, hurriedly cleared, hurriedly cultivated and prematurely exhausted by farmers who had never troubled to use any manure or fertilizers. Utter consternation reigned among the farmers, and the rural population were consumed with a speechless fury. Dire distress prevailed throughout whole States and districts. The people were still too scattered to have developed a very coherent radicalism, and their leaders were too individualistic to form a genuine bloc. However, they were feeling their way; they wanted to find where they stood, and they turned to Mr. Franklin D. Roosevelt for guidance.

The latter found himself in the position in which

Jefferson had been placed in 1799. He could not reject the support offered him by the discontented farmers and irritated masses; without them it was impossible that he should be elected, and he intended to be elected. But if he placed himself at their head, if he gave them a programme and helped them to organize themselves into a solid bloc of radicals and malcontents, he would find it very difficult to govern them afterwards.

For the first time for decades, a candidate for the Presidency of the United States resolutely set out on a tour of the country. Mr. Roosevelt chartered a train, into which he packed his family, his advisers, his secretaries, his journalists and the notabilities who desired to support him. Then he started his campaign. He patiently proceeded to all the agricultural centers which were the rallying points of rustic radicalism. He stopped his train at them. He mounted the platform, supported by his wife and his eldest son, who was a tall, handsome man with winning manners. He clasped all the hands which were held out to him; he smiled in all the faces which were turned towards him. And he made speeches. For every place, he had his speech carefully prepared; it was made up partly of noble and soothing generalities and partly of very warm, very direct and very personal compliments addressed to the local radical leader. He reviewed the career of the radical leader, enlarged upon his generosity, his disinterestedness and his activity on behalf of the disinherited of this world; he praised him from every imaginable standpoint, and, if he were within reach, he pressed him to his heart and embraced him. He only abstained from praising his programme and saying that he himself subscribed to it. He drowned every practical radical problem beneath a flood of approbation and sympathy. He enveloped the politician in a vast embrace and so prevented him from making a dangerous move. Then, amid the applause of the men and the emotion of the women, he vanished. He had won the votes of these honest folk and he had not made them any concrete promise. He had not compromised his future.

The whole of this electoral campaign in the rural districts was conducted by Roosevelt with an ardent discretion and a sinuous and reticent prudence which soared high above politics and proved him to be a veritable statesman. In spite of the temptation to present a big programme, in the face of an adversary capable only of mumbling the old formulas, and when the pressure of millions of electors urged him to pose as a bold popular tribune, he kept a tight rein on his imagination, his eloquence and his Press. He won over the discontented districts, one by one; he gained the support of the radical leaders, one by one; but he did not organize a radical bloc and he did not form around himself any radical headquarters staff.

If he had not, like Jefferson, the good fortune to be able to throw the malcontents a continent to feed on, he had at any rate the skill to rally them all to his support, and never to allow them to forsake him or to form a party, an organism or a unit. American radicalism remained scattered, fluid and subject to the influence of the soil. It had no precise form and no doctrine. And the Government can still shape it to its needs, according to the time and the circumstances.

LINCOLN AND ROOSEVELT, OR THE ART
OF EXPLOITING CRISES

It is, however, becoming more and more difficult to
satisfy this radicalism or even to persuade it to have
patience! If Mr. Hoover had remained in power, there
would have been reason to fear a vast American peasant
rising; the Quaker President, with his pinched mouth
and his damp, nervous hands, had the gift of irritating
the humble folk, even when he tried to be affable with
them. His measures were always taken at the wrong
time, and his optimistic predictions were not fulfilled
and exasperated the masses. His exhortations to keep
calm were so clumsy that they seemed deliberate prov-
ocations and his plans for amelioration or assistance
invariably led to disastrous complications.

He had never understood the example of the man
who, with Washington, Jefferson and Wilson, is one
of the four greatest inventors of America — Abraham
Lincoln, whose wooden face and cramped personality
surprise Europeans whenever they see his effigy. How
did this provincial lawyer, who had never been very
successful, either in business or love, whose political
situation was by no means strong and who was surrounded by jealous or arrogant counselors, — how did
this man, whom nothing had prepared for the rôle of
dictator, contrive at the critical moment to gain the
popular confidence, the most absolute power and, finally,
the most unforeseen victory? This is the most curious
spectacle in this history of America, full as it is of contrasts and contradictions.

As Washington had perceived the rôle of Anglo-

Saxon logic in America, as Jefferson had divined the importance of space for this people, Lincoln saw how to turn to account the need for a crisis which exists in every American.

The English are always bewildered by it. When they land in America, they fancy they are among their own people, and they indulge themselves in this illusion until the day when a sudden shock shows them their mistake. The American who accepts Anglo-Saxon logic and customs in his daily life is not faithful to them every hour of his life and, in connection with the most important problems, he suddenly abandons them. When his most essential interests are at stake, he seems to stop acting as an Anglo-Saxon and to rely upon more profound and personal resources; in short, the American, in every grave contingency, is attracted towards a crisis, whilst the Englishman is fascinated by passivity. When a problem becomes increasingly complex and serious, the Englishman tries to leave time and the course of events to solve this problem. The American, on the contrary, instinctively inclines towards a violent reaction and enjoys an explosion.

His wars, his revolutions, his most important elections, his great economic epochs have always been crises. The American is only himself and in full command of his strength, daring and courage, if his life includes an element of excitement and "drunkenness", which does not at all appeal to the Anglo-Saxon of the Old World. Both his social and his private life are attuned to this fantastic rhythm, which is either superimposed on the ordinary rhythm of Anglo-Saxon customs, or else violates them and is responsible for the complexity of the American character. In business and in sentimental relationships, Americans constantly refer to the "showdown" — an expression which translates into the domain of private life that need of explosion and relief of tension of which public events in the United States afford so many examples.

The foreigner who stays in America some little time is surprised to hear so frequently an expression which is almost unknown in England. Whether it is in reference to a pretty woman or a big banker, a working carpenter or a music student, a German-American or a Chinese laundryman, from time to time you are told: "No, you can't see him to-day; he has had a nervous breakdown and has to take care of himself." A surprisingly large number of citizens of the United States, male and female, have at some stage of their existence had a nervous breakdown and retired from the world in order to take care of themselves. When a financier loses his fortune, when a singer is hissed, or, on the contrary, has just had an unbroken series of triumphs, he or she has a nervous breakdown. In order to insure the normal functioning of his physical nature and the regular pursuance of his activities, the American must from time to time have his explosion, his rupture, and his breakdown.

Perhaps it is somewhat presumptuous to try to probe the causes of this tendency. It seems, however, as if the climate were largely to blame. Without even going as far as California, where the perpetual summer charms, stimulates, overtaxes and exhausts the vegetable, animal and human species, it is easy to see that in the United States, the extreme and stimulating climate, which prevails from the west to the east and from the north to the south, and which excites an exaggerated vitality, cannot fail to produce also a growing exhaustion. In place of the damp, soft and unchanging atmosphere of England, where, from winter to summer and from summer to winter, the differences of temperature are very slight, and where the human being is, in June and December alike, bathed in a steamy soup of fog, more or less cool, more or less warm, America offers the most violent contrasts from one season to another, and in certain seasons, spring and autumn, the falls and rises of the thermometer are positively terrifying. In New York, in October, it is quite a common occurrence for the thermometer to rise five or six degrees centigrade between ten o'clock in the morning and four o'clock in the afternoon, and then fall abruptly seven or eight degrees between four and seven. In California, at sunset, the thermometer drops suddenly four or five degrees. In the dry, clear atmosphere of the United States, these startling variations of temperature act as a perpetual stimulus to the vitality of the people.

It is the same with the course of the seasons. In New York and Boston the spring comes in a few hours; the night before, the snow still lay twelve inches deep on the ground. You get up in the morning, and at the end of the street you hear a barrel organ playing and a bird chirping on a tree. You open the window and warm sunshine floods the room. The sky is a brilliant blue; in a few days, in a few hours, the earth, the trees and all nature usher in a summer which will perish as abruptly as it came, giving place to a cold, sparkling autumn, abounding in abrupt alternations and icy gusts of wind.

Apart even from temperature, the atmospheric conditions of the American continent would inevitably bring about a modification of the race, for there prevails in the United States, and particularly on the East Coast, a state of electric tension which we do not know in our humid Europe. In New York you sometimes get an electric shock when you touch the door handles; and sometimes, when you start to telephone, a queer sensation reveals the fact that an *aurora borealis* is upsetting all the telephonic and telegraphic communications of the district. In the summer and autumn, those tremendous electric storms, which suddenly burst over the continent and terrify people, exceed anything that we experience in the Old World. The nerves are excited and overtaxed, the whole frame is charged with electricity and, for a man in this state, an explosion becomes an indispensable relief, just as accelerated activity becomes a necessary habit.

Abruptly transplated into this climate, the Anglo-Saxon has adapted himself to it; he has kept his Anglo-Saxon everyday external life, but inwardly he has developed new habits and needs. Contact with other races and crossing with foreign strains have exposed him to unwonted influences, and because this vast and opulent continent offered him immense riches, gave him unlimited resources and invited him to feed copiously, he turned his back on the frugal and monotonous English diet. For two centuries, declare the American ethnologists, the human being in the New World has been steadily eating more and more, becoming stronger in every respect and acquiring a growing potential. Whereas the working-class Englishman never tastes fruit or green vegetables for eight months of the year, the American of Chicago eats fresh fruit all the year round; he has the finest melons in the world, grapefruit that look too good to be true and gigantic asparagus. Some nations are better cooks than the Americans, but no nation has so rich, so varied and so abundant a diet.

Filled with a surfeit of energy by his land and his climate, and exhilarated by the air he breathed, the American at first had to use all his physical strength in constructing, with the aid of the hatchet, the pickax and long days behind the plough, this virgin country, where everything had to be made, forests had to be cleared, roads had to be traced and towns had to be built. He toiled hard with his hands and with the sweat of his brow. He expended between 1630 and 1900 all that superabundance of strength which nature had lavished on him. But, with the years and the decades, his country finally became stocked, equipped and refined. The machine began to relieve man of the most arduous labors and most irksome tasks. Gradually physical exertion disappeared from the lives of almost all Americans. They no longer had occasion to employ and exercise all the physical strength which they were inwardly accumulating; office work and intellectual occupations replaced bodily activities at the very moment when their diet was becoming more and more choice and abundant. The economic indigestion which is troubling America and the entire world has its counterpart in the life of the people; in spite of the sports and the violent and systematic exercises in which the Americans indulge when they can, they still retain an invincible craving to use up a strength which no longer serves any need.

Thus they welcome any crisis which gives them a shock, calls for a sudden effort, completely sways their nerves and at length exhausts those reserves which have been too long stored up within them.

The whole course of the history of the United States proves this. The problem of slavery was an old problem; it in no way called for a hasty solution; it had been waiting more than a century, it could have gone on waiting, and, above all, it could have been solved far more wisely if it had been solved by degrees; however, the country had to have a war and the nation was set on adopting a violent and radical solution. Lincoln, who had grasped this fact, led the people and was followed, for he turned to account that theory of a crisis, so dear to the American people.

The World War exercised an irresistible and magnetic influence on the American people. Not a single shrewd, wise and well-informed individual could, from the out-set, have any doubt that, if the war went on, the United States would be incapable of evading their rôle, and that this rôle would be a very big one. However, owing to the Anglo-Saxon logic which ruled the country and to which Mr. Wilson bowed unresistingly, the problem was treated as one of those which time would solve and which there was no need to tackle in a hurry. The whole presidential campaign of 1916 was pacifist and dilatory. Wilson triumphed on a programme which extolled neutrality and abstention. However, neither he nor the country could avert the final explosion, which brought the United States into the war on the side of the Allies. This was not the outcome of a gradual evolution; it was a swift and sudden right-about turn. It was logical, but it only came about through a crisis; action became possible only on the day when the whole country was seized with a sort of delirium. From that moment the rôle of the President was easy; the opposition disappeared; a fleet was fitted out; an army was formed; and, in a mood of quivering ecstasy, the whole country embarked on that formidable adventure which three years later it was at a loss to understand. Wilson, in a sudden flash of instinct, had contrived to utilize the crisis ideology of the American people.

This art of utilizing crisis is also the great talent and the chief idea of President Franklin D. Roosevelt.

From 1921 onwards, the Republicans, who were then in power, had tried to shield the country from emotions and to blunt the sharp edges of all events. Whatever happened, the President summoned the journalists, offered them cigars, slapped them on the back and engaged them in affable conversation. They chatted like old school chums in the peaceful atmosphere of the White House, far from the industrial, banking and agricultural centers, before a stately and peaceful luncheon at one of the embassies and after a game of hand ball or tennis, in which the President had, without much difficulty, beaten his Postmaster General, or his Assistant Secretary of the Navy.

To the journalists he would say: "Yes; things are not yet all one could wish, but they are already getting better. Last week five hundred more railway cars were loaded in the State of Nevada; and it has been brought to our notice that Keokuk has paid its taxes with far greater ease than last year. One can't say definitely that business will recover in June, but there will unquestionably be a marked change in November and towards next February you will see! We must not encourage the people in exaggerated hopes, but we must keep up their *morale;* prosperity can only return if every one trusts in Providence, in the Government and in prosperity. You may tell your readers that everything is going on nicely. Prosperity is just around the corner."

With these encouraging words, which were generally embellished with a few figures and statistics and, on great occasions, with a few graphs, the President rose to his feet, clasped the journalists by the hand, occasionally asked after their families, and dismissed them. Faith-fully, on the following day, the whole Press of the United States administered to its public the soothing syrup which the President had prescribed. All the omens were good; everything was going to be all right, every one would do his bit, and God, with the collaboration of the Republican Party, would insure the final and complete prosperity of the country.

These delightful and comforting pronouncements were Mr. Hoover's special method, and to this method the ex-President remained faithful to the end. In spite of the growing numbers of unemployed, in spite of the fact that the economic situation was getting worse and worse, in spite of the closing of the banks, scores and later hundreds of which were unable to meet their liabilities, Mr. Hoover, with a smile which became more and more strained, continued to proclaim the approach of final and inevitable prosperity and to pronounce benign oracles in benign accents. After he was defeated, he still went on doing it.

For all that, catastrophes were impending, as Mr.

Hoover himself knew. In the face of a hostile Congress, of a discontented people and of impatient foreign nations, he was beginning to have some difficulty in preserving his serenity. The elections had shown that he no longer conformed with the country's ideal and that he had lost the confidence of the masses. Neither Mr. Hoover nor his Party could be under any delusion on this head: if worse complications were to be avoided, it was imperative to devise some new measure with the least possible delay.

It seemed quite natural to Mr. Hoover that he should address to Mr. Roosevelt a letter, couched in polite terms and tinged with cordiality, in order to tell him that, in the difficult times through which America was passing, only the union of all good citizens and the collaboration of all men of good will could safeguard the vital interests of the country. He declared himself, therefore, resolved to talk with Mr. Roosevelt and prepared to come to an understanding with him, with a view to pursuing a policy which should insure a painless transition from the policy of the Republican Party to the policy of the Democratic Party. Mr. Hoover's letter was full of good will.

Mr. Roosevelt dispatched him an exceedingly cordial and exceedingly prompt reply. He assured him of his zealous and undying determination to defend the interests of America at all times, in all places, and no matter who should be in power. He promised Mr. Hoover the benefit of his assistance, his support and his knowledge, but reminded him that, in view of his total ignorance of all the most important international and even national problems, concerning which neither he nor his Party had been kept informed by the Republicans, he was not at the moment in a position to offer any suggestion which would be useful or might be relevant. He wished Mr. Hoover good luck and good health.

Mr. Hoover did not regard himself as beaten, and, as the fatal day drew near, that day on which the autumn payments of the inter-Allied debts fell due, payments which the Powers had neither the desire nor the intention of making, and concerning which the United States had once given them vague, contradictory but gratifying assurances, Mr. Hoover returned to the charge. With a laudable concern for honesty, he deemed himself under an obligation to do something to help England, and perhaps France, and he knew that it would be difficult to obtain from Congress a moratorium or any concessions whatever in favor of the European debtors, for Congress was in a peevish mood, and a President who has just been beaten at the elections does not enjoy much credit with parliamentarians. Mr. Hoover, therefore, taking advantage of a journey which Mr. Roosevelt was making to Georgia for reasons of health, begged him to be so kind as to stop at Washington on the way, so that they might talk things over.

Mr. Roosevelt replied that his respect for the Constitution, which did not allow an ordinary citizen, even if he were the future President of the United States, to interfere in public affairs, inspired him with some uneasiness concerning the rôle which Mr. Hoover so kindly proposed to him, but that, none the less, he would overcome his reluctance and, since Mr. Hoover desired an interview, he would interrupt his journey to call at the White House. This he did, and, not without emotion, people saw the past and future Presidents of the United States shake each other by the hand, after which they retired to Mr. Hoover's study, where they remained closeted for some time.

They were then seen to emerge and to shake hands again. But this was all that was seen. Mr. Hoover had begged Mr. Roosevelt to lend him his support and influence in order to obtain the gracious coöperation of the Democratic members of Congress, but Mr. Roosevelt, with a sigh or a smile, or, more probably, both a sigh and a smile, replied that this was beyond his power; he could not impose his will on the elected deputies of the people. Mr. Hoover thereupon remarked rather stiffly that this attitude would render it impossible to arrive at any satisfactory settlement with Europe regarding the debts which matured on December 15th, and that it would also render impracticable any speedy modification of the prohibition law. Mr. Roosevelt raised his eyes to heaven and withdrew.

Immediately upon his return to his hotel, he told his secretary to expedite the preparations for his departure, and he arranged to leave by the next train. Consequently, Mr. Ogden Mills, Secretary of the Treasury, whom Mr. Hoover sent to beg Mr. Roosevelt to reflect once again, and to entreat him to make the move which would enable Mr. Hoover to speak in the name both of the present and the future Administration, found no one left at the hotel save servants and subordinates.

Mr. Roosevelt was extremely sorry, but he had been obliged to set off at once. And he left Mr. Hoover to reflect upon the impending catastrophes.

Mr. Hoover reflected during the whole of that winter. The situation was getting worse every day. Every day banks collapsed, every week the number of unemployed increased, and every day the Federal Government found itself in a more difficult predicament. The country no longer had any confidence in the President; it distrusted the Senate and the House of Representatives; the bankers and the big financiers had become so unpopular that it was wiser not to mention their names. The newspapers railed incessantly, the unemployed organized demonstrations and, from one end of the Union to the other, the atmosphere was pervaded with bitterness, mistrust, anxiety and irritation.

By dint of going from bad to worse and from worse to worse still, events had reached a critical point; all the banks in the State of Michigan, one of the largest states in the Union and one of the most industrial — the State of Mr. Ford, in fact — appeared to be on the verge of simultaneous bankruptcy. The Governor, in alarm and hoping thereby to save the banks, had closed them, a step which had not produced a very good impression on the public of his State or on that of the rest of the country. The banking scare spread far and wide, and sinister rumors were current concerning the credit of the United States and the fate of the dollar.

It was now February, still some weeks before the inauguration of Mr. Roosevelt, and during this time a great many disasters might happen. Mr. Hoover felt that he ought to draw Mr. Roosevelt's attention to this situation and ask him whether he did not deem it advisable to intervene. They exchanged messages, telephone calls, telegrams and notes. They were both very cordial,

very confident and very disinterested, but it seemed
evident that, on the one hand, Mr. Hoover, who was on
the eve of his retirement, could not take upon himself
responsibilities which would hamper his successor or
resolve upon measures the application of which would
bind Mr. Roosevelt; while, on the other hand, Mr.
Roosevelt was not legally entitled to lend his predecessor
the support which alone would have enabled him to make
head against circumstances. Mr. Hoover hesitated for
a long time to declare a national moratorium, in order
to save at any rate those of the banks which could be
saved and to preserve the national gold which, during
these elaborate discussions, threatened to retreat *en masse*
to foreign countries. Mr. Roosevelt overflowed with
sympathy for Mr. Hoover; he sent him moral encouragement, but he did not give him any direct support.

"Any one would say he was expecting a catastrophe,"
declared some Republicans.

Others went so far as to suggest: "Any one would say
he was wanting it."

Thus all sorts of perfidious and sinister designs were
attributed to Mr. Roosevelt, whilst the telephone was
ringing from one end of the United States to the other
in search of an official who would agree to proclaim a
national banking moratorium and in this way save the
gold of the United States and Wall Street. As the end
of February slowly drew near and the catastrophe
rapidly approached, as the panic spread with the swiftness of a cyclone, two honest Israelites, Mr. Lehmann,
Governor of the State of New York, and Mr. Horner,
Governor of the State of Illinois, were at length discovered, who were quite willing to sign on behalf of

their two States — the most important States in the Union — a moratorium of the banks. All the other Governors signed after them.

It only remained for Franklin Delano Roosevelt, on the day of his accession to power, to publish a proclamation that all the banks in the United States would be closed for one week.

March 4, 1933, the date of Mr. Roosevelt's entry upon his office, was a day of national catastrophe. All the banks were closed, and any one who had not taken his precautions, even if he were a millionaire, had to scour the streets in search of money. The hotels refused to give out any coin, and the railways were at a loss how to cope with the transportation of hundreds of thousands of passengers, who had come to Washington for Roosevelt's inauguration and were now stranded in the Capital, without return tickets, without money and without credit.

One might have sworn that Franklin Roosevelt had expected this catastrophe.

He had not wanted it. But he had not tried to avert it. He was too wise not to know that his people preferred a sudden shock to the slow process of drifting on to the rocks from which they had been suffering for the last eight years. Hoover had wanted to soothe the nation and he had exasperated it. Roosevelt, in order to obtain complete power and to win the sympathy of the whole nation, took care not to spare them the abrupt shock of reality. His political instinct warned him that, in view of the widespread discontent, in view of the insuperable difficulties which beset business men and the Federal Government, in the face of the discouragement which was gaining ground every day, the right method was not to mitigate the shock of this slow decline, but to make the country feel it and appeal to its latent energies by sounding the alarm.

From the beginning of March, 1933, Roosevelt banked on catastrophe! He did not prevent the closing of the banks, he did not check the fall of the dollar, he did not conceal from the country any of the problems which beset it on all sides; but he tried to rouse it from its lethargy and to gain its confidence by stirring up its latent vitality. He succeeded. After the week during which the banks were closed, the dollar proved itself stronger than before, and, when Roosevelt announced that he did not intend to maintain the dollar at its gold value, though the foreign countries were distracted, the New York Stock Exchange celebrated the occasion by a rise of quotations such as had not been witnessed since 1929.

Franklin Roosevelt succeeded in gaining over his people such a dominion as can only be acquired by statesmen capable of controlling and exploiting the deepest tendencies of a race. In order to save his country from decline, he fed it on crises. As in 1860, as in 1917, America is drunk with a vitality which has always been able to insure her ultimate victory.

THE TASTE FOR GREATNESS IN AMERICA; WILSON'S METHOD AND ROOSEVELT'S METHOD

With more temerity and with a secret apprehension, President Roosevelt further appealed to one of those profound national instincts which all his immediate predecessors had neglected and which the Republican

Party mistrusted, for it did not seem to have any link with eighteenth-century American traditions.

The Republicans have proclaimed that the Americans are the most virtuous people in the world. They have no doubts on this head and they repeat it constantly in their speeches, in their articles and in the editorials of the *Saturday Evening Post*, the purest mirror of the Republican soul. According to the Republicans, the Americans are so virtuous that they are ingenuous and cannot meet a European without being cheated by him. The noble and unfortunate American, in order to escape this lamentable extremity, is obliged to take refuge in his ivory tower and guard himself, as far as he is able, from all contact with this crafty and corrupt outside world.

The Republicans even maintain that this was Washington's theory and that, in his "Farewell Address" to his good people, he exhorted them to shun all outside ties and all harmful contacts. From that time, the Republican Party, the faithful heir of the old Federalists and of Washington, has never ceased to denounce all international embroilments in which, according to them, the Americans lost their purity, their time and their money.

The advice which Washington, at the beginning of the Napoleonic Wars, gave to his three million American farmers and fishers no longer seems pertinent to the hundred and thirty million capitalists, industrialists and agriculturalists who now constitute the American people; but this doctrine has remained an obsession with the Grand Old Party, as it likes to call itself, or the "elephant", as it is nicknamed. And no one, with the exception of Theodore Roosevelt, who was not himself very orthodox, has dared to contend against this current. From 1919 to 1933, the Republicans took advantage of the hostile reaction against the Democrats and the World War to proclaim their doctrine anew, and they succeeded in getting it acclaimed by the people. For a time any one might have imagined that it was one of the essential articles of Americanism.

Perhaps it is, on the same grounds as Anglo-Saxon logic. But it suits only American daily life; it does not suit that other being who is concealed within every American, that hero of the great days, who revels in crises and likes to turn the world upside down. The citizen of the United States has always borne within himself not only the soul of an emigrant but the instinct of a crusader. He has preserved a traditional mistrust of that Old World in which his ancestors could not stay and which drove them out and could not understand them, but he has also preserved a craving to return to it, to put it to rights and to dazzle it by his magnanimity, his justice and his greatness. The American does not trouble his head very much about the outside world, but he cannot resist the attraction of glory and he has an instinctive taste for the majestic. He delights in gigantic monuments, vast enterprises, ambitious programmes and idealistic outbursts. This element does not altogether harmonize with the other features of his character, any more than his craving for crises harmonizes with his Anglo-Saxon logic; and it is easy to misconstrue, it is possible to deny, this longing for the sublime, which obsesses the American people in its hours of exaltation.

Few of America's great men have taken note of this

curious trait in her character. Washington was certainly unaware of it, and Jefferson ignored it, whilst John Adams, whimsical and clear-sighted, had apparently divined it but did not know how to turn it to account. In the nineteenth century, liberal ideas and the task of economic organization did not afford any opportunity for giving free scope to this instinct. The wars in which the United States engaged — the War against England in 1812, the Mexican War in 1846–1848, the Civil War in 1861–1865, the Cuban War — were somewhat sordid, and the memory of them was not flattering to the national pride.

It is, therefore, only just to render Woodrow Wilson this much homage: he realized that the American people were consumed with a thirst for greatness. Wilson was not Julius Cæsar; he in no way resembled Alexander the Great; the startling talents of Bonaparte and the brilliant and vociferous qualities of Mussolini were alike denied him. He conveyed the impression of a distinguished pastor, just descended from the pulpit of a church frequented by good society, rather than of a great statesman; but he had made a careful study of the history of the United States, and his intelligence, which was both stiff and abrupt, had occasional flashes of genius. He realized that the war would interest the United States, if it seemed to them the most difficult and stupendous enterprise that imagination could conceive. He divined that the country needed a gigantic task. And he gave it this dream.

It is true that the American intervention in Europe was a great enterprise and that it had vast consequences, but it also seems that a more limited, more prompt and

more skillful assistance would have produced an equally
decisive result at less expense. Without four million
young Americans quitting their homes to enroll beneath
the standard of their country, without two million of
them crossing the ocean, the victory could have been
won, and Germany forced to sign a peace acceptable to
the belligerents. The Allies would have reaped a less
costly triumph, but America would not have become
conscious of her greatness. It would have been a successful diplomatic and political operation, not a national
revelation. In spite of his blunders and his clumsiness,
in spite of his defects and his ignorance, Wilson did
succeed in giving his country that lesson in imperial
greatness which it craved, which no other American
statesman had been able to afford it and which transformed the nation in the course of a few weeks into
the most imposing power in the world.

The Republicans disowned Wilson. They did not want
to take advantage of the standing in the world which
the Democrats had won for their country. They re-
jected the League of Nations, the tangible monument
of American influence; they withdrew into themselves,
retreated into their banks, and proclaimed their intention of confining their attention and solicitude to the
internal interests of their own country. We have seen
and we shall see what were the results. But it must be
admitted that, from 1919 to 1930, American public
opinion encouraged the Republicans most of the time
and followed them all the time. People were terrified
at the thought of what Wilson had done. They imagined
that through his fault they were saddled with crushing
responsibilities and exposed to vast and needless dan-

gers. They were thankful to feel themselves at a safe distance from the furnace, back in their own continent, where they lived in their own way and were free to deal with all their local problems as they pleased and to solve them without bothering about the rest of the world, of which they desired to know nothing. America was overjoyed to feel that she was back in her shell, and all, from the radical intelligentsia to the old-fashioned patriots and the honest folk in the street, inveighed against that mad epoch when they had embarked on the senseless crusade which was to put Europe in order. It was far better to stay at home, cultivate one's land and earn one's living.

No politician tried to stem this tide of opinion.

It was Franklin Roosevelt who, for the first time, in his electoral campaign, began once more with subtle skill and almost feminine audacity, to talk about the outside world.

The failure of the Republicans was obvious; they had not solved any of the national problems; they had damaged the international prestige which America enjoyed in 1918; they had let the world crisis drift from bad to worse, as if it in no way concerned the United States, and, when it had almost engulfed America, they had tried to apply local remedies, which were both feeble and ineffectual.

For the first time since 1919, Roosevelt ventured to say, cautiously but plainly, that the fate of the United States was linked up with the fate of the world, and that the restoration of prosperity in the United States had to be envisaged as part of a world crusade. He knew that Congress detested remarks of this sort, for Congress is elected by the States and districts; not by the universe; he knew that the American journalists did not like this way of talking, and he knew that the people were no longer used to it. None the less, he had the courage to tell the people the truth and to prepare them for an international collaboration.

Amid the anxiety of the country, amid the depression which is harassing its business men and industrialists, amid all the eddies which are agitating the political world and preventing it from reflecting upon great questions, Franklin Roosevelt is trying to make his nation realize the imperial rôle which it is called upon to play, in virtue of its position between the Atlantic and the Pacific, in virtue of its size and of the importance of its one hundred thirty million inhabitants, and in virtue of that eager and exuberant vitality which it owes to its race and climate. He is trying to show it that its financial problem, its industrial crisis, its agricultural ruin, its customs policy, are parts of other, larger aggregates, in which it must play a leading rôle if it wants to keep its prestige and recover its equilibrium.

In order to succeed in this enterprise, the President is at the same time forced to maneuver, for he has to avoid wounding the susceptibilities of Congress, and yet to speak plainly in order to rouse the people. His every gesture has to be exactly calculated. His every word has to possess a carefully weighed significance and as rich a sonority as possible.

If he succeeds, he will have roused from its lethargy one of the greatest of the civilized nations and he will have revived in his country a profound and fruitful tendency.

"Franklin Roosevelt," people said in August, 1932, "is a weak man. He is a sick man who has been able to vanquish his infirmity, who will be able to vanquish his adversaries, and who will then have exhausted all his strength. He will collapse in the presidential chair."

He occupies the presidential chair, but he has not even seated himself upon it; ever since the beginning of March, he has been on his feet. He has done the work of ten men; he has displayed a physical energy which a young and healthy man might envy. He has succeeded in doing what none of his predecessors during the last ten years were able to do: he has dominated Congress, he has secured prompt and definitive votes.

"Franklin Roosevelt," people now say, "is an adroit politician; he has outwitted all his adversaries, he has even outwitted a great many of his friends, but he is more politician than statesman, for he does not appear to have any programme, and his actions do not betray any coherent views; he is groping his way, and soon it will become plain that he is only guided by circumstances. Franklin Roosevelt is a blind man, who can perceive objects which are near to him and avoid abrupt collisions, but he does not look ahead; he has no principles, no far-sighted plan; none of his hurriedly improvised measures will bear lasting fruit, and it will soon become apparent that he has merely been chasing his luck, armed with a smile and determined to grasp at good fortune no matter whence it came or upon what terms it was to be had. He is not a great man, but he is an astute man."

Roosevelt's Method

It is true that Mr. Roosevelt's most conspicuous quality is tact, and, as he has succeeded a number of Presidents who prided themselves on possessing neither tact nor refinement nor subtlety, he seems odd. He shocks a number of worthy folk and he disconcerts a good many politicians.

But the method he is employing is entirely logical and it is highly appropriate to the circumstances.

It is impossible for a President of the United States to have a definite programme at the beginning of his administration.

He is thrust into power by a party which has prepared for the elections a document known as a "platform." This document is, in fact, very insipid. It is composed, or rather concocted, by the augurs of the party, whose chief anxiety is not to offend any important group within the party and not to tie themselves to anything compromising. As the "platform" must at the same time ring like a clarion call, it is, in its own way, a very subtle and exquisite stylistic exercise. It must, in substance, be very vague and noncommittal, it must not bind the party and the candidate to anything positive, but it must give the impression of warmth, generosity, courage and the most daring initiative. It must also be careful to follow closely the platform of the other party, to reply to all its objections, to satisfy the same groups of citizens and to go one better than the promises of the adversary. In short, the platforms of the two parties are parallel and identical. Their only difference is in wording and tone.

Some years ago a newspaper amused itself by organizing a platform competition among the students. It was a case of drafting the best Republican platform and the best Democratic platform. In all the universities of the country, the young people exercised their prowess. The most successful were those who used the same principles for two versions which were identical in substance and only differed in phraseology.

Once established by the party committee, once ratified by the party convention, these texts become sacrosanct, and the candidate is bound to respect them, to conform to them, and to treat them as Gospel, if he means to be a real leader of the party and to insure the loyalty of all his electoral troops. If he is clever enough, the platform does him the service of enabling him to avoid any declaration of principles. On any ticklish point, he refers his questioner or his interrupter to the party platform, retorting with a smile: "What is the use of asking me questions like that? Read our platform." If the platform contains the desired answer, all is well; if it makes no mention of the subject, it is still better, and the party has every reason to applaud its candidate.

It often happens that the platform of a party has been drawn up by a group of old men or veteran politicians who have no special liking for the candidate or indeed hardly know him. He himself is at this moment wholly taken up with the discreet and exhausting preparatory efforts which he has to make, in order to insure that he shall be nominated a few days later as party candidate; he has no time to devote to such details and he does not devote it. The platform is drawn up behind his back; it often serves as a means of teasing him or

giving him a lesson; sometimes even it is meant to keep
him in check. It often records the conflicting aspirations of groups and districts which have been unable
to agree and have purposely concocted an ambiguous
text. In short, it is primarily and essentially a parliamentary document, excellent for quoting at critical
moments, indispensable during the whole electoral period, inevitable for the weeks immediately following,
but forgotten by every one at the end of ten months and
devoid of all meaning or importance in the second year
of the Presidency.

The convention which selected Mr. Roosevelt as Democratic candidate was a stormy one; in it the most contradictory views were represented and the most bitter
struggles for influence secretly waged; and the platform
reflected these things. It was more courageous, more
dangerous, more compromising and also more hypo-
critical than is ordinarily the case with documents of
this nature. Mr. Roosevelt had to bear this in mind,
and, during the whole of the year 1933, the first year of
his Presidency, he will profess a pious respect for his already obsolete programme. He will not abuse it, for on
one vital point he has evaded the obligations assumed by
his party in the summer of 1932. The Democratic platform talked solemnly of the necessity for the United
States to have a sound currency and to respect it. Carter
Glass, Senator and expert on banking, who had secured
the adoption of this phrase, understood thereby that the
Democratic Party undertook to defend the dollar and
its gold value to the last ditch. As for the rest of the
Democrats, each of them interpreted it to suit his own
fancy; and, when the critical moment arrived, Mr.

Roosevelt was not hampered by this Sibylline text. He acted as he saw fit, and he got the majority of Congress to approve his action. When Carter Glass accused him in the Senate of having betrayed the party programme, he produced the impression of a collector of postage stamps interrupting a stormy session of the Stock Exchange in order to discuss the value of a New Caledonia stamp. None the less, Roosevelt was sensible of the criticism.

The platform of the Democratic Party debars the President from having a personal programme concerning the problems of the day and it does not allow him to reveal his views. He may lay as much blame as he likes on the sacramental text; he is bound to respect its form.

Besides, this suits him very well. In the whirl of events which are sweeping along himself and his country, this shrewd politician, with his subtle flair and delicate tact, utilizes tendencies rather than principles. He has no recourse to doctrines, but he carefully examines the realities on which he can support himself in order to make headway. He tries to discover the living instincts of the nation, which will enable him to stimulate its energy anew, revive its optimism, and launch it once more upon its career of work, happiness and creation. Franklin Roosevelt is not a doctrinaire; he trusts to intuition, and what he understands best is not the economic world, nor the administrative machinery, nor financial problems, nor the workings of diplomacy, nor world politics: his true element is the American people; it is of them he thinks, it is on them he relies for support, it is to them he looks.

With a delicacy of touch perfected by wide experience of men, with a courage strengthened by a long struggle against disease, with a determination which the gravity of the situation has only confirmed, he is laboring to revive in the American people those great and fruitful forces which have saved the country at every critical moment in its history.

Following the great inventors who made the personality of the country — Washington, Jefferson, Lincoln and Wilson — he is trying to create not a new machine but a passion.

PART TWO

LOST AMERICA

LOST AMERICA

In 1919 England, France and America had just won the greatest war ever waged by man.

England and France dominated the world. America dominated her allies, who could refuse her nothing, for she was their money-lender and their supreme resource. Her statesmen were the arbiters of the peace; her financiers made loans and laid down the law to the world. The dollar god reigned supreme.

In 1933 America went bankrupt; she let the dollar collapse. She could not prevent Japan from laying hands on Manchuria, nor force France to pay the annuities of her war debt, nor compel England to stabilize her pound.

In 1933 the United States perceived that for ten years they had been on the wrong road, that they had squandered their power, wasted their capital, allowed their farmers to exhaust the land and ruin themselves, their industrialists to get into debt, their railways to flounder in insolvency and their banks to become bankrupt by their own extravagance. In 1933, the wealthiest people in the world witnessed the closing of 32,000 banks and many of them were able to reopen only after a complete reorganization. It felt that its international prestige had vanished, that the national confidence was shaken and that penury was threatening the country, a portion of whose population was already without any fixed means of livelihood.

What had happened in the United States between 1919 and 1933?

Why did Franklin Roosevelt appear as the savior of a people whom unskillful pilots were guiding on to the rocks?

CHAPTER I

THE WRECKERS, THREE WOODEN KINGS

In 1919 all America exclaimed: "Let us have done with Wiggle and Wobble." — "Back to Normalcy."

The Wiggle was Mr. Wilson, the Normalcy was Mr. Harding.

It was certainly wrong to regard Mr. Harding as a normal man, that is to say, on a par with men in general, for Mr. Harding was exceptionally handsome. His wife said: "When I look at Warren Gamaliel, I feel as if I were looking at a king." And this was the opinion of other women too; it was the opinion of all the American ladies between 1920 and 1922; it was the opinion of the politicians. Warren Gamaliel Harding was a good, handsome, honest man.

But he was unfortunate. His goodness betrayed him into weakness; his easy-going nature led him to make compromises, and his handsome figure made him a prey to the devouring passions of women and the vicious intrigues of men. Warren Gamaliel Harding was a victim.

He was the victim of his wife, who loved him too much to leave him in peace and to admit his right to live the pleasant little *bourgeois* life which he craved; he was a victim of his friends, who respected him too

much not to exploit him to death. He was a victim of
his party which, without any regard for his qualities,
without any concern for his imperfections, without
being able to see his limitations, laid upon him a crushing burden and led him to the brink of a catastrophe
from which only a merciful Providence saved him by a
sudden and opportune death.

No one has ever done justice to President Harding.
Some have tried to make him a true hero [1] who has
been slandered too long and is worthy of laurels and
shrines. Others depict him as the willing tool of swindlers, knaves and criminals, the patron of base little
schemes and the accomplice of vile traffickers.

In reality, he was neither the one nor the other, but
simply a weak, commonplace, honest and conscientious
man, whom the women refused to leave in peace, whom
the old gentlemen led astray by their flatteries, and
whom politics murdered by casting him for an absurd
rôle.

The Republican Party is a very big party led by a
group of eminent men, worthy in every respect of the
esteem, admiration and gratitude of the civilized world.
It saved the American republic between 1860 and 1867,
and it produced great spirits like Theodore Roosevelt
and Lincoln; it represents an Anglo-Saxon industrial
aristocracy, with a great deal of dignity, consistency and
good sense. It is one of the greatest political institutions
in the world and one of those whose finances are the best
managed. It owed its glory to the rôle which it adopted
at the time of the conflict between the North and the

---

[1] "A second Lincoln," said his former Attorney General, Daugherty.

South. It was the party of Union at any price, the party of the North, the liberal and anti-slavery party. It waged a bitter war, and by its weight, its virtue, its guns, its human masses and its wealth, it crushed the South, which was attached to its slaves and to its aristocratic, agricultural and archaic civilization. The triumph of the Republicans spelled the triumph of the *bourgeoisie*, the apotheosis of political liberalism and the accession of industry to power. It was also the moment when the North, and, more particularly, Yankee New England, began to set the tone for the whole of the United States.

From that time the Republican Party reigned supreme. The war had been costly, but it did a great service by creating national unity; it enlarged the agricultural and industrial markets, and while insuring the predominance of the Nordic elements, it allowed the establishment of protective customs tariffs and the rapid advance of industry. It led straight to opulence. The Republican Party, which was in power from 1865 to 1912, with very rare intervals, proceeded to exploit the country systematically. At a period when men's minds were swayed by economic considerations, it was clever enough to be a party in which economic interests always took precedence of political problems. By this means it evaded the danger which ordinarily threatens political parties; it could not be accused of being either reactionary or radical; it was republican, which soon ceased to have any meaning save "well-disposed to those who make money and who are eager to help others to make it."

The Republican Party distrusted general ideas, and

it is not possible to credit it with a doctrine; some of its leaders were regarded in Europe as reactionary, others as liberals, others as radicals. According to circumstances and the trend of opinion, the party moved in the direction which seemed to it most profitable, and it would be useless to try to discover a strict method in its conduct. It none the less obeyed a few persistent instincts: it never ceased to be a patriotic party; it always preferred to support itself on the Anglo-Saxon race, and it automatically practised the policy of Louis-Philippe, who gave first place to the rich, but strove to make it easier for the poor to become rich.

After 1860 the Republican Party was the party of the rural and urban *bourgeoisie* in the United States. It grew in size and strength, thanks to the prosperity of this class; it languished when this class suffered, and, if ever this class should disappear, the party would be doomed to extinction. As long as this class exists, the Republican Party will return to power at regular intervals.

In 1920 it felt itself on the point of recovering the power, which it greatly desired, for the Democrats had for eight years filled all the public offices, and during the war these honors had been particularly lucrative. The industrial North was eager to supersede the agricultural South in power and honors; the lawyers of Boston and Philadelphia fretted and fumed when they saw their colleagues from Richmond and New Orleans giving themselves airs and setting the tone in the Federal courts and in the Department of State. People were tired of Wilson, with his professorial idealism and his political religiosity; they wanted a practical and economic policy, a sound and solid policy which would pay.

During the war America had made a great deal of money, and now people wanted to keep this money and enjoy it in peace. They wanted peace as soon as possible and a peace which would wipe out the memory of the war; for the popular enthusiasm for this crusade had vanished as quickly as it had come, and now that the result was known and obtained, it was disappointing. Most disappointed of all were the two million young Americans who had been transported to Europe in order to fight and who had suffered, above all, from seasickness on the voyage, mud in the trenches and the tedious and squalid routine of garrison life in the devastated towns and among the impoverished populations. They took a gloomy view of the war and Europe. The opposition elements which had, since 1917, been roughly handled and repressed — pacifists, radicals and Germanophiles — exploited this lassitude; they also turned to account the discontent of the people who, in their ignorance of European problems, could not understand and distrusted the Treaty of Versailles. Finally, they took advantage of the suspicions of Congress, which could not admit that America was interested in anything save their reëlection and their electors.

The elections of 1920 were prepared in this atmosphere of bitterness and discontent; people wanted to give Wilson a lesson, to get rid of the Democrats, to break off all irksome ties with Europe and to prevent the return of a troublesome individual like Theodore Roosevelt who, in 1912, had jeopardized the unity of the Republican Party and given the Democrats an opportunity to enter into power. They wanted to be happy and rich and not to bother about anything else.

The Republican Party exploited these passions which it had not created.

It could not be held responsible for this state of mind.

But it was quite willing to profit by it, to exploit it, and to make it the basis of its policy. That group of patriots and of wealthy and enlightened capitalists who dominated the Republican Party and wanted to serve their country, undertook at once to please the crowd by a negative or egotistical foreign policy, and to gratify their patriotic instinct by causing the glory and influence of American economic power to shed its luster far and wide. The United States desired henceforth to take no responsibilities outside their own territories, but they did not like the world to do anything without consulting them; they were so great that their interests could not but be constantly at stake, in every country. For the purpose of carrying out this double and doubly difficult policy of political abstention and economic expansion, the Republican Party selected, in succession, Mr. Warren Gamaliel Harding, Senator and journalist, of Marion (Ohio), Mr. Calvin Coolidge, ex-Governor of Massachusetts and lawyer, of Northampton (Massachusetts), and Mr. Herbert Hoover, Secretary of Commerce and mining engineer, of Palo Alto (California) and London (England).

Mr. Harding was a handsome man. Tall, well-made, straight as a poker and stalwart without being heavy. He had a boyish smile which, in his youth, had won him the hearts of all his comrades and of all the old people; later, that of Mrs. Harding and of a number of other ladies and women; later still, that of the electors and, finally, that of the Senate of the United States, however hard this last heart may be. Finally, by dint of smiling, Mr. Harding was elected president of the United States.

Mr. Harding was not stupid or vicious or dishonest or vulgar or foolish or corrupt. He had many qualities which won him the affection of all those who were brought in contact with him, but he had one which rendered all the others useless, dangerous and out of place. Mr. Harding could not resign himself to being detested. That is why he ought never to have engaged in politics. It is also why he ought never to have married. He belonged to the human race not to politics, to the feminine sex, not to Mrs. Harding.

Mr. Harding married, and this was his first misfortune. He was at that time residing in a little town in Ohio, where he was manager of a modest and fairly successful newspaper. He was loved by all the small folk around him, and his obscure existence was a very agreeable one. Mrs. Harding, for her part, belonged to one of the great families of this little town, and her head was full of great passions and great though petty ambitions. The first of these latter was to marry the handsomest man in the place, Warren Gamaliel Harding. And she managed to extract the consent of her father, who had no desire to see his daughter marry a paltry journalist, son of an obscure country doctor, just as she managed to extract that of Warren Gamaliel himself.

She married him and from that time she directed the life of her husband with merciless affection, zeal and care. Whatever any one may say, and even if she did not actually give him a dose of arsenic at San Francisco in August, 1923, it was she who killed him. From the accounts of his newspaper down to the special train which conveyed his coffin across the United States, she managed everything. During this last triumphal journey she was so busy managing everything that she had no time to weep.

She had the gift — peculiar to women — of sacrificing herself to her husband to such effect that she immolated him too on the altar of her sacrifice.

On the same altar she would appear to have slain the League of Nations, or, at any rate, American participation in the League of Nations.

This was Warren Gamaliel Harding's second misfortune. Although he was the son of an insignificant country doctor and had not distinguished himself in his studies; although, in short, he was a provincial politician and owed his elections to his manner of smiling first and saying nothing afterwards, Harding had a fairly shrewd intuition of the political needs of a great people. He was pushed towards the Presidency of the United States by his wife and by his friend Daugherty, a clever and ardent local politician, and he was installed there by the group of his fellow Senators who for two years had been doing their best to kill Wilson. The Republican clique in the Senate had accepted Harding, for it knew that he would never risk unpopularity, hatred and criticism. It regarded him as a convenient tool for carrying out its programme: namely, the complete destruction of all that Wilson had worked for, including collaboration with Europe and the League of Nations. Harding felt that this was madness. He had inscribed in his programme American participation in the Court of Inter-

national Justice, and he liked to employ formulas which
left the door open for an agreement with the League
of Nations. The Senate would not tolerate this, nor yet
Daugherty, nor yet Mrs. Harding. It was Mrs. Harding
who finally coerced him. He yielded to pressure and he
changed his formulas; he renounced his programme.[2]

Thus it was that the greatest Power in the world refused both to contract political alliances, which would
have given Europe a sense of stability after the turmoil
of 1914 to 1918, and to collaborate in the peaceful solution of the problems raised by the war. By common accord, the Senate, Mr. Daugherty and Mrs. Harding induced the President to refuse to negotiate any other
treaty than that incredible document by which the
United States made peace with Germany without signing the Treaty of Versailles. It is said to have been Mrs.
Harding who dictated this line of action to her husband.

One of the objects of Mr. Harding's admiration was
Mr. Hoover, and Daugherty shared this predilection.
Mr. Hoover had just organized the food supplies for
Belgium and the invaded provinces of France; he enjoyed a great prestige, and he passed for a liberal. The
intelligentsia of America regarded him as one of the
greatest men of the age; the *New Republic* and the
pink salons of New York helped to promote his success. Mr. Harding, who was not a liberal and perhaps,
at the bottom of his candid soul, regretted the fact, felt
himself attracted by Mr. Hoover. The latter always
gave the impression of being in such a bad temper that

[2] See "The Inside Story of the Harding Tragedy", by Harry M. Daugherty,
pp. 173–176.

Mr. Harding, who was always in a good temper, was bound, by the law of opposites, to be fascinated by this man, whose mouth was too small, his stomach too large, his skull too round, his hands moist with perspiration and his face puffy with enthusiasm.

Thus it was thanks to the honesty and the conscientious scruples of Mr. Harding that Mr. Hoover recovered the good graces of the Republican Party, which had borne him a grudge for having served under Wilson. He entered Mr. Harding's Cabinet as Secretary of Commerce.

Mr. Harding's Cabinet served the Republican Party as a sort of Pandora's box, into which were packed higgledy-piggledy: Mr. Hoover, the liberal, who was to collapse in 1932 beneath the blows of the indignant radicals and liberals; Mr. Hughes, the distinguished Baptist lawyer, who was all for morality, prohibition and the International Court of Justice, and who was one of the last American statesmen to wear whiskers; Mr. Denby, who was never anything save Secretary of the Navy; Mr. Daugherty, fat, coarse, cunning, unknown to the world at large and too well-known, it was said, to America, who was the intimate adviser of Harding and the intimate enemy of the Senate (he was Attorney-General) ; Mr. Fall, an ex-Senator, whom the Senate revered and who, as Secretary of the Interior, signed those famous leases by which private companies acquired the right to exploit petroleum fields hitherto reserved to the Navy, — leases which apparently procured for Mr. Fall, in the first place, a sum of one hundred thousand dollars remitted to him by Mr. Doheny, the beneficiary of the leases, in the second place a great deal of notoriety,

and in the last place a few months' imprisonment; Mr.
Mellon, one of the chief bankers of the world, who
combined the most trembling timidity with the most
imperious temper and whose name was, in turn, synony-
mous with sound and intelligent prosperity and, later,
with the most stupid and perilous inertia.

This oddly assorted Cabinet, which was a faithful reflection of the mind of Mr. Harding, in whom were
blended all the most honest desires and the most dangerous illusions, continued, none the less, to function har-
moniously for some time. But it would have been para-
doxical for any permanent understanding to subsist
between Mr. Hughes, who passed for a man of
the world and a saint of the Baptist type, and Mr.
Daugherty, who passed for neither the one nor the
other; between Mr. Hoover, who aspired to be everything, and Mr. Denby, who could be nothing; between
Mr. Fall, who was cynical and brutal, and Mr. Mellon,
who was optimistic and bland. All these elements, which
co-existed quite happily in Mr. Harding, were incapable
of coöperating in his Cabinet, and very soon all these
great men were pulling different ways. This marriage
of heaven and hell, of puritans with adventurers, of
provincial politicians with international financiers, of
Quakers with Baptists and Episcopalians, could not possibly result in perfect harmony.

Mr. Daugherty was imprudent. He admitted it himself in an excellent book. He had a friend, Jess Smith,
who sold groceries and presided over the "Elks" of Ohio.
The Elks of Ohio were not horned beasts but honest
citizens, anxious to drink in peace, far from their wives,
and to serve their economic and political interests by

good-fellowship. No harm in that, and no discredit to
Jess Smith, Daugherty's friend. No harm, either, in the
zeal of Jess Smith, who was commissioned to receive
secret and discreet contributions for Harding's electoral
campaign. The trouble began when Jess Smith had an
attack of diabetes, and the trouble became serious when
Jess Smith shot himself dead with a revolver, after having burned his papers. Malicious tongues declared that
he had been concerned in various scandals and that Mr.
Daugherty was implicated. It was alleged that Mr. Smith
had availed himself of his intimacy with Mr. Daugherty
to obtain facilities for the benefit of liquor smugglers.
A number of scandalous stories were related, and the
Senate took advantage of these to get rid of Mr.
Daugherty, who was requested by President Coolidge
to hand in his resignation.

All this happened long after the death of Mr. Harding. But people claimed to discover some connection between the death of Mr. Harding and these incidents.
However that may be, poor Mr. Harding, harassed by
the threefold and exhausting domination of his wife, his
friend Daugherty, and the Senate, showed signs of
physical and moral fatigue. He still smiled and still
shook any hand which was extended to him, but he had
the air of craving forgiveness, and, since no one knew
for what, this was highly embarrassing. Unpleasant
rumors began to circulate. The Senate began to gossip,
or rather, to shout, for the United States Senate always
gossips at the top of its voice. Despite the solid prosperity
of the country, a radical bloc was formed in the Senate,
which rendered the conduct of the government extremely difficult. Worse still, the good *bourgeois* Old

Guard showed signs of discontent and nervousness. It was, in fact, Mr. Harding's method to attract to himself friends and enemies indiscriminately and to settle the opposition by means of cordiality, whilst his confidant and intimate adviser, Daugherty, was in the habit of settling the opposition by more summary and energetic methods. This difference of methods gave rise to *quid pro quos* and contradictions highly damaging to the Administration, and Mr. Harding was conscious of a rising tide of hostility. It made him ill.

It was arranged that he should make a journey to Alaska, which ought to have rested him, but he was so obsessed by the fear of being hated and of having given offense that he transformed this holiday into a succession of speeches, appeals and supplications on his own behalf. The summer was very hot, Mrs. Harding very nervous, the problems of this base world more and more complicated, and the season not propitious for the consumption of oysters and mussels.

The upshot was that Mr. Harding suddenly died. It will never be known which of the causes enumerated above was primarily responsible for his death, and the question is still under dispute in the United States, so that it would be presumptuous for a foreigner to pronounce an opinion.

Mr. Coolidge, who succeeded him, had a bad digestion.

Mr. Harding was a Baptist, Mr. Coolidge a Congregationalist.

Mr. Harding came from Ohio, Mr. Coolidge from Massachusetts.

Mr. Harding was greatly beloved by the Senate, but the Senate had not much confidence in him.

Mr. Coolidge was not loved by any one, but the Senate had confidence in him.

Mr. Harding had never been able to resign himself to saying no, and he died of it.

Mr. Coolidge could never resign himself to saying yes, and this earned him the reputation of being a great man.

Mr. Harding had never succeeded in bringing to a successful conclusion any important transaction, for he was too anxious to please everybody.

Mr. Coolidge was such an adept at displeasing and seemed to bring such cool and confident efficiency to this task, that he was never able to secure positive results of any importance.

Because he lacked mistrust, Harding ate out his heart in impotence and ended in melancholy.

Because he was mistrustful to excess, Coolidge was entrenched in impotence and attained the most joyous contentment.

By opposite methods and means, the two men rendered the State similar services, but Harding was punished for them, while Coolidge was rewarded. It was said of Mr. Harding that he was blind and weak, and of Mr. Coolidge that he was prudent and strong. However, both were content to follow events from a considerable distance, to conform to the wishes of the Senate with some slight modification and to serve as best they could the economic interests of the American *bourgeois* class and of American business men in general.

To tell the truth, Coolidge was not without wit. By dint of holding his tongue, he had finally become keenly conscious of the absurdity of himself, of others and of

life. One spring day, when he saw Senator Borah on
horseback, proceeding at a gentle trot beneath the tall
trees, Mr. Coolidge remarked in a thoughtful tone,
"Must bother the Senator to be going in the same direction as the horse." Another day, when he was walking
with a friend past the White House, the friend asked
jestingly: "I wonder who lives there?" — "Nobody,"
retorted Coolidge; "they just come and go."

President Coolidge would have liked to feel that he
was doing something, that he was useful, and that he
was contriving to solve some of the problems of international politics, since this seemed to him the rôle of
the President of the United States. He was interested in
the Russian question; he wanted to avoid clashes with
Japan, but the Senate was deaf to his arguments on this
head, and as soon as he was President, he was given to
understand that he would not be allowed to do as he
pleased. He did not forget the lesson, and henceforth
he made little attempt to obtain from Congress results which, after all, he did not greatly value. International politics had small interest for him; he knew
nothing about them, and, though he had no actual
antipathy to foreigners, they seemed to him a long way
off and not very interesting, and he preferred to hear
nothing about them. Moreover, in common with Mr.
Mellon and a large number of Republicans of his type,
he professed the doctrine that the less the Government
intervenes in the life of the nation and the less it meddles
with the affairs of its citizens, the more chance there is
that the country will be prosperous, happy and contented. He did not see any grave objection to the obtuse
and negative attitude of Congress. He said one day:

"Why shouldn't I hold my tongue? I have never been
hurt by what I have not said." Apparently he also
thought: "I have never been hurt by what I have not
done."

Nevertheless, Mr. Coolidge had no lack of courage.
During the strike of the Boston police in 1919, when
he was Governor of Massachusetts, he mobilized the
State Guard and adopted an energetic attitude towards
the strikers. A storm of protestation was raised throughout the world, but Calvin Coolidge did not budge. When
the chairman of the American Federation of Labor sent
him a telegram, appealing on behalf of the strikers,
Coolidge replied simply: "There is no right to strike
against the public safety by anybody, anywhere, at any
time." He refused to be dissuaded from sending this telegram and he never forsook his silence, his stubbornness
and his inflexibility. In the end, he won the day: the
strikers were dismissed, a new police force was formed
and Coolidge owed to his energy a national prestige
which, combined with his silence, with Mr. Stearns'
money and with a certain amount of luck, won him the
Presidency of the United States. He came into power at
the very moment when America was reaping the fruits
of the war and when, amid the other weakened, ener-
vated and anxious nations, she seemed a colossus of
strength. He saw that the situation of the United States
was extremely favorable, and he had the wisdom not to
spoil it by any untimely initiative.

He had the sagacity to allow the bankers to make
money, the industrialists to make new motor cars, the
speculators to speculate on the market and the whole of
the American nation to become drunk with prosperity.

It was reserved for the most frugal of Presidents to govern the country at a time when the delirium of optimism and prosperity was at its height; it was reserved for the most taciturn statesman in the world to hold his tongue whilst the air reverberated with the loud trumpetings of prosperity and whilst, beneath a dazzling sky, the clouds which heralded the storm were beginning to gather. In the spring of 1927, copper lost in a few weeks thirty-three per cent. of its value, and the market for raw materials began to show signs of perturbation, whilst the agricultural situation grew worse from day to day. But in New York, the Stock Exchange was raising a din which drowned any disquieting rumors; the whole country was absorbed in speculation; the industrialists were inventing new methods for compelling the public to purchase their products; the newspapers were boosting American prosperity, and the Rotary Clubs were chanting its praises in chorus and trying to make it more real and stable by insisting upon its immutable sovereignty in the United States. The little lawyer from Vermont, who occupied the White House, was silent. What could he have done amid all this uproar? Since people liked to get excited, it was not for him to interfere. None the less, he had an inkling of the storm which was impending, so much so that, when he was asked if he was willing to stand for the Presidency again, he replied: "I do not choose to run." And nothing more could be extracted from this man whose lips were set in the form of "no."

At that time it might have been said that the Republican Party was drunk with its own sterility.

For eight years it had held power, and in hardly any

domain had it achieved positive results. International relations were still in a state of chaos. The question of the inter-Allied debts had been subjected to a provisional settlement, which most people realized could not be a lasting one. The orgy of banking prosperity was pursuing its course without supervision or organization. Not a man or an institution did anything to check the riot of delirious production. To the sound of the songs of the Rotarians and amid their acclamations, the chariot of American prosperity advanced.

In a corner of a large official building in Washington was ensconced a stout man with piercing little eyes, who had for ten years been waiting for his hour and who hastened to snatch at the opportunity much as a frog snaps at a piece of red cloth or a fish bites at an earthworm.

Mr. Herbert Hoover was not a politician, and the politicians did not think that he could ever become one. But he was energetic, intelligent, ambitious and very clever at creating a machine; it seemed to him that, with the aid of this machine and a few formulas, he would be able to govern the United States.

Whilst Mr. Harding had the gift of popularity and was good-natured to a fault, whilst Mr. Coolidge raised unpopularity to a fine art and rudeness to affability, Mr. Hoover had a talent for unpopularity, an instinct for tactlessness and a craving for rudeness. Nevertheless, he mastered himself sufficiently never to push his unpopularity or his tactlessness or his asperity to such lengths as would have given them glamour and distinction.

He seemed neither to love his fellow-men nor to un-

derstand them, which, in the eyes of some, gave him
the air of a leader. He appeared neither to love ideas nor
to understand them, with the result that in certain
circles he gained the reputation of a practical man. It
seemed as if nothing amused him and everything vexed
him, with the result that many regarded him as a great
man raised high above his fellow citizens, his contemporaries and the masses.

As a matter of fact, Mr. Hoover possessed hardly any
positive quality save a certain rigidity of mind and a
certain tartness of character, which enabled him to
fight and kept him fighting to the last. As he was not
sufficiently clear-sighted to perceive his limitations and
as he was not sufficiently wise to discern the complexity
of the political game, as he was not sufficiently proud to
despise the exercise of power, nor sufficiently humble to
deem himself the inferior of any one on this earth, Mr.
Hoover, as soon as he found himself possessed of wealth,
decided to occupy the chief administrative post in his
country, and pettily but vigorously, methodically but
obtusely, he labored towards this end.

He had made his fortune in China, in England and in
Australia, but he remained American. He had traveled
the world over to no purpose; he had acquired neither
a taste for the exotic, nor a liking for the foreigner, nor
intellectual or artistic curiosity, nor international friendships. After twenty years of wandering, Mr. Hoover
brought back nothing from all these foreign lands and
picturesque adventures save a large fortune, an immense
antipathy to everything which was not scientific, philanthropic, economic and American, and a stupendous confidence in himself. He had no great learning, as he well

knew, and his career had not made him one of those intellects which probe the mysteries of things; he was not an industrialist, and he had never had occasion to build up a big creative enterprise or to manage a large staff of engineers and workmen. He was not a politician, nor yet a diplomat who has mastered the resources of social and individual psychology and the rôle of psychic factors and of material interests. But he knew himself to be the king of the modern world, and he felt himself superior to the politicians, the diplomats, the industrialists and even the scholars, for all his life he had been a *salesman.*

In the modern world, where human ingenuity has rapidly succeeded in bringing to light the treasures once so jealously hidden in the earth and in exploiting them with such amazing skill, the problem is no longer to find gold, silver, iron and coal, but to sell them. The appetites of men have remained timid and their digestions slow; before the immense Gargantuan repast which science and industry spread before them, they are awkward, intimidated, embarrassed. The industrialist, the scholar, even the banker, had ceased to be kings; the commercial traveler reigned supreme, the salesman dictated the laws.

It was at this juncture that Mr. Hoover made his appearance on the stage of American politics. Economic life was congested; politics were congested; social life was congested. In the midst of its triumph the Republican Party was very conscious that clouds were gathering on the horizon, and it began to be troubled about the future. After the good Mr. Harding and the wise Mr. Coolidge, it would doubtless be prudent to offer

the American people a man who would convey more
impression of activity, greatness and strength, a man
who would enjoy a vaster personal prestige and a more
cordial popularity. Doubtless the best politicians of the
party, the senatorial Old Guard, as well as the most
sagacious of the Republicans, the wary bankers, had
their doubts concerning the mental, moral and personal
qualities of Mr. Hoover. They did not regard with the
eye of favor this tradesman, who had begun by living
away from his country, who had returned to it during
the war in order to serve under a Democratic President,
who had passed for a Democrat and had been regarded
for a time as the probable Democratic successor of President Wilson. People bore Mr. Hoover a grudge for having flung in his lot with the Republican Party in 1920,
when it was clear that the Democratic Party was entering upon a period of eclipse; people also bore him a
grudge for having immediately aimed at the Presidency
and for having played his cards extremely well. For he
certainly had played them well. As Secretary of Commerce he had not wasted his time. He had reorganized
this ministerial department, which had hitherto possessed little importance or popularity; he had linked it
with the Department of State and had organized a body
of commercial attachés in foreign countries. He had
done everything in his power to extend American markets outside the United States and to systematize American industry. His ministry was at once a vast industrial
publicity agency and a laboratory of economic dictator-
ship. Under his energetic guidance, industry, it was
claimed, was becoming modern and systematic, and
salesmanship was becoming intense and scientific.

People were saying this on all sides, and no one contradicted them. This was the time of the great American financial and industrial boom. Shares were rising on the Stock Exchange, every one was speculating for a rise, and even if Mr. Hoover sometimes overrated the praise bestowed upon him by his friends and admirers, this was useful to American speculation and therefore it was eagerly applauded. The launching of Mr. Hoover, carefully prepared by Mr. Hoover in accordance with his thirty years' experience of the launching of mining and financial enterprises, was generously assisted by the bulk of American business men, who were then at the zenith of their power, their enthusiasm and their optimism.

Hoover the technician was applauded everywhere. No one could resist the torrent of his popularity and even his faults were glorified into virtues. If any one said: "But the man is cold, awkward and dull." — "Quite so," replied the Hooverites. "Mr. Hoover is a technician. Would you have him resemble a pretty woman?" If any one suggested: "But he knows nothing about politics and, after all, a President of the United States is supposed to concern himself with politics!" — "Oh, yes!" they retorted, "that is true, and it was a mistake. If our Presidents had paid less attention to politics and more to technical science, America would be richer, happier and more powerful."

Finally, if any one exclaimed: "But there is nothing human in Mr. Hoover!" — "So much the better," they replied. "He is a real technician, without any weaknesses."

It was thus that in 1928, to the slogan of "Hoover and

Prosperity", Mr. Hoover was elected by the most impressive majority that the country had ever experienced. By twenty-one million votes against fifteen, Mr. Hoover defeated Governor Smith, who was, none the less, recognized by all as the most judicious and the most skillful and reasonable politician in the United States. After the reign of the normal, represented by Mr. Harding, after that of good sense, embodied in Mr. Coolidge, began the reign of technics, in the person of Mr. Hoover.

Never was there such a disaster. Immediately on his election and before entering upon his duties, Mr. Hoover had begun his official life by a vast friendly and business tour across the States of South America. It was a "gesture" and a reminder to the world both of the Monroe Doctrine, by which the United States reserve for themselves a sort of protectorate over South America, and of the desire of the United States to conquer new markets. In regard to the South American States, it was both a display of friendship and an indication of economic anxieties. It might, in short, be the opening of a new era in Pan-American relations.

This it was not. Mr. Hoover was not much good at the South American languages. He did not understand the psychology of the South American peoples. He was entirely ignorant of the inner workings of their political life. Some of the rulers of the States were polite, others were cold, a few were positively rude. Here and there people took the trouble to be cordial, but on the whole, Mr. Hoover returned far from satisfied, leaving behind him a disagreeable impression and having obtained no concrete results. Compared with the Prince of Wales, he might have been a traveler in pneumatic plugs come to sell his wares to pretty women who were expecting a representative of Jean Patou or of Mlle. Chanel.

Mr. Hoover returned home in order to be installed as President of the United States. On a cold, rainy day, which did not, however, subdue the enthusiasm of a frantic crowd or the brilliance of a splendid pageant, Herbert Hoover, thirty-ninth President of the United States and first technician in the world, was installed in the White House. That day he smiled. And he continued to smile until towards the middle of October.

Immediately upon his installation, Mr. Hoover began to build up his machine, and his first step was to organize a body of journalists, who every morning read all the newspapers published in America, cut out all the items which concerned him, pasted them in a large album, and compiled a summary of them in a few pages, with notes and appendices, so that the great technician could, when he repaired to his office, see what his country and his Press thought of him. In this way he would always know where he stood.

Alas! He did know. On October 19, 1929, shares on the New York Stock Exchange suffered a sudden and disastrous fall, and the country began to get uneasy. Mr. Hoover saw that public opinion was wavering. He immediately announced that this crisis would be of short duration and that they must go straight ahead: "Prosperity is just around the corner."

At the end of a few months, prosperity was still just around the corner. Industry, in its turn, reflected the embarrassments of finance; agriculture began to raise lamentations, and there was talk of unemployment. Mr.

Hoover summoned the journalists to his presence and declared to them that the depression was an attack of nerves and that it must be combated by confidence and optimism. In order to prove it, he smiled at them and assured them that business would recover in the autumn.

The spring passed, the summer passed, and Mr. Hoover's first prophecy was fulfilled: everything was going badly, and every one was saying that everything would get better. But in the autumn of 1930 Mr. Hoover's second prophecy was not fulfilled: everything was going rather worse, and people began to get tired of saying that everything would go better. People were still saying, "Prosperity is just around the corner," but it had become a national joke. In vain did Mr. Hoover read the Press; it only told him unpalatable truths; in vain did he smile; a void had formed around him and his mirror showed him only a forced grimace. The industrialists were cold, the financiers were nervous, the farmers were furious. And they all turned to the technician and asked him: "What's to be done?" But the great salesman could do nothing.

The world refused to buy.

The production of steel dropped, the shares of the United States Steel Corporation dropped, the price of corn dropped!

And Mr. Hoover himself fell from the full height of his popularity into the mud.

"Do something about it," people said to him. But he could not do anything, for he had no idea what to do. He had never been a creator, an inventor, a philosopher, a scholar, nor yet a politician. He had never been anything but a technician, a machine for putting into practice what others had invented before him. And other people were no longer inventing anything. In the years 1930 and 1931 the best minds of the Republican Party were sunk in apathy, its prophets were nonplussed, its doctrines were turned to ridicule.

It is very unjust to put all the blame on Mr. Hoover. He was only the priest (the high priest) of a cult of which the others were the prophets. Why then reproach him for having stammered, held his tongue and failed to give replies, when his prophets, the oracles of the Republican Party, were themselves mute and vanquished by fate? The only peculiar and specific fault of Mr. Hoover was that he had a face and personality apparently destined for the vengeance of gods and men. But for this, people ought to have been grateful to him rather than resentful.

During the collapse of 1929–1932 he was at his post, and he duly played his part as the priest of mute gods.

Let us now turn to those prophets who failed Mr. Hoover at the critical moment.

CHAPTER II

PROPHETS OF STEEL

THE Republican Party called itself "the Grand Old Party", and it was right; there was grandeur in it.

Ordinarily the public only sees in the political parties a syndicate for purposes of exploitation, and it is true that every political party, if it is to last, must exploit some passion or instinct in the public, but, according to the quality of the passion or the instinct they exploit, the political parties are deserving of more or less high esteem or more or less profound contempt.

The Republican Party of the United States was not content to exploit those minor jealousies which modern theology is pleased to dub "class instincts" and "class struggles"; nor did it flatter the patriotic passion in its most elementary form, but it set itself to discover in the most intimate recesses of the American soul tendencies and cravings which it alone knew how to satisfy.

The Democrats were a vanquished party, crushed by the defeat of 1860, a party of Southerners, poor, dirty and humiliated, a party of peasants and of small folk who distrusted life. The Republicans were a triumphant party, who believed in their own victory and in victory in general, who had faith in existence and in the value of life. They were a party of *bourgeois,* of bankers, of people who were rich or who intended to become rich; they believed in the universe because they believed in themselves.

The Republican Party enhanced the pride of the American people at a moment when the American people wanted to be proud, and it drove the people forward at an epoch when destiny was driving it forward. It helped the people to realize its strength and to turn it to account; it revealed the vastness of the nation's resources and kindled its ambitions. With the aid of Lincoln and Theodore Roosevelt, it roused the American people from its torpor and made it conscious of its national rôle. But for the Republican Party, America would never have become the formidable and imposing empire whose power was revealed to an astonished world during the War of 1914 to 1918.

But, after all, this was the least of the services which the party rendered to the country, or rather, it was their more external and frivolous aspect. The pride of the American people is not a sort of metaphysical gift or an intellectual concept; it is a sort of physical gift; one might almost say that it is a material halo and that it is somehow connected with the texture of the American skin. The American people is far less conscious of its strength when it contemplates its gigantic warships, either upon the ocean or upon the screens of its movies, than when it surveys its ubiquitous bathrooms and swimming pools. The people of the United States is proud of its comfort.

Each nation has its own type of comfort. For the Frenchman, it is a well-served meal and a bottle of old

wine; for the Italian, it is an old house with paintings
by old masters; for the English it is their afternoon tea;
for the Germans, it is abundance of beer and sausages.
For the Swede, it is perhaps the inevitable palm tree
which adorns their railway stations and testifies to their
energy in challenging destiny; for the Americans, it is
undoubtedly their bathroom.

America is both torrid and glacial. The harsh climate,
the immense country in which the scattered human beings had to grapple with overwhelming tasks, the soil
which was at once fertile and rapidly exhausted, — all
these things gave the colonist a lofty idea of his rôle
and obliged him to take great care of his body, which,
in this struggle with virgin nature and this close contact
with a merciless climate, would soon have succumbed if
it had not been the object of special attention. In our
old Europe, the farmer takes such good care of his land
that it is eager to repay his efforts, and the inhabitant
and his country, the farmer and his climate, end by becoming adapted to one another. There is no need for
the man to pay great attention to his body. In America,
a man must always pay attention to his body and wash
and tend it; and so the American, like the Swede and
the Norwegian, instinctively feels himself an aristocrat.
Deprived of that close intimacy between people and
things which constitutes the happiness of French rural
life and makes the French peasant what he is, the
American can never be a peasant. He may be a bum,
he may be an industrialist; in either case his body, which
has to defend itself against an environment to which
it is never adapted, is the body of an aristocrat.

The Republican Party was cunning or lucky enough

to see this and bear it in mind. It encouraged industry
and everything which was calculated to afford the
American that protection against things which he
needed. The Democratic and archaic civilization of the
South remained a rural civilization, whilst that of the
Republican North rapidly became an industrial civilization, a harsh and brutal civilization, with immense
black and chaotic towns, where gold reigned supreme
and shone with a dull luster, but where every house
rejoiced in a bathroom, where the kitchens all had gas
and electric stoves, and where even the poorest found
a whole system of machines and implements to protect
them against nature.

The French *bourgeois* has more servants, but he has
not those innumerable minor requirements which the
climate has developed in the American, nor yet all
those delicate implements which civilization has bestowed on him. Hardly had he landed amid all sorts of
new, hostile and overwhelming things, than the citizen-
to-be of the United States, newly arrived in a country
almost ignorant of man, succeeded in enlisting all sorts
of objects against the dangers of the outside world. By
this means he became an aristocrat after his fashion,
without the red-heeled shoes of the old French aristocrats, without exquisite manners or dazzling eloquence,
without systematic haughtiness or professional pride,
but from the mere fact that his body was in greater
danger and demanded greater care.

The first two centuries of North America were hard,
and the life of the Canadian is still arduous, but, since
the industrial development of the United States, the
whole American population has gradually grown ac-

customed to these physical refinements and they have become an essential part of their civilization. Before he has mastered the English tongue, the Calabrian immigrant to New York forms the habit of shaving, washing, eating fruit and bathing himself. He owns a motor car and he has a radio for which he pays in weekly instalments. He then feels himself an American, and it does not worry him that his stew is badly cooked or that his shirt has holes, since his trousers are pressed twice a month and his tie was purchased on Broadway.

This curious civilization, consisting of visible and tangible comfort and of luxury in dress and toilet, and contrasting so strikingly with the rudimentary and sketchy character of the national culture, symbolizes the twentieth-century Republican America, ruled by Harding, Coolidge and Hoover.

But, above all, it is the America of the great modern American prophets, and of the most famous of them all, — Henry Ford.

Henry Ford has a little head and small bones. His family comes from Ireland and his features betray the fact. He is sprung from the people, but he was never a proletarian. He comes from Europe, but he belongs to America. His parents would not have done anything very important in Europe, and he himself would not have done anything special in a world whose material needs were less and whose intellectual demands were greater.

If he had been born in a small country, Henry Ford would have ended by making watches or machines for perpetual motion. He would have languished in the background of some gloomy shop, and people would

have said of him: "What a nice boy, and what a pity
he should be a little crazy and good for nothing!" He
had the good luck to be born in a country where his
physical dislikes, his weaknesses and his exigencies ranked
as virtues. He had the incomparable fortune to be born
in a country which abounded in space, whilst he himself was fascinated by space, much as children are
fascinated by toys, butterflies and flowers, which they
long to touch, break and spoil. Henry Ford was an
American who could not dispense with physical refinement, and he had the genius to push this refinement
into a domain where no one had pushed it before; he
bestowed upon the American populace, at once slave
and queen, that space amid whose immensity it was
groping its way like some clumsy and microscopic creature, intoxicated and crushed. Thanks to Henry Ford,
this space was put within the reach of all, and, as
the great kings distributed domains to their vassals,
so did he distribute to his good people the immense
territory of America, like a garden in which they
might disport themselves. His motor cars, sold at low
prices, allowed every one to travel everywhere and
every day.

The Fords were Americans of recent date; they had
come from Ireland and had bought a farm near Dear-
born, Michigan, in the north of the United States,
close to the Canadian frontier. Ford, senior, was a good
farmer, who cultivated his lands well, took good care
of his cows, his pigs and his poultry and was kind to his
five children. Henry, his eldest, was an odd child, who
did not mind work but detested animals and had little
affection for the land. In Europe he would have been

a sort of monstrosity; in the New World he was one of those innumerable denizens of the rural districts who may live for decades on a farm but, for all that, will never become peasants or country folk.

Little Henry Ford was clever with his fingers. He was a good worker and he liked handling tools. One day when he was seated with his father in the cart which was conveying some merchandise to the neighboring town, they met a strange machine which was blocking up the roadway; it was a road engine. Little Henry got down, looked at it and was so filled with wonder that the men in charge of the engine invited him with complacent condescension to feel and examine it. He walked round it ten times, climbed on to the seat, was shown the handles, levers and chains. The men explained to him its working, made the engine whistle and the wheels revolve, and when Henry set off again with wide-open eyes and gaping mouth, he had just experienced the greatest emotion of his childhood. Henry Ford had discovered the glory of the machine in this old rustic engine, at the bend of a country road.

Afterwards he dreamed of it. He could not resign himself to life on the farm. He left for the town when he was fifteen years of age. He entered a metallurgical company, where he received two and a half dollars a week, and where he was ecstatically happy. He went on to another company and gradually his mechanical education was completed. He had all the necessary gifts: clever, delicate and supple fingers, a sober intelligence, interest in the concrete and an incapacity of perceiving the abstract, and an imagination puerile in the face of ideas and creative in the face of objects. Lastly, he was

serenely indifferent to money; he neither loved it nor
despised it; he was neither ashamed of it nor proud of
it; he rarely gave it a thought and then only when he
received it. He would have been a model workman if he
had been a workman; but he was not a workman. Nor
was he a scholar; at no time did the mysteries of human
or material life have any attraction for him. He was a
mechanic, who loved to feel the movement of objects
and to create that movement. The rhythm of life in
things interested him infinitely more than the rhythm
of life in men, and his obsession was to create this
quivering motion and render it universal.

He never ceased to dream of his road engine. In spite
of his father, who wanted to get him back onto the
farm, in spite of the difficulties of the lean years and the
charms of family life, he frequented the factories more
and more and stayed in the town. He had entered the
employ of the Edison Company at Detroit, and, while
working there, he caught a glimpse from time to time
of its great chief, who filled him with a mute veneration
and whose least words he drank in eagerly. He believed
rather less in God; he believed more distinctly in something new.

But his road engine still obsessed him. At that time
people were beginning to talk of the motor car, and
whilst he was working at the Edison Company he set
himself, during the hours he was able to steal from his
work and his wife, to make an automobile. People
laughed at him. He, Henry Ford, the farmer, was
making a machine which was to move without horses!
Month after month he worked at it, and the year 1892
passed without his having achieved any results. Finally,

in April, 1893, as spring was approaching, Henry Ford, one gray and rainy day, invited his wife to contemplate his prodigy. Mrs. Ford, who was a cautious woman, took her umbrella and planted herself on the edge of the pavement, whilst Henry produced from the shed a strange object made of iron and wicker, which, under his manipulation, emitted strange sounds and finally set itself in motion; in it Henry traveled around the block of houses, followed by Mrs. Ford, who, majestically sheltering herself from the rain beneath her open umbrella, did her best to keep pace with this grotesque machine.

Such was Henry Ford's first expedition in a motor car!

Soon after he found capitalists who supplied him with the necessary funds for setting up a factory.

And soon after he quarreled with them, because they wanted to make money and reap big profits, whilst he wanted to build motor cars and make small profits. In vain did he try to explain to them what he had heard Mr. Edison say: that the way to make money was in mass production. The shareholders did not understand, and he parted from them in 1902.

So Ford returned to Mrs. Ford and his garage. He took his machine to pieces, tinkered at it and altered it. Finally, in December, 1899, he entered his automobile in a contest against a famous racing motorist. To the general surprise, he won. He found a partner, and he built two mysterious machines; he entered them in another race and he won again. These successes, combined with the extraordinary shape of the machine, which looked like baskets on wheels drawn by skimmers, had

attracted the attention of the public. Henry Ford began to be the fashion. Whereas between 1899 and 1902,
in his first company, he had laboriously produced twenty
cars, he was able in 1903 to found the Ford Motor
Company with a capital of one hundred thousand dollars, of which twenty-eight thousand were paid up.
Then, in 1910, he erected a new factory, and in 1908–
1909 he started making the famous "Model T", the
traditional Ford, high-built, tinny and steamy, fast and
ungainly, capable of making its way anywhere and of
outstripping all the other cars of that time; capable
also of stopping for no reason and of resisting all the
efforts of reason, mechanics and art to get it going
again: in fact, that Ford which America dubbed "the
flivver" and which was the object of so much derision
that it became a national habit, a sort of patriotic toy,
a feature of the American character.

Of these cars Henry Ford constructed twenty thousand in 1909, half a million in 1916, a million in 1921.
On May 18, 1922, he constructed the six millionth car
of this "Model T." By 1927 he had produced a total of
fifteen million. In 1927 he was said to be worth two
billion dollars, whereas in 1919 the capital of the Ford
Company had amounted to only one hundred million
dollars and in 1900 Ford himself had possessed no more
than a few thousands. His assembling plants, of which
he had thirty-five in the United States and twenty-five
in other parts of the world, turned out two cars a minute. He was the supreme potentate of the motor car.
He was the most powerful industrialist in the world.
No one could intimidate him, no king or government
could frighten him, and the power of international

finance, which seems to dominate our modern world, only excited his ridicule.

In 1921, Wall Street, which was watching him out of the corner of its eye, thought that it was going to succeed in bringing him to his knees. A serious economic crisis was brooding over the United States. Ford had to meet liabilities to the tune of seventy-five million dollars and he had only twenty million in hand. A good-natured banker took the train and journeyed to Detroit. He saw the industrialist, who received him kindly and with whom he discussed the topics of the day. The visitor mentioned that the banks would have no objection to making Mr. Ford a generous loan, to which Mr. Ford vouchsafed no reply. Then, growing bolder, the banker confided to Mr. Ford that the banks were quite prepared to furnish him, for the purposes of his business, with an excellent treasurer, who would be an advantageous substitute for the one whom Mr. Ford was at that time employing. Thereupon Mr. Ford rang for his servant and, with perfect politeness, asked him to conduct the gentleman to the door. This was the end of direct relations between Ford and Wall Street. Mr. Ford met his liabilities. He stopped abruptly all his orders for raw materials and unloaded his stock of cars on his agents. By this means he secured sufficient money at one stroke to extricate himself from his difficulties.

Then he bought a newspaper for the purpose of denouncing the bankers and the Jews.

Mr. Ford, in fact, after he became great and powerful, conceived a passion for ideas. It was not entirely his fault perhaps; probably the journalists were more to blame than himself for this mania; but, with age and glory, this weakness became more and more pronounced; he was not content to be one of the most fascinating idols of the United States; he was a talking idol, an idol which pronounced oracles.

Mr. Ford has a gospel. He declares that industry must never be a means of making money but a method of service. Any one who serves does in the end make money, but any one who concentrates upon making money soon ceases to serve and even to succeed. The only way to serve, however, is by mass production and at very low prices, at the same time paying a very high wage, so as to secure intelligent and energetic workers from whom remunerative service can be demanded. This morality of production also ranks in Ford's estimation as a social morality, for, by paying one's workmen well, one not only creates factories with a rational output but also a society capable of absorbing the products of these factories. In order to arrive at these results, all that is needed is a bold and practical mind; the rest is child's play.

Mr. Ford's creed has been summed up by himself in four principles:

1. An absence of fear of the future or veneration for the past.
2. A disregard of competition.
3. The putting of service before profit.
4. Manufacturing is not buying low and selling high.

Mr. Ford wanted to serve humanity and to wed the man to the machine. He entitled one of his philosophic essays: "Machinery, the new Messiah." In fact, he saw in the machine the salvation of humanity, once crushed beneath the weight of arduous, mean and fruitless drudgery, but now able to stand erect, since the machine is there to do all the dull and dirty work.

Ford is not a merchant whose main anxiety is to sell his goods, nor an engineer who aims at constructing an elegant and exquisite instrument, nor a scholar who devotes himself to solving a theoretical or general problem. In short, he has no love of money or of ideas or of refinement. He is the high priest of a new god, the prophet of a new religion.

To his partners, who pestered him in order to persuade him to sell his cars at a higher price, he opposed an invincible obstinacy. He was the first to make cheap cars, and he boasted of wanting to "put the mob in automobiles." Thus Ford was a philanthropist. But Ford also said to his agents, when they told him of the complaints of purchasers who grumbled at being able to buy only cars of one color: "Any customer can have a car painted any color that he wants, so long as it is black." And he refused to give way. Ford was just as much concerned for the machine as for the man, and when man pleaded for variety and the machine demanded uniformity, he decided in favor of the machine.

Why should he not pay heed to the demands of his machines? Did he not say to a journalist who came to question him about his ideas: "I make no difference between matter and spirit; they are different degrees of fineness of the same thing"? This did not mean that Henry Ford was a materialist. For a long time he took pleasure in going to church. Then, with age and exhaustion, he contented himself with listening to the sermons supplied him by the radio, but he always insisted that he enjoyed them and that some day he would have a church built in memory of his father and mother; and he declared that, after all, he believed in God and in Jesus Christ.

Ford did not try to destroy either gods or men, but he introduced among men a new creature, the machine, and among the gods a new deity, machinery. In his eyes, only the machine can content and guide humanity; it must supplant the other forms of civilization and reveal to man his duties and his rights. He was so convinced of this that even agriculture seemed to him merely an illusion destined to disappear very soon. The farmer had no reason for existence; he did badly and slowly what could be done better and more rapidly by well-trained industrial staffs. The uncouth farmer, who is, moreover, idle for part of the year, ought to be replaced by intelligent workmen, who would attend to agriculture as and when required, with intelligence, efficiency and method, and go to the factory for the rest of the time. For the factory is the center of Ford's life and intelligence, since the factory is the marriage of man to the object, the enthronement of the object in man's life. And when people protested against this barbarous creed, Mr. Ford pointed to his factories, which stretched as far as the eye could reach, to his immense and luxurious mansion, to the endless file of his workmen and the moving sea of their motor cars, and replied: "Look!"

America looked, she bowed and she admired, speechless with an enthusiasm which was not merely veneration of success, but was blended with gratitude, fervor and a secret sense of complicity.

America admired when Mr. Ford changed his model

and succeeded in launching another; she admired when he set to work to build luxury cars; she admired when he also undertook the conquest of the upper regions and embarked upon the construction of aëroplanes and the exploitation of aëronautic companies. She admired him when he patronized Mr. Hoover, her technician ruler, and when he started his collection of American antiques and national curios. She admired him in the illustrated supplements of the newspapers and in the dithyrambic articles in the reviews; she admired him in his own books and essays; she admired him as she knows how to admire, with candor, generosity and vim. She admired him because he had brought the motor car into the lives of the small folk and because he had enabled the whole immense population of the United States to enjoy that vast and virgin space which once separated peasants, farmers and townsfolk and which now bathed them like a cool sea, into which they could dive without drowning, in which they could swim for their pleasure, and which they could enjoy with every movement they made. She venerated him because, under his influence, the other great industrialists, his friends or his rivals, his imitators or his enemies, were soon obliged to follow his example, to lower their prices as he did, to raise the salaries of their workers as he did and, as he did, to launch upon the market immense series of objects which were of careful, indeed perfect manufacture, but produced in masses and destined for the masses. Ford set the American crowd in motor cars, and others made the American crowd the most refined crowd in the world, — a crowd with watches, radio sets and silk shirts.

He was admired until the day when he had to close

down a part of his factories and dismiss a third of his
workmen. Then people began to examine his methods.
Everywhere they saw gigantic factories half closed or
working at reduced speed; they saw those enormous
plants half-empty of workers and titanic workshops,
destined for an unlimited output of goods which the
world could no longer afford and refused to accept,
completely idle. The day came when people began to
ask whether Mr. Ford, by systematizing his production,
replacing half his workmen by machines and making
those he kept work like machines, had not ended in a
delirium almost as dangerous in its way as that of the
Bolsheviks; they began to ask whether his madness was
very different from the Russian madness.

By dint of systematizing and organizing the factories,
the staffs employed in the United States had been reduced to such a point that, even if prosperity returned,
it would be impossible for all the discharged people to
find jobs. And serial production had been developed to
such a point in the manufacture of motor cars and
footwear and in various other branches of industrial
life that, as soon as the crisis was overcome, it would
need only a few months of unrestricted output to produce a fresh glut on the market, which would inevitably
bring about a fresh crisis before much time had elapsed.

During a very brief space of time, it seemed as if
there were plenty of room in America for both the
machine and for man. America was then at the zenith
of her glory, and the splendor of her industry irradiated
the world. This period is ended. The world has shrunk
back into itself; it is ruined and no longer wants to buy
anything; the glory and prosperity of America seem

to be undergoing an eclipse, and in the silent suburbs of
Detroit, in the poor and gloomy outskirts of Pittsburgh,
the machine lies forsaken, while, a little farther on, man
is dying of hunger.

Mr. Ford explains the drama thus: "It is not the
fault of my system," he says; "my system is the best
possible, but it has not been applied with sufficient
accuracy." However, the people of the United States
have just refused to continue the experiment; they have
turned down Mr. Ford's great technician friend; Mr.
Hoover has fallen; he has ceased to be President of the
United States and to be an oracle. He has withdrawn
into private life.

The professors in their lectures, the journalists in
their articles, and even the essayists, are beginning once
more to speak of the virtues and wisdom of handiwork.
They cite the example of France, Italy and other countries, once denounced as backward but now envied, for
they are less industrialized, less "standardized"; their
agricultural life is still independent and real, simple and
rustic, so that a stoppage of industry does not bring the
whole economic life of the country to a standstill.
Detroit, with its inconceivable destitution, is a tragic
spectacle. It would seem as if heaven, after having allowed Mr. Ford to witness the apotheosis of all his plans,
was determined to make him see the futility of every
human conceit, and as if suddenly a supreme and ironic
architect had shown him the other side of the picture.
The American crisis of 1929–1933 is not the bankruptcy
of world capitalism, but it is certainly the acid test of
Mr. Ford's methods. The machine is crushing man, and
man is cursing it.

Man is succumbing beneath the weight of the machines. But even this is not the most tragic spectacle afforded by modern America.

Whilst in our old Europe, science, with its methods and its hypotheses, is an incomparable stimulus to the human spirit, and young men and great scholars are thrilled with delight in its lucid exactitude, in America, on the contrary, great scholars, students and young people are far more conscious of the warm and sensuous contact with reality which science puts within their reach, and they devote themselves to scientific study in the hope of learning how to handle animate and inanimate matter more intimately, forcefully and effectively. American scholars, their pupils and their students are instinctively realizers; they make tools, machines and appliances. They do not so much fill their minds with their knowledge as fill their homes with objects to which their science relates.

Thus a strange void remains in the very heart of their personality! One is conscious of it in Mr. Ford, whose intellectual adventures have been sometimes grotesque, as in the case of his peace crusade, when he crammed upon an unseaworthy boat a number of old ladies and a miscellaneous assortment of dubious individuals. He had the good fortune to fall ill at Christiania, and to leave the expedition without undue difficulty, for he did not incur more ridicule than he was able to quench with the aid of his fortune.

A certain candor, a lack of logic, and a strong animal vitality protected Mr. Ford against himself and against his doctrines, but one of his fellow prophets furnished an example of the normal and tragic culmination of this destiny.

Mr. Eastman had invented modern photography; he had launched it in America and he had made it an immense adventure. He had spread the fame of the Eastman kodak into regions whither the fame of Alexander, of Napoleon or of Jenghiz Khan had never penetrated. Mr. Eastman had acquired an immense fortune, and, in his pleasant town of Rochester, he was a king. He reigned there with a splendor which shed its radiance upon all. Thanks to him, the university prospered; with his aid, a school of music had been founded; he maintained a conservatory and an opera, and all around Rochester and in all the United States, a whole constellation of universities and other institutions testified to the munificence of Mr. Eastman.

In his vast mansion, the staircase was adorned with flowers whose perfume penetrated into every room, and an organ, played every day by some expert, celebrated for Mr. Eastman's benefit the pathetic inventions of the human spirit. Here, in this huge, opulent and somber abode, Mr. Eastman dwelt with his genius and with a few intimate friends.

One day these friends were horrified to hear of his death.

After dinner, Mr. Eastman had retired to his study and had asked not to be disturbed. And he had committed suicide. He had prepared a very careful will and a very lucid statement. In it he said that life had lost all interest for him and that he had no more use for his own life, since he had put into practise all the useful ideas he had conceived, and had successfully carried out all the useful schemes he had planned. He killed himself, therefore, because he had nothing better to do. He tried to destroy the void which neither the fragrance

of the flowers nor the notes of the organ, neither the
memory of good deeds nor the workings of a powerful
mind, which had controlled billions of dollars, human
lives and the destiny of whole towns, had been able
to fill.

The death of this great prophet made a big sensation
in the United States. Then it was forgotten.

This was a mistake. Mr. Eastman is a symbol. Just as
the machine and the factory came to a standstill because there was nothing to feed them on, so Mr. Eastman's intelligence stopped short because it had closed
round a void. Perpetual association with machines had
robbed him of all his perceptions. This doctrine of mass,
this religion of production, if carried to its logical conclusion, would culminate in such a rigorous asceticism
that it would become fatal. People realize this now, and
are almost astonished that they were able to put up
with it so long.

They forget that it was coördinated and perfected,
thanks to the financial theories of the Republican Party,
and that the apostles of big American finance supplied
the people those violent emotions which Mr. Ford,
enamored of the pure joy of the machine, refused them.

CHAPTER III

BAR GOLD OR GOLDEN CALF

IN the twentieth century the world admired three great forces: the German army, the English navy and the American dollar. The heavy gold dollars, the light, firm paper dollars and those mysterious and formidable checks, which transmitted the prestige and influence of the dollar from one end of the globe to the other, swayed the passions of men from 1920 to 1930.

The dollar god was the great post-war god, when the German army was vanquished and the English navy was seeking new gods.

The dollar god was a powerful and imperturbable deity, which inspired in men, as becomes a deity, both awe and trust. Whilst the mark was indulging in feverish paroxysms, whilst the franc was perishing of inanition, after a few tragic convulsions, whilst the pound itself, after a long and serious illness, was obliged to amputate arms and legs and forfeit a third of its value, whilst all the small fry of foreign currencies were capering in every direction, the dollar god reigned immutable over the stock exchanges and over the dreams and desires of men; it attracted to itself all the speculators, all the workers and all the *rentiers*. It was the standard to which everything was reduced. The entire world kept its ac-

counts in dollars, and the world had, like America, acquired the habit of estimating everything in dollars.
In the clubrooms of America, solemn-faced gentlemen
wag their heads and say: "Oh, yes, So-and-So is worth
two million dollars!" And women exclaim: "What a
fine fire we have just seen! It was a five-million-dollar
blaze." And the father of a family declares with tender
pride, not in a vague and literary sense, as in Europe:
"That million-dollar kid of ours!" or, "He looks like a
million dollars." The dollar was the standard and common measure of everything.

From the deserts of Africa to the frozen tracts of
the Arctic, every region and every race, every nation and
every class bowed before the dollar god. Even Red
Russia, which we are taught to think of as austere and
disinterested, paid its tribute. The American engineers
received favored treatment from the Bolsheviks, and
when Mrs. Otto Kahn, the wife of the great New York
banker, went to visit the museums and curiosities of
Soviet Russia, the Government placed at her disposal
a special train and accorded her royal honors throughout her tour.

Bankers and bankers' wives were admired in the Rue
de la Paix, in Unter den Linden and in Timbuctoo. The
American banker spent the winter in Egypt, the spring
on the Riviera or in Paris, and June in London, where
he had himself presented to the King of England. Incidentally he had an interview with Mussolini, a blessing
from the Pope, a breakfast with Einstein, an evening
with Primo Carnera, an afternoon at the races with
Lord Derby and tea with Mlle. Chanel. The American
banker, high priest and representative of the dollar god,

reigned over the world and over America from 1920
to 1930.

His empire over America dated from farther back
and was connected with the party game in the New
World. The twentieth century had enriched the United
States and had encouraged the growth of a rich, active
and robust middle class. The bankers, being the richest,
most active and most robust, as well as the best-informed
members of this class, naturally set the tone; and as
they supplied the money to keep politics going, politics
could not do without them. They steered its course.

American politics in the twentieth century did not,
in fact, represent a battle of ideas, as in numerous
European countries, where parties with set programmes
wage bitter war against one another; nor was there any
acute class conflict, for the sense of class did not exist
in this new country, where every citizen had sufficient
naïveté, pride and respect for tradition to believe himself capable of arriving in a few years, by his own efforts,
at the summit of the social scale, if he worked hard
enough and had luck. American politics represented the
conflict of rival groups which wanted to gain power
or keep it and who tried, without any great intellectual
scruples but without deliberate dishonesty, to promise
the voter what they thought he wanted. Apart from
a few details, apart from a few traditional principles,
which were pompously announced rather than strictly
obeyed, the two parties in their proclamations tried to
gain the ear of the public by similar means. The victory,
therefore, inevitably went to the one who offered most
or offered it best. Politics was the art of handling men,
of presenting one's merchandise to them in an at-

tractive light, and of organizing a strong, brilliant,
adroit and docile team. The country was, according to
the Constitution, governed by the President and Congress, but the President and Congress had to obey the
instructions which their party gave them, and the latter, in its turn, was led by those who provided it with
the means of winning the game, of fighting and holding out, by those who had the sinews of war — the
financiers.

Every one knows that these money-lenders have
played a decisive part in the national and international
politics of the United States. Any one who has the
wisdom to offer and pay a big sum on behalf of a candidate for the Presidency or the Senate, or to the party
funds at a critical moment, may afterwards aspire to
a political post proportionate to the "effort" he has
made. Perhaps he will be a member of the Cabinet, as
happened to Mr. Mellon, who had financed the campaign of the Republican Senators of Pennsylvania
against the League of Nations and Mr. Wilson; perhaps
he will simply be "intimate adviser", as was the case with
a collaborator of Mr. Coolidge and as some really prefer,
for it gives them a mysterious power, much prestige
and no responsibility; or he may perhaps be sent on
vague and important missions to a foreign country, as
happened to Colonel House, a Houston banker and
Wilson's principal backer. In any case, he will have his
reward. Between 1920 and 1930, the compact group of
these capitalist money-lenders played a decisive rôle in
American politics. Without ever appearing in the front
of the stage, they made the laws, they secretly drafted
customs tariffs, controlled foreign policy and dictated

the appointments to many of the principal offices. They commanded all the avenues of power and, in fact, no young politician could be elected to office in America unless he had first been nominated in the "Primary." This is the name given to the elections which take place before the national elections. No ambitious young man can be a candidate for a great party unless he passes this test, and if nominated, his campaign expenses are usually supplied by his wealthy backers and friends.

Thus the *bourgeoisie* keeps a tight hold on its politicians, who always need its help; and the bankers keep a hold on the *bourgeoisie,* in whom they inspire respect and fear. The names of Rockefeller and Morgan are better known in the United States than those of Julius Cæsar and Hannibal; they are uttered more often and with more veneration than those of the recent Presidents of the United States. They possess for the people a more universal significance than the names of Hoover or Coolidge; and they fill the minds of old and young with dreams which no President of the United States could ever inspire in the masses. They are a living force, not the symbol of an office.

The great financiers of America are interested in political life, but they do not enter it, or only reluctantly. They merely touch it with the tips of their fingers and with distaste, although they like to play a hidden rôle in it and are quite determined to have it under their control. From time to time, they interest themselves in a politician who attracts them by the wisdom of his views, the charm of his personality or his skill as an angler. They then support him for the pleasure of the game.

They have their candidates, as a great English lord has his race horses.

The most brilliant epoch of American high finances was in the years 1919–1925. The capitalist had at that time immense sums at their disposal, for the profits from the war had not been squandered. They even had the ear of the country; the Americans do not like ideology as an everyday article of diet; they enjoy it from time to time, like exquisite cooking or alcohol, when they need emotion and uplift; but they object to it for daily consumption. Now Mr. Wilson made the mistake of feeding them on it, and of doing it in a tone which smacked of his university courses and his public lectures. People were tired of all that, of his League of Nations and of his crusade for democracy; they had had enough of all this justice, all this fraternity, all this philosophy and all these professors. They wanted facts and figures.

Under Mr. Harding the professors vanished from the scene. They were replaced by the experts, and the experts were bankers.

There was Mr. Dawes, who came to tell the French how they could make the Germans pay them without harming the Germans; to assist him he had Mr. Young and Mr. Robinson. Mr. Dawes was a Chicago banker, Mr. Young was a New York industrialist and financier, Mr. Robinson was a California banker, and all three were men of very distinguished minds, although the result of their efforts did not after all fulfill the hopes of the universe.

Then Mr. Young came back, and he brought with him Mr. Traylor, a Chicago banker, and once more he

gave the Allies a plan for securing payment, and to
Germany an agreeable and innocuous method of effect-
ing the payment. It was a very good plan, but we
know what happened to it.

Then Mr. Parker Gilbert, a banker, who is now a
member of the Morgan firm, installed himself in Berlin,
where he presided over the payments made by Germany
when Germany felt disposed to pay.

Then Mr. Gates W. McGarrah came to explain to
Europe how to reorganize her finances, and he was en-
throned at Basle.

The bankers reigned supreme in the world. They also
reigned supreme in America, where Mr. Harding had
taken Mr. Mellon, the biggest banker of Pittsburgh, as
Secretary of the Treasury, and it looked very much as
if Mr. Mellon, for all his taciturnity, was doing just as
he liked, although Mr. Harding made long speeches.

The dollar and the American bankers reigned over
Europe and over the United States. They had their own
creed, their conception of the universe and their outlook
upon destiny. They were not professors, but they too
had their system.

In good American society, a few years ago, the following anecdote was being circulated. A famous billionaire,
who has a fine estate in the island of Mount Desert,
off the coast of Maine, decided one year to give this
island, which is frequented by the upper ten of New
York and Philadelphia during the summer, a network of
roads, which was greatly needed. He sent for a contractor and signed with him a carefully drafted agreement. The agreement was so careful that at the end of
a year the contractor came to the famous billionaire

and said to him: "I can't go on; I'm losing twenty thousand dollars every month; let me have a new contract."

"No, my friend," replied the billionaire, affably, wisely, and piously, "we signed the contract in all good faith, and you must carry it out; you won't get any other. But, as I am a Christian, I will refund you the amount of your losses, if you will show me your invoices; and let this be a lesson to you to make your contracts more carefully in future or to keep a closer watch on your workmen."

The poor fellow argued to no purpose; he made no impression on the billionaire.

American big finance of the post-war period had a brutal and virile fashion of being rich. It scorned ideology; it took little interest in diplomacy; even politics it looked upon as bunk, and the Government as a necessary evil which it must try to reduce to the minimum and confine within strict bounds. All would be well, they said, if only things were allowed to take their own course and people were allowed to make money. No ideology, very little diplomacy, and that, above all, a gentlemanly diplomacy good for dinners and official receptions, and the least possible government. Such was the formula. Everything was to be related to economic life, everything reduced to the sound, immutable, simple and fruitful laws of political economy. Thus, with courage, optimism, work, a little luck and a lot of money, they could gain more money, be happy and, incidentally, make the world happy, since prosperity is infectious, and, by procuring it in the first place directly for oneself, one procured it afterwards indirectly for others.

Under the influence of this group, the United States,

which was already being driven in this direction by time-honored traditions, became less and less interested in European political life. America did not sign the Treaty of Versailles; she repudiated the pact of guarantee promised to France, she scoffed at the League of Nations. She stopped sending official representatives to the big international conferences. She contented herself with "safeguarding American interests": that is to say, with dispatching to the Old World bankers whose duty it was to listen to what was happening and whose right it was to say "No," if they thought America would lose anything by the decisions. These species of diplomatic eunuchs, who were not diplomats and often had large families, were called "unofficial or official observers", and when one considers the rôle they played during these critical years, one is equally astonished to think that there should have existed intelligent and honest men willing to accept this rôle and great nations willing to tolerate such proceedings.

America had, in principle, renounced all foreign policy. Such was the pure doctrine of Mrs. Harding, and therefore of Mr. Harding; such was the impeccable doctrine of Mr. Coolidge. Such was the aspiration of Mr. Hoover. But as America did not like to leave the world without some compensation and some benefits, she not only sent the world "observers", but also encouraged her great banks to bestir themselves, to export capital and to acquire interests all over the world. America refused to have political dealings with foreign countries, but she made investments in foreign countries.

The American people did not sufficiently trust its statesmen and politicians to send them abroad; it did

not sufficiently trust its diplomats to authorize them
to do anything active and positive in the world; but it
had such immense confidence in its bankers that it allowed them to go wherever they saw fit, they and the
money of the country, and to do as they liked on their
own initiative but with the discreet backing of the
Government. The National City Bank; the Bankers'
Trust; the house of Morgan; Goldman, Sachs; Dillon,
Read and Company and the Mellon National Bank acquired interests and lent money in every corner of the
globe. And Mr. Hoover's first gesture, once he had been
elected, was to tour South America, not as a President,
nor even as a politician, but as a merchant examining
the markets with a view to extending his business. We
have already noted the list of America's banker representatives in Europe between 1920 and 1932. Need we
add that the United States ambassador in London was
first Mr. Dawes, a Chicago banker, and then Mr. Mellon,
a Pittsburgh banker? And that Mr. Eugene Meyer,
banker and millionaire, was entrusted with the task of
saving the country by means of the "Reconstruction
Finance Corporation", of which he was appointed chairman. Mr. Edge, financier and millionaire, was ambassador in Paris; and the wealthy capitalist and big
financier, Ogden Mills, was the last hope of the Republican Party in 1932. The big banks seemed the pillars
of American greatness.

The most tragic shipwreck of modern times was that
which engulfed the reputation of Andrew Mellon, for,
of all the bankers of the United States, Andrew Mellon
had stood out as the leader of this great movement, and,
from 1920 to 1930, it was regarded as a clear, indis-

putable and self-evident truth that, ever since the foundation of the United States and with the exception of the first Secretary of the Treasury of the United States, Alexander Hamilton, who had genius, the United States had never known a Secretary of the Treasury comparable in wisdom, judgment, shrewdness and luck, with Mr. Andrew Mellon, Secretary of the Treasury under Mr. Harding, Mr. Coolidge and Mr. Hoover, formerly chairman of the Mellon National Bank at Pittsburgh and archetype of the powerful American banker.

This was the general opinion from 1920 to 1930. In 1931 a game was in vogue which consisted in some one asking: "Who is Andrew Mellon?" and in some one else replying: "The man who died of good health," or "The man whose success was a failure," or, more simply, "The man who stayed too late."

Mr. Mellon is a little man with eyebrows which spread all over his face. His looks, his words, his movements cannot get past these eyebrows. When he talks, when he stammers, when he addresses you, he looks at your dog, if, by good luck, you have a dog, or at your shoes if you have no dog. If your shoes are hidden, he does not know where to look, and he does not look at anything. If he sees that you are listening to him, it embarrasses him; and if you are not listening to him, it annoys him. One day, after he had just concluded a long political speech in honor of Alexander Hamilton, his illustrious predecessor and patron saint, a polite and embarrassed journalist came up to him and said:

"I am quite ashamed of my audacity, Mr. Mellon, but I should be very grateful if you could let me have the text of your speech. No doubt I was badly placed, for, though I listened as hard as I could, I couldn't hear what you were saying."

"So much the better," retorted Mr. Mellon, and he made off with his speech and never saw the journalist again.

Mr. Mellon does not like talking, but he likes acting. And, in the course of his life, he has acted a great deal. Behind his eyebrows he thinks quickly and shrewdly, and he decides quickly and clearly. He has flair, resolution and courage. He had them from the outset of his career and he kept them to the end. To his courage he owed the brilliant beginning of his career, and to his courage, no doubt, he owed its long duration. When he was twenty years of age, his father, a Scotsman who had emigrated from the south coast of the United States in order to settle in Pittsburgh, where he had made a handsome fortune, decided to give his two sons a nice little sum to enable them to have a business of their own. Andrew was the elder and the manager. He agreed with his brother to found a timber business, which started off quite well. A few months later the father was dumb-founded to see his sons arrive and ask him for work.

"Why, what's happened to your business?" he asked.

"We've sold it," they replied, "because we are sure that a crisis is impending."

The father was delighted. His sons had perceived before himself the signs which heralded the storm. In his enthusiasm he took them immediately into his bank, and after a few years he left Andrew at the head of his business. Andrew Mellon was at that time not yet twenty-five years of age. Under his management, the bank prospered; he worked in collaboration with Frick, who was shrewd, able and as astute as himself.

Andrew Mellon had studied at Pittsburgh, but there was not much to be said about that. He was a man who liked reading, but no one ever knew what book he was reading. He had a taste for the arts and he bought pic-✓ tures, but he did not show them to any one. He was a good son and a good husband, but there was little to say about that either, for he did not like speaking of it. He was extremely powerful in the industrial world of Pennsylvania, he had constructed the first private pipe line for conveying petroleum into this region and he was a member of more than a hundred boards of directors, but of that he never spoke, or hardly ever, and it was wiser not to speak to him about it, for he inspired a profound awe among the people of Pittsburgh. He was very generous, but he did not like any one to mention his benefactions to him. He was very active in politics, always ready to subsidize a good cause and to assist his Republican friends to defend the party, but he objected to any one speaking of it. He was one of the most powerful financiers in the United States and one of the most studiously hidden. He had succeeded in everything he had undertaken, and he had even succeeded in passing unnoticed. He made so great an impression on the people of Pittsburgh, and those who came in contact with him, that they did not dare to speak of him, and he made so little impression on the people outside, who did not know him, that they never spoke of him.

In 1920, however, when the Republican Party, with the support of the *bourgeoisie* and the collaboration of

high finance, won the day and crushed the party of
Wilson, now infirm and defeated, the shrewder politicians felt that they ought to make room for bankers
in the government and that this would help them to remain in close contact with the party and the Administration. But there could be no question of taking any
one from Kuhn Loeb; they were too Germanic. The
Morgans were too well known, and Mr. Morgan would
not have consented. In the Bankers' Trust, the National
City Bank and the other New York banks, there was no
one who seemed quite suitable. No one at San Francisco,
no one at Chicago. But at Pittsburgh was this dark little
man, with his beetle brows and the air of a long-toothed
gray mouse, whose loyalty was as well known to the
party as were his skill and energy to the district.

As soon as he was elected, Mr. Harding, at the advice of the Republican Senators of Pennsylvania, invited Mr. Mellon to come and see him in his modest
little cottage at Marion. Mr. Mellon did not wait to be
asked twice; he set off then and there. Mr. Harding received him, and they had a long conversation. This
honor alarmed Mr. Mellon. He was prepared for it by
his knowledge of men and his experience of political
life, but his knowledge of men and of politics made him
averse to accepting it. Mr. Harding flattered him, patted him on the back, spoke to him of duty, fatherland
and civic obligation. Finally Mr. Mellon said, as he took
his leave, that he would think it over, and he set out for
the railway station on foot.

"Wait a moment," said Mr. Harding suddenly. "I
will send for my chauffeur and the car."

"No," replied Mellon, "no, no, I prefer to walk."
And he set off at a gentle trot through the summer dust,

with his gray overcoat over his left arm and his great
eyebrows drawn so closely together that his eyes were
completely hidden.

He thought it over and he accepted. He resigned from
the hundred boards of directors of which he was chairman or member. He retired from active life, from business and from his bank. And he settled down in Washington. There he toiled diligently and methodically. He
conscientiously attended all the meetings of the Cabinet
and was studiously attentive and studiously silent.

"What do you think about this question?" Mr. Harding, who believed in the wisdom of humanity and
loved the sound of words, would ask Mr. Mellon, who
was silent.

As a rule, Mr. Mellon was greatly embarrassed. Sometimes he was more fortunate; he had an opinion, and he
was able to reply promptly and positively: "Mr. President, I entirely share the opinion of my colleagues who
have just spoken."

However, he had his doctrine, and it would be unjust
not to make some mention of it.

Mr. Mellon maintained that every well-governed
State must keep its expenditure below its revenue. This
did not seem a paradox to him.

He thought that the national debt ought to be paid.

He thought that the best course for a Government to
pursue was to impose upon the country the lightest
possible taxes, in fact, only just enough to pay its bills,
and he forced Congress to adopt this policy.

He thought that the public credit should be untiringly
fostered and safeguarded, and he did not forget this
rule.

For the rest, he thought that the less a State governs,

the better the country prospers, and he strove to obey this maxim.

He began, to the great scandal of good politicians, by retaining all the distinguished officials whom the Democrats had placed in the Treasury. This caused a great uproar among the politicians, and his Assistant Secretary of the Treasury even tried to force his hand. The Assistant Secretary was dismissed. Thus the politicians learned from Mr. Mellon that they could touch what they liked, but that the fraternity of bankers was outside and above their sphere. They had to submit, but they bore him a grudge which was later to find vent.

Then Mr. Mellon set to work. The United States had at that time what was apparently a crushing debt, though really it was not at all heavy for so rich a country. Mr. Mellon succeeded in reducing it by nine billion dollars. Three times he reduced the income tax, and he ended by saving the American taxpayers, in the course of eight years, an expenditure of eighteen hundred million dollars.

He attacked the problem of the inter-Allied debts, and, despite the repugnance of the European Governments, despite the indignation and resistance of the European peoples, despite the indignant protests of the European Press, he managed to make them sign agreements providing for a regular payment of the sums which had been lent to them by the United States. He succeeded so well that he was afterwards able to prove to his fellow citizens that they had done a very good stroke of business, since France was going to pay them 2,734 millions, Belgium 302 millions and Italy 782 millions, whilst he proved to these foreign nations that America had been extremely generous towards them, since she had only demanded from France a payment of 1,680 millions, from Belgium 180 millions and from Italy 426 millions. That was splendid, and very satisfactory to everybody.

Unfortunately, it seemed as if on this occasion Mr. Mellon had talked too much. The Europeans knew the figures which Mr. Mellon was circulating for internal use, and the Americans knew the figures which Mr. Mellon was presenting to the Europeans, and, as these figures conflicted, he found himself cornered by his own statements. The newspapers poked fun at him, and jeered at "the gentleman who drafted Mr. Mellon's reports." But what did this matter to Mr. Mellon? He was rich, happy and securely installed. He liked Washington. He had ended by adapting himself to the city and he lived there very comfortably. He was in no hurry to leave. The little footpaths beneath the big trees, the little golf parties, the little receptions given by the old ladies, and the little gossips in a little circle of well-bred people — all this suited him very well. He did not lose his temper; he let his prosperity speak for him. It spoke so loud that people were bound to recognize him as a great man.

But one day it stopped speaking. People were becoming uneasy. Mr. Mellon assured them that it was all nothing. And he tried to check the downward trend of the market by a fresh reduction of income taxes. This was in the spring of 1930. The market stopped falling for a moment, but only to recover its breath; it very soon resumed its headlong progress towards catastrophe, and Mr. Mellon panted behind securities which were in full flight, bonds which were put to the rout and quotations which were in a state of panic. He was prodigal of optimistic and encouraging assurances; he announced, and he made Mr. Hoover announce, that all that was needed was a little patience, just a little more patience. "Prosperity is just around the corner." But there it stayed. Nothing helped to mend matters. Everything was going from bad to worse.

Then people began to notice that Mr. Mellon was a little gray man, that he stammered, that he lacked dignity, assurance and elegance, that he often made mistakes in the figures of his statistics and that he was getting old. They said it to themselves and they said it to Mr. Hoover. They even told him that the presence of Mr. Mellon in the Cabinet was likely to be harmful to the President and to his reëlection.

Mr. Hoover did not know what to answer. He does not like unpopularity. In relation to himself, he can put up with it, but in relation to others it seems to him intolerable. Moreover, he had no reason for being loyal to Mr. Mellon, who had done his best to block his way to the Presidency, and who had only rallied to his side for lack of anything better to do. He therefore intimated to Mr. Mellon that it seemed time he had a rest, or rather he tried to intimate this. But Mr. Mellon was somewhat deaf and refused to take it in. After all, he felt very young, power had given him a new lease of life, and it seemed to him that, after ten years at the Treasury, he would be a boy again. There was no hope of persuading him to quit. The case called for a desperate measure. Mr. Mellon was dispatched as am-

bassador to Great Britain, and America breathed a sigh
of relief.

But already all was lost.

In America and in Europe people had too much admired the big financiers who directed the dance of prosperity not to hate them when the catastrophe arrived.

Their assurance had astonished the world, and as long
as their assurance had guided the public along a path
which afforded possibilities of self-enrichment, it had
seemed on a par with the reckless daring of the
conquistadors. When it had ceased to be anything but
the portent of catastrophe, it seemed an insufferable
arrogance and the people thirsted for justice and
vengeance.

People scoffed at the creed which all had been putting
into practice for the last ten years with blind and con-
sistent faith. They were now incensed against both the
creed and its apostles.

It was then that Charles E. Mitchell became famous.

Mr. Mitchell is a big man with a big nose and a big
straight mouth, not fat nor heavy nor unctuous, but,
on the contrary, brusque, lively and spontaneous. But
his brusqueness is not the brusqueness of a general,
there is nothing youthful in his vivacity, and his spontaneity only charms the person to whom he is speaking.
He has all the good qualities, all the smartness and dash
of a commercial traveler who, after having cleared off
all his stock, has nothing to sell but gold mines and is
sure of selling them. He does not seem to be gifted with
an intelligence above the average, nor with any remarkable erudition, nor with any particular skill, and one

might well wonder what curious and capricious destiny saw fit to raise him to the summit of financial power and make him chairman of the Board of Directors of the richest bank in the world, the National City Bank, unless one had discovered, by means of comparison, that Mr. Mitchell possesses something that is lacking in almost all other members of American boards of directors: he loves the game he is playing and this game is good for his health. American boards of directors are filled with worthy gentlemen who have for the most part succeeded in a small way in a big business and who, because of this great adventure in which their small persons have been engaged, are filled with a great vanity and an infinite weariness. They would gladly have done with all these complications, but they dare not pocket their winnings and throw up the game, for the habit of business holds them in thrall, and the instinct of the game, which has survived enjoyment of the game, makes them loath to quit a contest in which they no longer hope or even desire to win, but in which they are afraid of losing what they have won already. They have stomach-ache, headache, and heartache.

Consequently, when they are confronted with a "high pressure salesman" like Mr. Charles E. Mitchell, who tells them flatly and vehemently what they would like to believe, who saves them the anxiety of looking ahead and spares them the trouble of grasping the final outcome of their actions, they feel for him an affection which may be exalted to a tender gratitude, and a trust as blind as love.

That Charles E. Mitchell was not intelligent afterwards became evident, but it must not be forgotten that he was intelligent enough to understand what his group wanted. On their behalf he created, launched, circulated and celebrated his famous theory of fruitful speculation, of a speculation automatically productive of well-being, prosperity and wealth. He upheld it in Paris, and in America he won numerous converts to it. It was, moreover, a brilliant theory.

Speculation on a rise, Mr. Mitchell maintained, consists in promoting a rise in the quotations of industrial shares; that is to say, in increasing their value: that is to say, in enriching those who have bought them. That is perfectly clear.

By reason of this very fact, those who possess these shares, and who have become richer, are able to buy more. They do not bury their money; they put it into circulation; they buy themselves motor cars, pictures, houses and jewels. This new money enables them to procure all the things they desire, and this gives industry a larger and hungrier circle of customers and a better market. That too is clear.

Consequently, speculation, by enriching the speculator, enriches the industrialist. It is not a swindle, since it really creates wealth; it is a social benefit. It is an indispensable state of mind in a rich and powerful nation. Without it there can be no money in circulation, no market for industry. The speculator, according to Mr. Mitchell's theory, was the true philosopher of the modern world. People ought to crown him with flowers and lavish civic honors upon him, and, above all, not discourage him, not hamper him or check the beneficent course of his philanthropic activities.

The public listened, rather bewildered and vaguely

uneasy. The journalists wrote and repeated these homilies, filled with admiration. They understood. Mr.
Mitchell was one of themselves; he said, in fact, that by
dint of talking of wealth, one created it. This was natural at a time when words were so powerful. Formerly
things and people created their words; to-day words
create things and the people for these things. For at
least a hundred and fifty years it was thus in politics.
Why should it not be thus with political economy and
finance?

Formerly wealth created the appearance of wealth,
the expression of wealth and the innumerable social,
verbal and administrative repercussions of wealth. Why
not admit that at the present day these repercussions, in
their turn, and the expression of wealth, by creating the
appearance of wealth, must end by creating the reality?
Thus, by dint of speculating for a rise, one would create
new wealth. Alleluiah!

America had chanted Alleluiah with Mr. Mitchell.
It had gambled on a rise. In the smallest towns of the
United States, in the obscure hamlets at the edge of the
forests, on the shores of the Great Lakes or among the
swamps of Louisiana, people gambled on a rise, and
eagerly watched the quotations on the Stock Exchange.
In little French towns, after the market, the drover of
oxen called in at the café to have a look at the New
York quotations. The old marquise, on her "At Home"
day, had on a table in the corner, by the side of the
cards for Boston and whist, the list of American quotations, which her banker made her read. The whole world
was speculating on New York and on the mirage of
New York's wealth. And Mr. Mitchell, at the beginning

of the autumn of 1929, explained to the French that things were going very well and that the principle of perpetual movement in political economy had been discovered.

A number of people, in the summer of 1929, asked themselves why it shouldn't be true and began to doubt their own doubts.

The autumn changed all that.

Mr. Mitchell and his colleagues had built up a magnificent machine, which was to make gold and which made it, but which suddenly collapsed, leaving only some dirty paper.

They had discovered a means of speculating several times on the same security and of multiplying each rise. Upon the various large and important corporations they had superimposed "Investment Trusts." The latter did nothing except invest the money which people entrusted to them. But they issued their own shares. And, when the shares which they had bought by way of investment rose, their shares rose too. A rise at one point of the circuit was sufficient to cause a reflected rise. This ingenious idea, by reflecting the image and appearance of wealth, was bound in its turn to augment it.

For some months it did augment it, but when the public began to doubt the industrial concerns on which the guarantee of the Trusts' securities was based, it lost all confidence in the investment trusts and in their securities, which were henceforward supported on a void. These securities dropped with a vertical fall. They might have been pebbles flung from a roof. In a few weeks, in a few days, some, and not the worst, tumbled from a hundred down to one, and did not even stop there.

Mr. Mitchell had not seen that, by multiplying movement, he had multiplied it in every direction, and that
he aggravated the importance of all financial, economic
and social oscillations. As the hope of wealth had sufficed to create real wealth, so the fear of poverty sufficed
to create real poverty and to destroy real wealth. Enterprises to all appearance capable of resistance were swallowed up in the panic. As confidence had created real
wealth from nothing, so loss of confidence transformed
real wealth into nothing. No one could do anything
about it.

Mr. Mitchell still smiled. In such cases, smiling is
a duty. Moreover, it is one's only chance of escape.
Mr. Mitchell smiled as Mr. Hoover smiled and as some
victims of the law smile above the cord which has
hanged them. He smiled and he talked, in the hope of
rallying the crowd to his support. But he was not easy
in his mind, for the shares of his own bank had dropped
considerably. He was surrounded by a rising tide of
hatred. People hated him because they had believed in
him. They hated him because of his smile. They hated
him because of his sonorous voice.

And it was this sonorous voice which caused his down-
fall.

The Senate had summoned the bankers to come and
explain their methods, and the Senate, very naturally,
was not well-disposed towards the bankers, the less so
since, knowing itself to be not very popular, it was in
quest of a scapegoat. It thought of the bankers and,
more particularly, of Mr. Mitchell, whom it honored
with a special invitation.

Mr. Mitchell made a point of accepting it. To tell the truth, he could not do anything else.

He repaired to Washington and appeared before the Senate. This was fatal to him. He was questioned and he replied. The Senators made long speeches. Mr. Mitchell spoke, in loud, clear and sonorous accents. And this was where he made a hopeless mistake.

As they listened to him, the Senators opened their eyes very wide, then they opened their mouths very wide, and finally, when they closed them again, their souls were filled with exultation; they beheld their prey. Charles Mitchell, the wretch, the scoundrel. . .

Mr. Mitchell had explained his methods. He had been precise, clear, formal and sonorous, as he always was. He had described the method which he employed in order to avoid paying too much in taxes. There is a curious law in America. Every one pays a special tax on the increase in value over the purchase price of any security which he sells. He has to declare this increase, and he pays a tax in proportion to its amount. He also has the right to declare his losses on such sales and these may affect his profits. In order to prove his losses, he must have sold the securities on which he declares a loss and not have repurchased them for thirty days.

This was a tax on speculation, very reasonable at a time when speculation was the great game of the American nation. But it was a dangerous tax, for it enabled the artful to contrive matters so that they need never pay these taxes. All that was needed was a few friends and a little dexterity.

This is what Mr. Mitchell did. He was chairman of such a big bank that he had a great many friends, and, touching to relate, his wife seems to have been one of his best friends. In 1929–1930, in order to avoid paying his income tax, he sold to his wife an enormous block of the shares of the National City Bank, his own bank, which he held, representing a total value of over three and a half million dollars. It was a fine stroke of business, and it yielded excellent results. Mr. Mitchell had no income tax to pay that year.

There would have been no great harm in that. A number of people did as Mr. Mitchell did. But he told the Senate all about it, which no one had done before. And the Senate leaped to its feet. It made speeches.

Mr. Mitchell had talked too much. It was a subject upon which he would have done much better to say nothing. For the shares of the National City Bank which Mr. Mitchell had sold to Mrs. Mitchell were not in his possession; they were deposited as a guarantee with Mr. Morgan, and Mrs. Mitchell had neither bought them nor paid for them. Concerning these two minor but delicate points, Mr. Mitchell's first declaration had been inaccurate. This was to cause him a lot of trouble afterwards.

Moreover, a number of other charges were brought against him, based on his declarations before the Senate.

It seems that Mr. Mitchell, as chairman of the National City Bank, had drawn a salary of some twenty-five thousand dollars per annum. But in three years he drew three million dollars in the form of bonuses.

It seems that Mr. Mitchell and his colleagues on the Board of Directors obtained from the bank advances to assist them in maintaining their position on the market, a bull position on a bear market, which is a very costly business. It cost the National City Bank a good round sum, a sum which the members of its Board of Directors borrowed from it and neglected to repay. This really made a very bad impression.

It also appears that the bank, on the occasion of a new issue of its shares, had induced the subordinate members of its staff to subscribe, and, in order to facilitate these purchases, had allowed them to pay by monthly installments deducted from their salaries. Unfortunately, the shares began to drop, and the employees continued to pay long after the securities had dropped well below the sums they had already paid. This, too, did not make a good impression.

Lastly, it appeared that the National City Bank had launched Peruvian loans upon its public, with much enthusiasm and flourishing of trumpets, at a time when it must have known that the Peruvian credit was dubious. The American financial attaché in Peru had warned the bank, which had refused to listen to him. It placed the loan with its public who, of necessity, presently saw the loan drop to zero. The effect of this revelation was deplorable.

The public could forgive Mr. Mitchell for deceiving the Government; perhaps he had done it for love of his wife. The public would have overlooked, though not quite so easily, the cavalier fashion in which the small employees of the National City Bank had been treated. But the public could not forget the tricks played on the public itself. Mr. Mitchell was disgraced.

He became the symbol of arrogance.

He became the symbol of the wicked banker. The banker became the symbol of evil.

The bankers no longer had it all their own way. America shook herself and turned over, like a sleeper awakening after a nightmare. She tried to pull herself together, but in America and throughout the world the dream continued.

On one of these occasions when America shook herself, the result was the closing of all the banks in the United States, an incident which gave a good deal of pleasure to the world but distressed the United States.

On another occasion, it caused the collapse of the dollar, which seemed to grieve the world and afford considerable pleasure to the United States.

After the German army and the English navy, the third of the great powers which the white nations had contrived to create collapsed before the eyes of the world.

And this was the beginning of an era and the end of an era.

CHAPTER IV

THE GRAVEDIGGERS

THE world was at first astonished at this sudden collapse. Then, upon reflection, people discovered that it was only natural. They had been waiting for it; they had foreseen it. For ten years, at least, a whole group of Americans never tired of proclaiming to the world the bankruptcy of the United States. They were patriots after their fashion, but their fashion of being patriots was to detest the United States, or at any rate the States as they appeared in 1929–1930, and, as these individuals lived in the United States and suffered from the United States, they infused into their denunciation an energy, a precision and a virulence which were very convincing.

It was a sort of religious war.

For some decades there had been signs of a decline of Protestant Christianity in America. At first the dogmas seemed to become blunt and insipid. Then the hierarchy had been seen to crumble. Finally, the morality had been subjected to attack. To tell the truth, it resisted, and the religious instinct, so strong and so general in the United States, seemed to take refuge and become concentrated in a kind of moralizing zeal which found expression in various ways in every region of the Union. All sorts of groups — young women, old maids, young

men, married men, etc. — made it their mission to impose on themselves or their neighbors some privation
or another supposed to be moral: abstinence from alcohol, renunciation of cigars and cigarettes, veto on the-
aters and Sunday sports, prohibition of games of chance
and of lotteries, etc., etc. But at the same time there
was growing up, in this intoxicating climate and under
the influence of this healthy, fortifying and abundant
diet, of this growing luxury and of this so greatly
vaunted liberty, an avid, white-skinned race, with a tall,
supple, feverish and pagan body. The more her moral
institutions tried to curb America, the more did her
life incite her to succumb to a voluptuous paganism.

Very soon there ensued a conflict, which was not, to
tell the truth, a conflict between heaven and hell, between paganism and Christianity, between God and the
devil, for neither the one nor the other intervened directly; it was a conflict between their contingent and
presumptive heirs: the "Rotarians", anxious to succeed
God, and the "Radicals", eager to supersede the devil.

In many little American towns, but, above all, in the
medium-sized and small towns, the two bulwarks of
order and morality are the Y.M.C.A. and the Rotarians.

The Y.M.C.A. is the last form assumed by Protestant
religious zeal in the Protestant denominations. Since
dogmatic preaching has become practically impossible,
since the hierarchy no longer interests any one, and since
the rules of morality have lost their clear precision, the
only thing left to do is to try to create on earth an
atmosphere of happiness and good will and to rear
a younger generation which shall live in this aureole
and see no other. The Y.M.C.A.'s are a combination of

hotel, gymnasium, school and club which radiate a
good nature suggestive of the commercial traveler, and
in a corner of which there cowers a poor, timid, nervous
and humiliated God. They do good; they get together
thousands of nice young men of small means and supply
them with a certain amount of comfort, of happiness
and of social life. They are sometimes rather clever;
sometimes even they become important, but they always remain ambiguous, and their goodness is often
vaguely redolent of hypocrisy.

They are supported by the churches, which supply
their staff and a part of their funds, and by the business men of the town, who give them the resources they
need. In fact, in every American town, north or south,
west or east, the commercial *bourgeoisie* is conservative
and does its best to be religious. It supports the Y.M.C.A.
and it patronizes the clubs of the Rotarians, Kiwanis,
Chautauquas, Moose, Lions, etc., etc., for they are
legion.

These are not true Freemasonry institutions, although
they have more than one tie with true Freemasonry.
They are commercial and moral associations. In every
town where they appear the Rotarians group the best
dentist, the best doctor, the best furniture dealer, the
best painter, the best baseball player, the best pastor,
the best theatrical impresario and the largest capitalist,
if it is possible to win his adherence. One day a week
they meet for lunch, and on this day they divest themselves of their ordinary personality and become Bill,
Tom, Dick, Pat, Walt, etc. They take each other by
the arm, they slap each other on the back, and they sing
in chorus. Between the courses couplets are chanted

with a vigor and zest far exceeding the vocal talents of the executants; then, at the end of the lunch, there is a short lecture and some friendly and useful gossip.

Just as Mr. Mitchell imagined that wealth could be created by believing that it existed and speculating on it, so the Rotarian imagines that goodness can be created by believing in it and speculating on it. He represents a romantic tradition of systematic and chromolithographic goodness, which seems out of date in our Old World but is well suited to certain American tendencies and to the American taste for advertisement. By dint of speaking well of his district, the Rotarian believes that he will attract to it tourists, factories and wealth, and that he will add to its charms. By dint of proclaiming happiness, goodness and human peace, and of extolling prosperity, he believes that happiness and peace will reign among men and that prosperity will become the universal rule. And, in order to make it still more sure, at his banquets he drinks water and sings — out of tune but at the top of his voice — college refrains and sentimental ditties.

It seems rather curious that in a modern nation any one should dream of preventing people from drinking what they choose, and that this veto should kindle in its partisans a mystic zeal. But it must be remembered that in a number of cults and creeds, religion is the almost exclusive domain of the female sex and that such men as play any part in it take on, when they enter the religious domain, a feminine psychology. This is particularly true as regards the Protestant cults, where such immense scope is given to sensibility, whilst the domain of the intelligence is often reduced to nearly nothing.

Now the secret enemy and perpetual rival of woman during the eighteenth and nineteenth centuries was undoubtedly drink. In his brief and monotonous life, man suffers from boredom. Rarely do his adventures give him sufficient delight to console or distract him. Rarely do his successes suffice to content him. Woman alone can afford him oblivion and pride, if only she is clever enough. But wine, beer, whisky and gin do not need any cleverness in order to make a man forget everything and make him proud of himself, even if, in the sequel, he has to expiate this pride by a number of humiliations.

In a climate as violent as that of America, the temptation of drink and the attraction of drunkenness are fatally irresistible to a number of weak natures. And woman, being stronger than man, less tired because she has less physical exertion to make, and more calculating, was swift to perceive all the harm which drink did to man and all the wrong which it did to woman. The feminine crusade against alcoholism and against all fermented liquor is of ancient date in the United States, and it has never stopped. But until 1916 it had not succeeded in mobilizing for its purposes a sufficiently large number of forces and groups to make it a national institution.

In 1916 the United States passed through a crisis which culminated in the establishment of prohibition. The churches knew themselves to be directly menaced by the decline of religious zeal. They were also conscious that the war had temporarily revived their strength and influence. In 1916, national industry, which had undergone a sudden and far-reaching development by reason

of the World War, had at its disposal vast sums and
felt itself mistress of the situation. It wanted to assert
its sway and to cure men of any temptation to revolt.

In 1916–1920 — thanks to the stormy events, which
were overexciting all emotions and making men more
malleable; thanks to the military service which was removing several millions of young electors; and thanks
to the universal craving for sympathy and heroism —
the women of the United States — mothers, wives, sisters, sweethearts — had at their disposal such influence
as they had never possessed before and were perhaps
never to possess again. They knew it and they took advantage of it.

Thus there was formed a bloc of zealous Protestants
who, seeing little hope of saving everything, wanted at
least to save public morality, of manufacturers who
wanted to increase the output of the human machine
and rid themselves of dangerous competition, and of
women who hated drunkenness and could not bring
themselves to tolerate so dangerous and so base a rival.
Certain of the big capitalists, such as Mr. Rockefeller,
advanced large sums of money to the Anti-saloon
League. The Baptist Church and the Methodist Church
took the thing in hand, whilst the Episcopalians continued cold, the Catholics were hostile, and the Jews
gave vent to shrill cries of indignation. The Federal
Government was not enthusiastic and the sensible people
were horrified, but the Government had other difficulties to cope with, and the sensible people in America,
as everywhere else, are not very numerous, not very
well organized and not very active. Prohibition gained
a swift and complete victory. It too was a form of
drunkenness.

Congress voted it, the President accepted it, the States ratified it and the courts enforced it. It forbade the citizens of America to drink beverages containing more than one half of one per cent. of alcohol. Thus beer and wine were ruled out, together with gin, whisky, brandy, and other strong drinks. All such things were sinful and evil. The bars were closed, the restaurants and clubs were forbidden to sell any "alcohol", private persons were not allowed to transport alcoholic beverages; even the doctors were not allowed to prescribe to their patients more than a fixed and very small proportion of alcohol. There was no longer any legal means of drinking wine and beer. Prohibition crushed the hydra of drunkenness and with it destroyed all alcoholic liquor.

It created the bootlegger. From every disreputable corner of the United States, from every frontier and every port, the bootleggers thronged, half bandits, half smugglers, always ready to sell you for an exorbitant price horrible liquids masquerading under familiar names and to swindle you without ceremony. The bar and the saloon vanished. The bootlegger and the "speakeasy" succeeded them. For the pleasure of drinking delicious liquors was substituted that of drinking forbidden liquors and of cheating the Government. It was a case of finding your man. Every citizen, figuratively speaking, had his bootlegger, as he had his tailor and his dentist. Every citizen, including those who, for their neighbor's good, had voted prohibition, paid for the violation of prohibition. They paid taxes for the application of prohibition and paid the bootleggers who violated prohibition on their behalf. Similarly the police who applied prohibition at the same time trafficked in

liquors, either coming to an understanding with the
bootleggers and the restaurants to facilitate their trade,
or practising it themselves directly. Where before there
had been excess of liquor, there was now not only excess
of liquor but also social deceit, official corruption, sub-
sidies to brigands and political trading. It became a social organization, an institution and the biggest school
of vice that any nation has ever allowed to be set up in
its territory.

The young people, the artists, the upper classes, all
those who had a taste for independence and refinement,
were the most attracted by this fever of drink and adventure, but the whole nation shared in the game, in
the deception and in the debauch.

It continued for ten years. People drinking everywhere. The most respectable houses had been transformed into a species of bar, where one was offered the
most poisonous and atrocious concoctions. People hid
themselves in their cars, their offices or their studies,
in order to drink. Men concealed a flask of whisky in
the lining of their overcoat when they went to a ball,
and it was very necessary, for without it, some of the
prettiest girls would have declined to dance with them.
Every one did it, every one said it, every one saw it,
and the absurd carnival continued.

Prohibition was an institution; it was a part of the
American creed, and the Protestant churches could not
forsake it without inflicting upon themselves a crushing
defeat. They preferred to wait; they tried to palliate
the evil.

But more and more, in optimistic America, where
every one insisted that progress was guiding men towards

happiness, temperance and virtue, towards reason and prosperity, a blind, grinning prohibition, red with wine and red with blood, fingering an unclean, mud-stained gold, was proving to all that the modern world too was able to create new and infamous vices and to revive all the old forms of hypocrisy.

It was easy to laugh. But some races do not laugh. In America, where the Anglo-Saxon race reigned supreme, where it imposed an ethnical discrimination and maintained a certain atmosphere of dignity, discipline and optimism congenial to itself, the other races suffered. True, they did not all suffer equally. The Italians, though little esteemed, adapted themselves to the situation. They made money and gradually rose to prosperity. Even the Irish, who have always been suspected and disparaged by the American aristocracy, had long occupied such a strong position in municipal politics that they seldom had anything to complain of and did not complain now.

But the post-war epoch was a very hard one for the Germans of America. From 1900 to 1915 they had enjoyed a great prestige and were looked upon as among the best citizens of the United States. Their seriousness, their love of work, their thoroughness, their culture and their beer were all equally admired. They were invited to the universities and the halls were adorned with portraits of the Kaiser. They had been just a little intoxicated by all this. Everywhere German clubs had grown up, everywhere Germanic groups and Goethe societies had swarmed. Therefore, when the fateful days of 1914 to 1917 arrived, they felt strong enough to resist the trend of Anglo-Saxon opinion. They showed courage, they fought for Germany, but they were defeated. And they found themselves at once disarmed, persecuted, despised and suspected. From 1919 to 1930, despite the rapid recovery of Germany and the growing estrangement of America from her former Allies in the war, the Germans were still little esteemed and felt themselves in a position of inferiority in the United States.

The Jews found themselves in similar case.

The frenzy of suspicion provoked by the War had placed the Jews in an unpleasant position. From 1917 to 1919 every one in America suspected every one of foreign name of being a spy, but it was German names which primarily aroused the vigilance of the patriots and the animosity of the chauvinists. Now many of the Jews in America had German names. They suffered the fate of the Germans. No sooner had this scare blown over than another and a still more serious one sprang up. Russia, amid an orgy of bloodshed, succumbed to Bolshevism, and this catastrophe was everywhere attributed to the Jews. America was deeply moved, both on account of the old sympathy of the Americans for Russia and because of the Bolshevik risings which broke out in Canada in the months following the Peace. There was a violent reaction in America, which took the form of barring the entry of Russians into the country and keeping an eye on the Jews.

Without being tragic or even critical or demonstrably painful, the position of the Jews was humiliating. Certain universities began to restrict the annual number of Jews admitted as students. In the schools of medicine, in particular, the rules were very strict. At the spas, in the hotels and in the fashionable places of resort, the Jews were cold-shouldered even more than before the war.

The protestations of the Germans and the discontent of the Jews grew and multiplied, and they soon became rallying points for groups of independent and indignant spirits, social reformers, intriguers, messiahs, lunatics, ladies in quest of a salon, editors in quest of a genius, impresarios in quest of prodigies, and snobs in quest of distraction.

A literature of revolt and protest grew up in this country of conformity and contentment. In the realm of Anglo-Saxonism, a Judaic Germanism, fed upon lamentations, lyrical effusions, cynicism and brutality, became a sort of fashion.

It shall suffice us to mention here such of these writers as have exercised a profound influence on the public and are most typical of this revolt, in virtue both of their qualities and their defects.

Mr. Sinclair Lewis is the greatest of them, by reason both of his stature and of the sale of his books.

For the rest, he is a rather sad man, who was born of non-Germanic parents in the Germanic region of the United States less than fifty years ago, and afterwards pursued his studies at Yale University.

There he doubtless learned less than he did in the newspaper offices, where he spent a long period of probation, and whose atmosphere enveloped him ever afterwards. They acquainted him with the life and customs of the American people from New York to

San Francisco and from Chicago to New Orleans. They familiarized him with the tedium of the trains, the dirtiness of the carriages, the satiety of all adventures and the emptiness of the social round. The journalism of the modern world, the great journalism of news, which does not pretend to prove or be in quest of anything in particular, is a stupendous school of melancholy and disenchantment, for man only finds in proportion as he seeks, and the man who resigns himself to accumulating details without any great connecting link ends by living in a dull, absurd and nauseating world. Life is only tolerable in virtue of its swiftness and its aim. Where it stagnates without direction or goal, it becomes hideous; it is worse than death. Sinclair Lewis, journalist and graduate from Yale, suffered.

He suffered the more since, from the outset, he was a monumental writer, devoid of genius, talent, fluency and grace. His first books were dull and tedious and they had no success. Then he wrote "Main Street", which was the most tedious of all his books and which had a triumphal success. "Main Street" was the story of an American Emma Bovary, a woman of some refinement, or at any rate imagination, who feels herself born for an ardent and complex life, but whom her husband, her love affairs and destiny are perpetually plunging back into the wretched daily routine, dirty, monotonous, disgusting and disillusioning. Everything is ugly around her. The little town is hideous, her neighbors are grotesque, their life is foolish and ridiculous, their souls are mean, and even their good nature is revolting in its stupidity. She loathes them and she loathes America. She cannot endure anything on this earth, but least of all can she endure her own country. And so her empty, futile, feeble life pursues its course.

The book is long and tiresome. It is heavy and mechanical. It has no charm either of fancy or of a fine story, or of tragedy or of hard and sparkling realism. The only thing to be said in its praise is that, with all its faults and all its tediousness, it is a book which a great many people have read. It brought Mr. Sinclair Lewis into fashion. It made its advent at a critical moment, in 1920, just after the establishment of prohibition, in the reign of Mr. Harding, who had himself come straight from Main Street and was a tragic victim of Main Street. The book was very well timed and it caught on; it was read in America, it was translated in Europe, and Mr. Sinclair Lewis commenced his official career as denouncer of American civilization to the United States and to the world at large.

From that date, every two years or so, Mr. Sinclair Lewis has published a novel of some four hundred pages, compact, solid, heavy and severe. In turn he reviled business men in his "Babbitt", and ecclesiastics in his "Elmer Gantry"; and he brought to this task so much patience, perseverance and solemnity that he finally won for himself the Nobel prize and the first rank of popularity among American writers.

It was perhaps unfortunate for him that he thus gained an almost political popularity and became an institution. And it was doubtless unfortunate for America that she could recognize herself only in the clumsy caricature offered to her by Mr. Sinclair Lewis. It was certainly very unfortunate for Europe that she imagined Mr. Lewis's books to give an accurate picture of American civilization and to imply an admission of European superiority. This was certainly not the view of Mr. Lewis, nor yet that of his disciples and friends.

It is easy to convince oneself of this by perusing the articles of the *American Mercury,* the monthly review edited by Mr. Mencken, the best publicist of this group.

Mr. Mencken is a German-American, born at Baltimore and brought up in that region, where he also started upon his career as a journalist. Then, in 1924, together with Mr. Nathan, he became editor of the *American Mercury,* one of the most lively, picturesque and typical reviews published in the United States.

Mr. Mencken is a critic and his review is a critical review; he has written some excellent studies of Shaw, Nietzsche and the American language. He is not light, but his heaviness is not clumsy; he is not genial, but neither is he ill-humored; he is not very gifted, but he does not imagine that he is. In short, he has a distinguished mind, and he has introduced into the world of American letters and the daily life of the United States a fairly acute uneasiness and an insight more lively than penetrating. However that may be, he has succeeded in grouping round his review a faithful congregation of readers and a solid phalanx of writers. He is one of the most redoubtable forces which go to form public opinion in the United States, and here and there his polemics are lit up by flashes of brilliance. At the very outset of Mr. Hoover's presidential career he said of him, with an insight which was rare at that time, that he showed little aptitude for greatness, although "There were the makings of a grand failure in him."

Mr. Mencken has a gift for formulas, and a fairly

keen sense of the ridiculous and of all that daily life
lacks in order to be pleasant or exciting. He is very
much alive to America's shortcomings, and he says so
for the delectation of the inhabitants of what Waldo
Frank has dubbed "Our America." He does not, however, concede any superiority to Europe, and, if he
criticizes her less, it is because she interests him less.
Sinclair Lewis and Mencken are not the apostles of a
more spiritual and refined civilization, but the critics
of a world whose spiritual elements they do not understand and whose brutality has lost its terrors for them.
They pose as the apostles of an intelligent and expert
materialism as against a clumsy and foolish materialism.

The wisdom which they enjoin upon America is not
the wisdom of Abel but of Lucifer.

They have splendid sport. For the last twelve years
the conflict which has been waged has proved the
dialectical weakness and the intellectual inadequacy of
the Protestant clergy. They strove to impose prohibition
and so contributed to their own undoing, by accepting
responsibility for the most unpopular and most imprudent decision made in the United States in the course
of a century. At the same time, the clergy wore themselves out in vain and futile discussions, and selected a
field of controversy in which they were bound to be
beaten, to make themselves ridiculous. Instead of biding
their time and dealing calmly with the evolutionary
hypothesis, which has been accepted for a century by a
number of scientists, because it provides a convenient
though rather arbitrary means of linking phenomena,
the Protestant clergy became obsessed by this theory.

Some of their number saw in it an instrument of God and interpreted the whole of the Bible from this angle; others looked upon it as a weapon of the evil one and wanted to burn every book which even mentioned the subject. The conflict raged in the ecclesiastical councils, in the seminaries and in the newspapers. It raged in the courts of justice, when the pious inhabitants of Tennessee demanded and obtained the dismissal of a young schoolmaster who had taught the theory of evolution as though it were a proven scientific truth. A group of freethinkers and liberals collected funds in order to defend this martyr, and Darrow, the great radical lawyer of Chicago, set off to plead on his behalf, whilst Bryan, the famous Democratic politician, championed the cause of religion.

It was an epic and absurd trial; it was a burlesque Punch and Judy show, in which religion and science were equally mishandled by their defenders and covered with ridicule by their disciples. Darrow, who is an eminent lawyer, a man of intellect and feeling, but not a philosopher, quoted Darwin's theories in a mutilated form and presented evolution in a false and puerile light, whilst Bryan, impelled by his apostolic zeal and by the heat, after having delivered himself of long and passionate harangues, in which the Bible was made to appear a book of true stories for big children, ate and drank so much in order to keep up his strength and his enthusiasm that he suddenly died of indigestion.

From one end to the other of the United States the newspapers echoed the proceedings, and, from the elevation of their pulpits, the Baptist, Methodist and Presbyterian ministers thundered, some in favor of tolerance, some in favor of faith, some in favor of men, some in favor of monkeys, some in favor of Moses, some in favor of Darwin. One of them even took up with him into the pulpit a little monkey, which he tethered to the font; then, turning to his faithful parishioners, he asked them whether, in this vile and wretched creature, they recognized the ancestor, the father and the brother of man? The congregation was greatly impressed by this demonstration, and the American newspapers published photographs of the monkey and of the pastor.

Trials of this sort did not fill either the temples of worship or the Sunday schools, and for the last ten years a more and more serious moral crisis has been raging in the churches of America. In vain do they federate and lavish aid and support on one another; they are growing weaker. The number of communicants and of duly registered members diminishes month by month. Despite the committees of pastors, pious men and zealous women, immoral literature is extending its ravages; the colleges are becoming more and more free in their morals and impious in their doctrines; in fact, the number of moral scandals in the universities has multiplied with alarming rapidity. All the efforts that have recently been made to bring back the people to religion have failed one after the other, and, save in the Catholic Church, it may be said that discouragement is rife among the Christians of the United States.

Finally, the last symbol of defeat, prohibition is about to disappear. It is becoming impossible to defend it; the Government is anxious to get rid of it as soon as possible; even Congress has yielded before the popular indignation, which vents itself at every opportunity. The great capitalists, including the most illustrious of their number, Mr. Rockefeller, have publicly declared that they would no longer support prohibition. People are sick of hearing of motorists killed on the road because they refused to stop soon enough in response to the command of a prohibition agent; they are sick of hearing of pursuits across the sea and of houses being searched on the strength of a mere suspicion. They are sick of hearing of the prohibition budget, and they laugh at the stubborn propagandists who still chant the refrain of "prohibition prosperity." A defunct prosperity is dragging prohibition into its tomb, and thus ending the last crusade upon which the Protestant churches of America embarked before confessing themselves defeated.

Celebrations are being organized to mark the repeal of the Eighteenth Amendment. America might be fêting the return of a monarch to his kingdom. And even the police declare that, since the abolition of complete prohibition, the number of cases of drunkenness and of crimes of every description has notably diminished.

None the less, prohibition has left a huge void in its wake. The dollar is falling, the Republican Party is languishing, prosperity is defunct, and now prohibition, the image and symbol of another age, is vanishing in its turn. The return of wine and beer and other alcoholic liquors is not, as many people imagine, the end of a foolish episode and the return to normal life. It is merely the end of one moral crisis and the beginning of another and graver crisis.

The vestiges of moral authority which a great party, at once powerful and clumsy, aristocratic and dema-

gogic, conservative and timorous, had tried to impose
on the crowd are in process of disappearance. This is
not the fault of any one man; it is not the exploit of
any leader. The Democrats are not responsible for what
happened between 1919 and 1932; they cannot be accused of having selected in Harding, Coolidge and
Hoover three King Logs, who could not govern this
fiery republic without burning themselves; they cannot be accused of having forced the Republicans to
pursue in Europe a policy of flight and fear, whilst
displaying in financial matters the most reckless daring.
They cannot be accused of having hastened the moral
crisis and accelerated the ruin of Coolidge's "Rotarian
Republic", of Ford's industrial legend, of Mitchell's
financial charlatanism, and of the moral frenzy of the
Anti-Saloon League.

For all this the Republican Party is responsible, in
so far as men and associations of men are responsible
here below for their acts. They took over America at a
time when the whole world looked upon her as the
strongest nation in the world and the one most worthy
of hegemony. They left an America weakened, divided,
and rapidly losing her gold, her faith in God and her
faith in herself; they left nothing in America save
America.

PART THREE

AMERICA FINDS HERSELF AGAIN

AMERICA FINDS HERSELF AGAIN

AT the beginning of 1932 the Republican Party was counting on victory.

The Democratic Party was disorganized, divided, ruined and incoherent. It consisted of a large and compact rural bloc in the South, of a number of incongruous and dispersed urban elements in the East and North, and of groups scattered here and there in the Middle West and West.

The South, which has remained faithful to the Democratic Party ever since the Civil War, is rural, poor, conservative and piously Protestant: Baptists, Methodists and Presbyterians still predominate there. They favored prohibition. No Democratic candidate can dispense with the vote of the Democratic States of the South. But the South, despite its defeat, has preserved a point of view so peculiar and a humor so different from that which prevails in the rest of the country that it seems impossible to please it without displeasing the other regions.

The Democrats of the North and East are, in fact, either Irish or intellectuals who are irritated and repelled by the Republicans. The Catholic Irish do not look favorably upon Anglo-Saxon predominance, they are hostile to prohibition, and, without being radical, they exhibit leveling tendencies which have to be satisfied. They are very dangerous enemies to any one who annoys them, for they are past masters of the art of politics; but they are also dangerous friends, for the rest of the country, which is mainly Anglo-Saxon and Protestant, regards them with suspicion. A Democratic candidate cannot dispense with their support, but their enthusiasm may ruin him in the eyes of the country. If he is officially patronized by Tammany, the great Irish political organization in New York, he is irremediably compromised in the eyes of the country.

The other Democrats in the East are mostly intellectuals, who form a brilliant headquarters staff with few troops. It would seem that they could be dispensed with; but this is by no means the case, for they own a great many newspapers, they are often in a position to influence the Jewish vote — which is, in the United States, an important item — and they exercise over the big towns of the Middle West and West an influence which alone makes it possible to rally round the Democratic candidate the malcontents from the great plains, the Mississippi Valley and California. Now no Democratic candidate can hope to succeed without the backing of these radicals and these malcontents of the West.

Thus the Democratic Party, with its vague principles, its poor discipline and its weak central organization, has had little chance of getting a President elected, for it has been too lacking in unity to rally a national majority behind a programme or behind a type of man. The ideas and the human type which please the conservative, Protestant and Anglo-Saxon South irritate the Irish, Catholic and liberal Northeast, whilst they exasperate the Nordic citizens of the West, with his Germanic culture and his socialistic tendency. In order to win approval, the Republican candidate has merely to conform to one single ideal: that of the wealthy, honest, conservative and well-informed *bourgeois* of whom his party throughout the country mainly consists; whilst the Democratic candidate can hope for victory only if he is as versatile as a chameleon and as multiform as Proteus.

Moreover, the party exchequer is almost always empty. The Republicans have money, organization, Press, agents and method. They have a machine; and the machine, with imperturbable assurance, selects the Republican candidate, whether he be insignificant, unknown to the country and surrounded by dubious friends, like Mr. Harding, or negative and taciturn like Mr. Coolidge, or a political amateur, without eloquence, charm or skill, like Mr. Hoover. The Republican Party was confident that, having got Mr. Hoover elected a first time, it would succeed in getting him reëlected. The Republican Party was a machine, and once more the machine would triumph over men; it would secure the triumph of its friend, the virtuous and mechanical Mr. Hoover.

No one bothered much about the electoral problem in Republican circles. Mr. Hoover himself, after having suffered some hours of gloom and a good deal of anxiety, felt his cares begin to disperse. He was sprightly against his wont. To his intimates he murmured that, if things settled down a little, if there was a ten per cent. improvement in the trend of economic life, he was sure of being elected. Now, during this spring of 1932, there was a perceptible rise of stock exchange prices and a distinct improvement in industry. Mr. Hoover looked at his index figures; like a good engineer he consulted his diagrams; like a good mechanic he examined his curves, and he found that he had an excellent curve.

To tell the truth, there were a few shadows in the picture. Business had not yet reached the stage of radiant prosperity; there were some unemployed — over seven million, in fact, according to well-informed people; the question of the inter-Allied debts was still pending and a source of repeated recriminations between Europe and America; in Europe, despite homilies, splendid programmes, and pleasant conferences in pleasant Geneva, peace was in greater jeopardy than ever before. Discontent was raising its head in the United States; the farmers were protesting and striking; the ex-soldiers organized a pilgrimage of protest to Washington, where they camped in the streets and the public squares, filling the beautiful white capital with their din, their dirt and their discontent. The banks went on collapsing. And Mr. Hoover went on predicting vainly and monotonously the return of prosperity, which, unfortunately, was still waiting for the American people "just around the corner", and refused to quit this unfortunate legendary position.

The spring passed. Mr. Hoover had dispatched Mr. Mellon to London, he had got ready his troops, and, for support in the critical hour, he had turned to Mr. Ogden Mills, who was young, intelligent, active, bold and a past master of polemics. Mr. Mills was sprung from a patrician family of New York and was a rich and influential financier, such as befitted the gold capital; his appearance was suggestive of a stout and rubi-

cund English "gentleman farmer" just returned from
hunting the fox, capturing the creature and celebrating
his victory. He looked as if he knew how to fight, how
to win and how to exploit his victory. He was young and
he was ambitious. To him the assisting of Mr. Hoover
to power represented the accomplishment both of a
national duty and of a feat of skill; it meant securing
a position as his eventual successor; he would neglect
nothing towards this end.

To tell the truth, it was not an easy task. The country was tired of Mr. Hoover, of his forced, cheerless and
expressionless smile, of his style, which was like that of
an outwardly scrupulous commercial prospectus, of his
puffy and acidulated personality and of his vinegary
cordiality. At the moving-picture houses of the small
towns, when he appeared on the screen, he was hissed.
A mayor in the suburbs of Chicago was even obliged to
publish a notice in 1932: "The citizens of this town are
requested to remember that Mr. Hoover is President of
the United States and to abstain from disrespectful demonstrations when the image of the first functionary of
the Republic is shown on the screen for, when they
hiss Mr. Hoover, they hiss their country and themselves."
In spite of this sage advice, people hissed. Mr. Hoover
was the grand failure which Mencken had foretold.

However, the sound of the hisses did not reach Washington. In any case, they would hardly have worried
Mr. Hoover, who thought in terms of machines. He was
constructing his machine and he relied on his machine.
He was chief engineer, Mr. Mills was chief mechanic,
and, with a few other mechanics, all would be well.

All did go well at first. At Chicago, where the convention of the delegates of the Republican Party assembled, Mr. Hoover was re-nominated rapidly, simply and without any effective opposition.

In the lobbies, however, people had been saying that as a President, Mr. Hoover had been an out-and-out failure. He had been able neither to preserve nor to restore prosperity. God knows how far they were from the time when every one was reveling in optimism and opulence! Mr. Hoover had once said: "Ours is a country where there are no poor!" And he had added that an essential point in his programme was "two chickens in the pot for every American family." Now very few American families, in this spring of 1932, still had chickens; a great many had not even pots. As for poverty, the seven million unemployed could ask the President what he thought of their condition.

Mr. Hoover, the great internationalist, the great organizer, the great philanthropist, was completing his fourth year of office; these four years had left the United States in an economic, commercial and diplomatic situation far worse than that of 1928. The United States had raised its customs tariff, and the other countries had retorted by raising theirs. England, after a long and brilliant period of free trade, had adopted protectionism, and was pursuing a policy of economic expansion with the aid of her depreciated pound. In all the markets American industry was being worsted by German industry, English industry and Japanese industry.

Everywhere those political clouds were gathering which made a trade revival still more difficult. The relations between France and Germany, as a result of the gradual eclipse of Monsieur Briand, were becoming more and more tense, whilst in Asia the advance of Japan in Manchuria and her designs on North China were growing plainer every day. The danger of war was becoming obvious and near. Mr. Hoover had done nothing to prevent it. No problem was solved, no remedy was prepared.

Inside the country, while the economic distress was getting worse, and while the intellectual discontent was spreading, the people were launching a furious attack against the Anti-Saloon League and the Eighteenth Amendment. Society ladies, lawyers, doctors and numberless other groups and corporations organized themselves for the fight against prohibition and its devotees. They turned against it the arguments which had once been used in its support. "What waste of money!" they said. "Can't you see that all this prohibition administration, all these agents, these coastguards, these motor cyclists, these motor cars and these spies are a very great expense to the nation, which has no need to provide for swindlers and blackguards! We must revoke the Eighteenth Amendment. This will be an immediate saving and will shortly be a source of wealth. A tax on wine, a tax on beer, would be wonderful resources for the State, for people would be pleased to pay them. The abandonment of prohibition," said these crusaders, "is the first step towards prosperity. It will fill the coffers of the government, supply work to several hundreds of thousands of unemployed and cheer up the American people." A great many men belonging to the Republican Party thought the moment had come for giving up prohibition and at any rate removing that stumbling-block from the path of President Hoover.

But this was not the opinion of Mr. Hoover. Doubtless the Anti-Saloon League was unpopular, doubtless Mr. Rockefeller and various other illustrious philanthropists had made a point of disavowing it publicly and loudly. Yes, all this was true, but Mr. Hoover could not help having a secret weakness, a personal sympathy, for this organization. It fascinated him irresistibly; for it was like himself, it too was a machine. He finally inserted in the Republican programme a tame and worthless little phrase, which allowed inveterate drinkers to vote for him if they wanted and to cherish the pious hope for a return of wine and beer. But Mr. Hoover promised nothing and he smiled on the Anti-Saloon League. Mr. Hoover sent instructions to the convention; the convention received them, obeyed them, and even had the courage to clap and sing. In the interests of truth, it should be mentioned that it is natural to American political conventions to clap and sing, just as it is natural for an Italian to gesticulate with his hands when he is speaking and to a Frenchman to drink wine with his meals.

The machine had had Mr. Hoover re-nominated as party candidate. It was so powerful that it would certainly be able to get him reëlected President of the United States.

As had been foreseen, the Democrats fought. The Irish supported their great man, Governor Smith; the radicals backed Mr. McAdoo, who had the merit of being Wilson's son-in-law, and the further merit, still more important in 1932, of radiating discontent and bitterness. The serious and sensible conservatives, the people of the South, supported Governor Ritchie of Maryland, a handsome and worthy man who managed his little State well and, in its semi-obscurity, displayed the virtues of a gentleman, at the same time setting an example of good conduct, good tailoring and beautiful neckties. There would evidently be a fierce contest.

The Democratic Convention met at Chicago. Everything portended anarchy and violence. It was hot; the delegates were numerous, thirsty and rowdy, the streets were blocked by the crowds, and the corridors were full of gossips, schemers and jealous rivals.

It was certain that words and good arguments would be lost in the uproar and frenzy.

For that reason, the impresarios of Franklin Delano Roosevelt, the Governor of New York, did not try to speak in public. Mr. Farley directed operations for Mr. Roosevelt. From his room, by telephone, in two or three rapid and secret meetings, he executed his moves. Mr. Smith had made known his wish to be candidate once more. He had kindled the hatred of the radicals in the West, who detested his Catholicism, and the hostility of the Protestants of the South, who despised it. He had created a plain situation, which allowed of a swift and decisive maneuver. Farley seized his opportunity.

This maneuver was executed briskly and discreetly. It was based on the mainsprings of politics, hatred and misunderstanding. It succeeded all along the line. Mr. Roosevelt was nominated presidential candidate of the Democratic Party.

He was ready. His agents and friends did not lose a minute in taking the convention in hand. Smith left the field vanquished and vexed, Ritchie retired discreetly and politely, McAdoo squared his chest to make it seem broader, for he is tall but very thin. The other great party men, stunned or content, kept quiet. Mr. Roosevelt, who, as soon as he got the news, came by airplane from Albany, New York, greeted the convention and made a lively impression. In flagrant opposition to established custom, the Democratic programme was on this occasion clear, definite and tolerably bold. It declared itself openly in favor of repealing the prohibition law, and it submitted a novel and daring programme of remedies and new measures for coping with the economic crisis. There was vigor and vim in the Democratic proclamation. Compared with the stale and hackneyed padding which made up the Republican declaration, that of the Democrats was like a red banner waving in the sunshine.

This was only the beginning of Mr. Roosevelt's audacities.

According to a principle established by wary politicians, nothing could be more dangerous to a candidate for the Presidency of the United States than to show himself too much and to speak too much. He must leave it to the Press and his friends to build up and color his legend for him. Else, in the course of a long round of speech-making, he is bound to let slip some incautious phrase and lay himself open to criticism or wound the susceptibilities of some influential politician. He thus wreaks his own undoing, and all that is left for his adversary to do is merely to utter a few simple, lucid and crushing aphorisms, which complete his discomfiture.

Mr. Hoover was fully determined to employ this method. He intended to hold his tongue and to outmaneuver Roosevelt by his silence. Besides, after all, he was President of the United States. He was the great technician of modern times, the great engineer of America; he ought not to be expected to perform great feats of eloquence, and further, in times of crisis, it was well to set an example of economy in everything, even in eloquence. He decided not to talk and to watch his adversary. Moreover, everything was going well; prices were rising, and the barometer was set at "fair."

Unfortunately, three events occurred that summer which gave Mr. Hoover a disagreeable reputation.

First of all, prices stopped rising. All along the line, industries and banks had to admit fresh losses and a new wave of depression. Mr. Hoover had said: "Give me a rise of ten per cent. and I shall be elected." Instead of a rise of ten per cent. he had a new drop of ten per cent.

What with the worsening of the economic situation and the heat of the summer, the unemployed were becoming restive. They organized a procession of agitators, who were to proceed to Washington and submit their grievances, their complaints and their suggestions to the Government, the President and Congress. This grotesque, dangerous and turbulent mob, although not really very numerous, filled Washington with its din, its dirt and its exploits. The ex-soldiers, or individuals who claimed to be ex-soldiers, installed themselves in the city. They were everywhere, they besieged Congress, they besieged the White House. They gave Mr. Hoover no peace. Finally, he could endure this persecution no longer, and he ordered the troops to evacuate these people, who were spreading disorder through the capital. The operation was performed vigorously but with some slight brutality. Some of the demonstrators were injured, some were very roughly handled, all were indignant. They were still more indignant when an announcement of the Government accused them of being "Reds" and ex-convicts. After this, their discontent reached such a pitch that when Mr. Hoover's Secretary of War, in order to settle the matter, came to speak to them at their national convention, they hissed him as though he had been merely a bad turn at a music hall, and they declared war to the knife on President Hoover. This meant that a vast and organized crowd detached themselves from the Republican Party, to which it normally belonged, and went over to the Democratic Party.

To these two omens was added a third. The State of Maine elects its governor at the beginning of September, a good two months before any of the other States. Now the State of Maine is normally Republican, but it is not always so, and the political augurs of the United States were wont to say: "As Maine goes, so goes the country." For years Maine had been consistently Republican. In September, 1932, although the Republican Party had taken infinite trouble, and although Mr. Ogden Mills had proceeded to Maine in person in order to organize Mr. Hoover's campaign and had addressed meetings there, in Maine the Democrats got a majority and a Democratic Government was elected. In a few hours the betting, which had until then been favorable to Mr. Hoover, turned in favor of Mr. Roosevelt. Roosevelt was recognized as a redoubtable candidate, and the possibility of his success was admitted. Mr. Hoover felt cold shivers down his back. To a number of electors who prefer to vote for the winning candidate, Maine gave their cue. Mr. Hoover knew it. He recalled the famous American proverb, "Nothing succeeds like success," and he trembled.

He was considerably cheered when he read in the newspapers of the vast tour which Mr. Roosevelt was projecting. Despite his infirmity, Mr. Roosevelt had resolved to charter a special train and to traverse America from end to end, in order to address the inhabitants of the different localities, make himself better acquainted with their needs and win their support. When he announced his plan, the Democratic leaders shook their heads and the veteran politicians flung up their hands towards the heavens, in which direction Mr. Hoover too cast a look of gratitude.

Mr. Roosevelt could not fail to ruin his chances: his health would give way, his speeches would be too daring, or else they would be too dull. In any case, it was impossible for him to please everybody, and, in view of his infirmity, it seemed likely that this reckless peregrination from one end to the other of the United States would end in a tragedy.

However, Governor Roosevelt was undismayed. He set off in his special train with his wife and his children, his nurse and his doctor, his friends and his advisers. He was surrounded by a staff whose most influential member was Professor Moley, of Columbia University, a respected criminologist with a shrewd brain. Moley prepared speeches to be delivered by the candidate. He furnished him with a stock of discourses on every subject, and these Franklin Roosevelt rapidly studied, sifted and ended by employing, according to the inspiration of the moment.

The train was full, the autumn was warm and rainy. The Governor went from town to town, smiling upon all, chatting with all, genial, kind and simple. The men came to shake hands with him, while the women showed him their babies, and gazed at this handsome, brave and disabled man with tears in their eyes.

He stopped everywhere, he made speeches everywhere. One day, when he arrived at a little town, a member of his staff with whom he was on very pleasant and familiar terms is reported to have said to him: "I hope, Governor, that here at last we're going to hear something new?"

"Certainly not," retorted the Governor, "you will hear what you have heard everywhere else. Nothing pleases a crowd more than a familiar air." And, indeed, that evening Mr. Roosevelt repeated his customary speech and, as usual, with great success.

Franklin Roosevelt's method is very simple. He seats himself carefully, rather heavily, in a big armchair, with his two elbows on the table, a large white handkerchief in the pocket of his waistcoat and his eyes turned straight towards the audience. Then he speaks in a grave, firm and musical voice. He is sober in his gestures, but he always takes out his handkerchief, and he always toys with it, thus creating, between himself and his public, a sort of bland, white wall, which softens the corners of his statements and the crudity of his views, without in any way detracting from the intimacy of the meeting. When he speaks, he is precise, his voice is pleasant, he rarely touches upon great questions and avoids too complex theories. However, he has to speak, and he does not hesitate to speak. He is no coward, and he knows that cowardice in politics is always punished. In all the Western States he was faced with the difficult task of winning over the radicals, whose vote was indispensable to his success, without alienating his conservative and Catholic troops in the South and Northeast.

Mr. Roosevelt accomplished this feat by a brilliant stratagem. In any center where there was a Progressive or Radical Senator, he arranged not only to have this Senator introduced to him but to devote a part of his speech to the man's character and career. He praised him and drew attention to the nobility of his life. He did not commit himself to any personal expression of opinion, he did not betray the secrets of his mind, he did not pronounce any articles of faith. No, he praised the Senator; in Nebraska he delivered a panegyric on Senator Norris; in California he extolled to the skies the famous Johnson, Wilson's great enemy and a disgruntled Republican, who was delighted with Roosevelt's words and transferred himself to his side with all his baggage and munitions. In New Mexico he saw Senator Bronson Cutting, and at each place he employed the same neat, simple and straightforward method. Nothing about principles, save a vague and general approbation, everything about the activities and characters of his radical friends. The towns, cities and villages were enraptured; the people thronged around Mr. Roosevelt's train. An immense wave of confidence surged over him.

When he was very hard pressed, he created a diversion. One day, in order to get out of a difficulty, he quoted the Pope. Another day he was ill, but he is an orator both too gifted and yet not sufficiently brilliant to run the risk of enthusiasm. Everything went off well. He won the radical crowds of the West by his personality, his smile and his gestures.

From every corner of the United States messages streamed towards him, while a vast silence enveloped Mr. Hoover. We must reply, declared all the shrewd and experienced advisers of the Republican Party in all parts of the country. And we must reply quickly. Mr. Roosevelt has had a huge success.

At length Mr. Hoover became alive to the danger. He decided that he too would set out on a speechmaking tour.

He started off. The autumn weather had suddenly turned dull and rainy. It was raining in Washington when the President set off; the leaves were falling, yellow and damp; in the gardens the last flowers of autumn were fading; the people were overcome with lassitude in the damp, warm autumnal air with its scent of decay. The melancholy train traversed the vast central plain, where it was raining. It arrived at Chicago, where it was raining. Mr. Hoover could no longer smile. His smile, strained to breaking-point, had ended by giving way or been washed out by the rain.

Mrs. Hoover, however, who specializes in Girl Scouts, smiled in his stead. She smiled from the platform at the back of the train and the journalists photographed her smile by magnesium light, and once the spark had been produced in the silver lamps which they employed, they threw the lamps on the rails. Mrs. Hoover gave a little scream; she sent for the journalists and gave them a good talking-to. How could they throw these electric

bulbs on the railway lines when at any moment a little
newspaper boy might come along with bare feet and
risk cutting himself? What carelessness on their part!
What lack of thought. She made them feel ashamed and
she also irritated them.

At Kansas City, whither Mr. Hoover repaired, hostile
demonstrations had been feared, and the hall had therefore been filled with all the Republican farmers who
could be mustered. There were ten thousand of them.
They gave vent to cries of joy when the President appeared, they uttered shouts of enthusiasm when he left,
and they punctuated his speech with admiring and appropriate exclamations. It was a good audience. The President had decided to venture a bold stroke. He attacked
Roosevelt and the Democrats without mercy. He declared that the country was in danger. He assured the
farmers of Iowa and Kansas that, but for himself, the
dollar would have collapsed, that the national currency
had been in deadly peril and that he, and he alone, had
saved them from catastrophe. He did not mince his
words, and the farmers, seeing him defend himself like
a stag at bay, uttered shouts of delight. They had at
length recognized Mr. Hoover's outstanding quality —
violence. This speech went the round of the American
Press, it went the round of the world, and it made a
profound sensation. Mr. Hoover was gratified; for the
first time since the beginning of the campaign, people
were listening to him, people were paying attention to
him. He employed the same vein in a speech delivered
in New York; he pointed out to the worthy citizens
of the metropolis the dangers which threatened them
if Governor Roosevelt were elected, and for their bene-

fit he conjured up a picture of New York as it would be if the Republicans were defeated. He conjured up visions of the grass sprouting between the paving stones of the city.

The people were stunned by his words. Up to this time Mr. Hoover's candidature had been imperilled. He had against him the radicals of the West, the Middle West and the East, the conservatives and the great bulk of the traditional Democrats of the South, but he still retained his hold on the *bourgeois* masses of the West and of the urban centers. These two speeches lost him their allegiance. They could not countenance a President of the United States who spread panic through the country for the sake of getting himself reëlected.

When Mr. Owen Young, chairman of the General Electric Company and one of Mr. Roosevelt's supporters, came to New York to speak on his behalf, he was received with acclamation and, in a calm, terse and clever speech, he had no difficulty in demonstrating the folly of Mr. Hoover's statements. He lulled the fears of the *bourgeoisie*, finance, industry and commerce. He invited them to join the winning side, and his speech rallied to Mr. Roosevelt's support the terrified *bourgeoisie*, whom nothing frightened so much as fright, and who detested President Hoover for having given them a fright.

As if heaven were determined that Mr. Roosevelt's triumph should be complete, Governor Smith, the only one of his friends and the only one of his enemies who had held aloof and who had been able neither to forgive him his maneuver of the spring nor yet to forget their old friendship, was persuaded to meet him. For both it was a question of pushing the candidature of Mr.

Lehmann, of whom they were very fond and whom they wanted to be Governor of the State of New York. But Mr. Lehmann was a Jew, and some people protested. Mr. Roosevelt, an Anglo-Saxon Protestant, and Mr. Smith, an Irish Catholic, found themselves fighting side by side on Mr. Lehmann's behalf. They began by embracing and they then succeeded in winning over the Democratic delegates who hesitated to choose Mr. Lehmann as their party candidate. The Irishman and the Anglo-Saxon were reunited around the Jew. At one stroke Mr. Roosevelt won for himself the whole Jewish vote and the bulk of the Irish vote.

His Press, admirably directed and manipulated by Mr. Farley, had carried out all the work of preparation in the most thoroughgoing fashion. The majority of the newspapers were for him. In fact, everything and everybody were for him. He had succeeded.

When polling day arrived, it was raining.

Mr. Hoover, utterly exhausted, in his house at Palo Alto, California, spent part of the afternoon reading telegrams. He had shaken so many hands that he had a large sore on his left palm. He had smiled so much that now he could only cry. He had talked till he stuttered and he had counted until he was delirious. As a buffet supper had been prepared in the dining room, his friends called in the evening to see how he was and to hear the news. They heard them. Mr. Hoover, very pale, emerged from his study and, without touching any food, came and shook a few hands. He then took a little turn outside, the students uttered a few shouts, and Mr. Hoover recovered a vestige of his smile.

In New York, at the same hour, Governor Roosevelt

made his way to his headquarters at the Hotel Biltmore in New York City. He was surrounded by all his staff. They flourished telegrams, all of them announcing victory. All the States, even the most Republican, were swept along in the Democratic torrent. There would be an unprecedented majority for the President, in the Senate, in the House of Representatives, in all the States, throughout the country.

⌡ In the end it was found that Mr. Roosevelt had won by a majority larger than any President of the United States had ever before obtained: twenty-two and a half millions, as against sixteen millions for Mr. Hoover. The latter had retained only a few States. The immense electoral domain of the Republicans had crumbled away beneath him. Never had there been witnessed so woeful a defeat. The radical West had forsaken him *en masse;* the conservative South had grouped itself unhesitatingly around Roosevelt; the industrial, intellectual, and Irish East had adopted Roosevelt as one man; the agrarian and industrial Middle West had done the same. All that remained to the Republican Party was Mr. Hoover, and all that remained to Mr. Hoover was the consciousness of a duty performed.

In the streets a drizzling rain was falling. The night was not very cold, and the crowds were stamping their feet in the mud. They were stationed before the screens on which the newspapers announced the results, and, as the results were slow in coming through, the newspapers displayed comic films in the intervals for the amusement of the populace. The crowd gazed patiently and silently. When it was announced on the screen that Mr. Hoover had telegraphed to Mr. Roosevelt admitting his defeat and had gone to bed, there was hardly any applause. When it was announced that Mr. Roosevelt had thanked Mr. Hoover, there was no applause at all.

The crowd displayed neither enthusiasm nor anger. It had just executed Mr. Hoover. It had just broken up a machine which had stopped working and invited a brave man to try what he could do with another. It did not applaud, but it went home, taking with it the memory of a man's smile.

CHAPTER I

A PORTRAIT OF ROOSEVELT

THE election of Mr. Roosevelt was a personal triumph. The people was determined to vote against a type of man it detested, against a group which had ended by making itself hated, and against an attitude which seemed intolerable.

Ever since the month of February, 1932, Mr. Hoover had fought without intermission. But the voices of the malcontents were loud enough to have reached various parties and a great many individuals. The Communists, who were enjoying a vogue at this troubled time, might have reaped a rich harvest; the Socialists, who had at their disposal large funds, beautiful women and a very handsome candidate, Mr. Norman Thomas, certainly counted on winning over several million voters. Actually the Communists secured 55,000 less and the Socialists about 170,000 less than in 1912![1]

On November 4, 1932, Mr. Hoover was swept from the field, and Mr. Roosevelt was the object of a veritable plebiscite. The people acclaimed him personally and at the same time paid their tribute to the type which he exemplified.

[1] In 1912, when the women had no vote and there were only sixteen million votes, Mr. Debs, the Socialist candidate, secured, in round figures, 900,000 votes.

It was to some extent the fault of the Republicans, whose method on this occasion lacked both wisdom and foresight. By trying to do too much, they brought about their own undoing, and, by trying to rid themselves of Mr. Roosevelt promptly and rapidly, they prepared the stage and the setting which was to serve for his apotheosis.

It is generally imagined that no more than the European peoples does the American people know the Presidents whom it elects. That is doubtless the reason why it elects them. Let us hope so, at any rate. Fifty million men and women, of all colors, of all races, of all kinds and of all descriptions, are called upon, every four years, to give their opinion concerning a man whom they do not know and whom they will never know, whom they have not understood and whom they never will understand. They none the less vote in large numbers and with alacrity, interest and sometimes even passion. They do not know who this man is, or what he wants, or what he will do; yet he excites their enthusiasm or their anger, their sympathy or their hatred. They see before their mind's eye, they carry in their imagination, an image which has moved them and has contrived to stir their passions.

The man himself counts for nothing in all this. His Press and his publicity agents have created for the use of the public the image of a personage, and it is this vision which is elected to the Presidency of the Republic. The relation between the man and the image is sometimes remote. In 1920, Mr. Harding ranked in the eyes of the pious crowds of America, of the Congregationalist and

Baptist, Presbyterian and Methodist pastors, who worked for his election, as "the normal man", a worthy, peaceable man, steady and thoroughly *bourgeois,* whilst his life and his adventures, his character and his career, were rather of the picaresque variety and full of picturesque episodes. His image had been toned down for presentation to the public. That of Mr. Hoover, on the other hand, had been colored up. The Press and industry drove him to be a personage, but they did not get him very far, and from 1920 to 1928, in order to secure his election, it was necessary to build up for him an entirely fictitious rôle — that of a bold and dauntless liberal, full of new ideas and initiative; whereas Mr. Hoover was, in fact, a timid and nervous conservative, sometimes shrewd but always instinctively inclined not to take action if action could be avoided. The fault of the Hooverian legend was that it subsequently made Mr. Hoover ridiculous. It is a mistake to overdo anything, even a halo. It is apt to throw too much light on the brow beneath it, and, when a man is bald, caution is advisable. The halo which Mr. Hoover was neither able to wear nor yet to doff with sufficient celerity attracted all eyes towards him and made him ridiculous.

The calumnies which the Republicans circulated concerning Mr. Roosevelt prepared the latter's apotheosis. Yet they had no suspicion that they were making a mistake, particularly as a similar tactic had succeeded in 1928 at the expense of Governor Smith, at that time Democratic candidate for the Presidency and Mr. Hoover's rival. Mr. Smith was a very great politician, whom the industrial masses loved and the upper classes respected and admired for his accurate political judg-

ment and his understanding of the various social forces.
Mr. Smith enjoyed great prestige. It was difficult to
attack him. It was impossible to attack him openly.

But it is always possible to slander a public man, if it
is done stealthily, modestly and anonymously. The Republicans discovered, what every one knew, that Mr.
Smith was a Catholic; they also discovered that Mrs.
Smith was rather stout, not very well-dressed and of
somewhat rustic manners. Add to this that Mr. Smith
was hostile to prohibition. Nothing more was required.

Immediately officious emissaries journeyed from town
to town, and along all the channels of Protestant
ecclesiastical life there spread vague, terrible, disquieting and distressing rumors: Mr. Smith, if he were elected,
would consult the Pope on every subject; Mr. Smith
would organize a visit of the Pope to the United States;
Mr. Smith would suggest to the Pope that he should
come and settle in the United States. Mr. Smith would
conspire to corrupt the young people of the United
States and to deliver them into the hands of the Pope;
Mr. Smith would not govern, he would be a mere
dummy, the Pope in disguise, a cloak for Antichrist. And
then it was added in a very low whisper: And, besides, if
you could only see Mrs. Smith! Mrs. Smith at the White
House!

There was nothing very noble in all this, there was
nothing even very serious, for all these rumors were
absurd. None the less, it was the hardest blow the Republicans dealt the Democrats in the campaign of 1928.
In vain did Mr. Smith struggle and protest and appeal
to Mr. Hoover's good faith; in vain did he appeal
directly to the latter. The only reply he got was: "Not

at home." Mr. Hoover did not know, the Republican Party did not know, the Republican Press did not know. No one knew, no one had heard, no one understood. And all this time the rumor traveled, spread and grew. It found its way into dull, narrow and feeble minds, that is to say, into the great human masses, who are constituted in the United States as they are in all the other countries. Entangled in these calumnies, which were too stupid to be answered nobly and intelligently, Mr. Smith, who was too human not to suffer from them and too decent to retaliate in the same fashion, lost millions of votes and districts and several States in the South which ought to have supported him but were estranged from him by this moral, anti-papal, anti-Irish, Protestant propaganda.

The chief instrument of this sublime achievement had been a woman lawyer, Mrs. Mabel Walker Willebrandt. She had worked so well that she was rewarded with a post of assistant to the Attorney-General, as well as by an important office in the Prohibition Government. She afterwards continued a career so well begun by obtaining the lucrative position of consulting solicitor to the association of producers of raisins (and of wine) of California. This she certainly deserved, for she had obtained a result which was of considerable value to the Republican Party: she had succeeded in exciting in a section of the American people a feeling of distrust of Governor Smith, which even his marvellous political gifts could not dispel and which even his generous mind could not forget.

When the candidature of Mr. Roosevelt began to excite the attention of well-informed people, the Republicans, who divined his strategic talents as a politician and already knew his gifts as a statesman, were anxious to finish him off quickly, and they had recourse to the procedure which had seemed so effective in the case of Mr. Smith.

The Republican newspapers, great and small, the organs with a large circulation and the local rags, began to speak of Mr. Roosevelt, and with one common accord they depicted him as a dangerous man, whose weak health, unstable character and ill-defined ideas made up a sinister and alarming personality. Franklin Roosevelt in the Presidency would mean the enthronement of disorder in the United States, the prolongation of the crisis for several years, and the exposure of the country to most serious upheavals. The rumor spread, the slander grew, and was tinged with pity, colored with indignation or tempered by esteem, according to the place and the time; but it was becoming a refrain and the public noticed it. This was a critical moment in Roosevelt's candidature. Another few days of this rumor and he was lost.

At this juncture, there suddenly appeared in all the newspapers of America neat and concise little paragraphs emanating from New York and announcing that the big New York bankers, knowing of the progress Mr. Franklin Roosevelt's candidature was making, were trying to thwart it by an underhand campaign of calumnies against his character and his programme. By an effectual counter-attack, Roosevelt's friends denounced Wall Street as the source of these rumors.

Wall Street was at this time detested. Wall Street was the scapegoat, it was made responsible for speculation, the crisis and all the muddle and depression of the country. The idea that these arrogant and guilty bankers were venturing to attack in this way a popular statesman excited the indignation of all. The incident was graven upon every mind. Mr. Roosevelt's personality, of which many were entirely ignorant, immediately became attractive and familiar to them. He was persecuted and he was attacked by Wall Street; he was therefore worthy of esteem. Between February and June, 1932, the whole of the Middle West and the West, which were resolutely hostile to New York and Wall Street, turned towards him. His legend was launched.

Thus the maneuver which the Republicans had planned against Governor Roosevelt, before he had been nominated as official Party candidate, recoiled against its authors. It had merely served to attract the attention of the great public to Franklin Roosevelt and to render him popular by contrast with Wall Street. He appeared as a martyr, a persecuted tribune and a great and misunderstood man, all of which things the crowd prefers to the greatest glory in the world.

And no one, moreover, believed that there could be any ground for distrusting Franklin Delano Roosevelt.

How could one distrust a man who belonged to the Roosevelt family?

The Roosevelts are Dutch and, in the hierarchy of races in the United States, the Dutch rank very high. They are a Nordic people, like the Anglo-Saxons; they are a cultured, intelligent, patient and tenacious race. They have contrived to preserve their peculiar characteristics down the ages, while yet adapting themselves to the country and maintaining close ties with the

Anglo-Saxons. The first Dutch occupants of what is now New York and the State of New York, the first landowners of that valley of the Hudson which the English took away from them, without, however, taking away their immense estates, rank in the United States as aristocrats. Although there must have been a great many poor or humble Dutch at the time when the colony of New Amsterdam was ceded to England by the Netherlands, the impression has remained in the American nation that the old Dutch stock was an aristocratic stock. Among its offshots were legendary figures, such as the Van Rensselaers, who had carved out for themselves along the higher reaches of the Hudson a sort of kingdom, of which they remained the rulers up to the end of the eighteenth century. The rest of the Dutch profited by the prestige of two or three families, and, as they were all industrious, worthy, tolerant and sociable, the epithet Dutch, or son of a Dutchman, was a social distinction in America. Not every one who chooses can be Dutch in the United States, although a number of Jews have had a good try.

The Roosevelts were not at first among the most illustrious of these Dutch families. They had lands, they were wealthy, they had a good veneer of culture and of social position, but there was nothing particular to relate or to extol concerning them. The first to attain to fame was Theodore Roosevelt, of Oyster Bay, the famous Republican President, whose picturesque physiognomy, impetuous and shrewd rather than profound intelligence, sudden, daring and fantastic adventures, and imperialistic and journalistic instinct, fascinated the American middle class from 1900 to 1915. He was

President; he wanted to give America a true sense of American greatness and of Roosevelt's genius. He revealed to the civilized nations — who were somewhat bewildered but quite sympathetic — the American sailors, the intensity of American life and the American, Teddy Roosevelt. The Kaiser received him very amiably, Oxford conferred upon him a doctor's degree and the students fastened a little Teddy bear to his doctor's robe, France was fascinated by him, a beautiful French princess translated his works and a professor of the Collège de France made him the object of his studies.

Theodore Roosevelt remained famous for this journey, for the laws which he got passed against the trusts, and by reason of his efforts to get himself reëlected a third time. He failed and the end of his life was melancholy; but the American people, who had not always approved him, whom he had sometimes vexed and often disgusted, retained a very pleasant memory of him as a not too distinguished, very vivacious and very likeable patrician. The humble folk loved his not too refined vitality, which was like their own; the great folk were gratified to think that one of their number had played so important a rôle. In short, the legend of Theodore Roosevelt was a splendid one and incomparably more illustrious than his life, though that too was fairly brilliant and very noisy.

This glory was reflected upon the entire family. Theodore Roosevelt had a strong family feeling and a very large family. He visited and was visited by his relations. He paid a great deal of attention to his wife, he did not neglect his children and he was on good terms with his cousins. In fact, the Roosevelts were a family after the European style, like many other families in

America. Such families preserve those habits of collective and continuous intimacy which are characteristic of our old families in the Old World, whereas the ordinary American family, while no less united or less real than the European family, is narrower in its scope. Father, mother and children — these are the American family. The executive power is in the hands of the mother; the legislative power is in the hands of the children; and the father has hardly any other power save that of going away, which is, after all, a good deal and all that he needs in a country where there is so much room. The American family is, for the most part, affectionate, cheerful and stable, though an optical delusion makes the Europeans imagine that it is bizarre and lax.

In the Dutch circles of the New World, the family has remained a family of the old style, in which the father possesses the authority, the mother the power, and the children a liberty governed by an unwritten, but subtle and explicit constitutional agreement. The Anglo-Saxon families have become merged in the terrestrial ocean and the social mass of the United States, in which innumerable Smiths, Joneses, Williamses and Adamses, who may be related but have lost all sense of kinship, rub shoulders without recognizing one another or knowing any other family save their fathers and mothers, their brothers and sisters. The Dutch families, on the other hand, have remained isolated and compact units, in which identity of name implies a sense of kinship and mutual recognition. When two Smiths or two Pierces meet in a train or in the street or in a club or in a drawing-room, or even in a bedroom, it never occurs to them that they are related. They are Smiths and Pierces, as they are human beings, by chance. When two Roosevelts or two Van Rensselaers meet, whether at a fair or on the ocean, they form a family group. They cannot deny that they belong to the same family. If they tried to do it, it would be the worse for them.

The Roosevelts, then, are a real family, and they have a solid prestige derived from the Old World. They are also one of the patrician families of America, thanks to Theodore Roosevelt, whose fame has shed its luster on them all. This Theodore Roosevelt, whom the American people liked to call "Teddy" or T. R., had a distinguished wife, on whom he lavished his love and his attentions, four lively and attractive sons, two daughters and a great number of cousins, most of them intelligent and distinguished — altogether, very likeable people. They were all on terms of intimacy with one another and formed a sort of Roosevelt clan, which the United States approved and admired.

Of all the family of Theodore Roosevelt, his daughter Alice was the most famous, and she thoroughly deserved it, by reason not only of the incomparable sparkle of her steel-blue eyes, but also of her keen and brilliant wit and the charming spontaneity of her manners. One day, on the occasion of a diplomatic dinner at the White House, when the reception rooms, the ante-chambers and the hall were crowded with ministers in uniform and officers in full dress, Alice Roosevelt was seen to arrive on the scene, rather late, by seating herself astride the banister and sliding down the first floor, where her bedroom was situated, to the ground floor. She collided with an admiral and a minister, as she came to earth, and since this was before aviation had become fashionable, it caused a great sensation.

Theodore Roosevelt had his legend and the entire Roosevelt family had a legend. It took up a lot of space in the newspapers, and it took up more and more space after 1900. Theodore Roosevelt, as long as he lived, figured incessantly in the newspaper headings. The same applies to his son, Theodore II, though he had less luck and less genius than his father; but his political career, the rôle which he played in the American Legion and his appointment as Governor of the Philippines, kept him in the public eye. Theodore's two other sons, Archibald and Kermit, also occupy important places in American life, the one in politics, the other by his hunting exploits and his charming personality. As for Alice, who became the wife of Nicholas Longworth, the most distinguished, witty and sagacious of all the members of the House of Representatives, after having been the liveliest young lady in America, she has become the most acute observer of national politics. She reappeared on the scene of the great political battles of 1928 to 1932 as adversary-in-chief of Mrs. Gann, the sister of Vice President Curtis, a worthy dame from Kansas, with a large notion of her own importance and odious manners, who wanted to take precedence of all the other Washington ladies. Mrs. Longworth sacrificed herself to the public weal and defied Mrs. Gann, all of which created a great sensation in the city of Washington where, before official luncheons, faultlessly attired gentlemen may be seen between ten minutes to one and one o'clock, pacing up and down before the house to which they are invited, in order that they may arrive at precisely the same moment as the principal guest. Into this atmosphere of scrupulous correctitude, Mrs. Longworth, and all the Roosevelts, imported a spontaneity, a fantasy and a sense of fun, which charmed a large number of spectators and interested everybody.

Certainly, Franklin Roosevelt is not an actual nephew of T. R., nor a near cousin of these illustrious Roosevelts, but they have a common ancestor in the eighteenth century and this ancestor has not been forgotten. Like all the Roosevelts, he was a good merchant. And he bequeathed to his family a sense of unity so strong that Elliott Roosevelt, brother of the famous President, was godfather to the young Franklin Roosevelt when he was baptized in January, 1882. Later, Franklin married the daughter of his godfather, who was led to the altar on the day of her marriage by Theodore Roosevelt himself, since Elliott was by this time dead.

If one desired to draw a distinction between the two branches, it would doubtless be found that Franklin Roosevelt's branch has, on the whole, more claims to social distinction, both because it has continued faithful to the political tradition of the family (it has remained Democratic, whilst after 1860, the other branch, that of Theodore, became Republican) and also because Franklin's mother belongs to the Delano family, which is linked up with the oldest traditions of the colony of New York. The Delanos were among those Flemish merchants who, about 1616, were the first to arrive in, to colonize and to exploit these regions, which were then almost unknown. They were, in fact, only frequented by a few fishers and a few daring traders, who tried, without any great measure of success, to do business with and swindle the red and naked savages who were the only other inhabitants.

Dutch on his father's side, Flemish on his mother's,

Franklin Roosevelt is a good Anglo-Saxon gentleman, reared in a wealthy *bourgeois* home in the country, where he and his family led a comfortable, athletic and simple life. His father, who was in business, made money and retired to a family estate in the middle of the Hudson Valley. He had had two wives and two sons, and he knew life. The circle of his acquaintances was large, but he had no personal ambition save happiness, and his great dream was to give a good education to his younger son, Franklin Delano, on whom he had based all his hopes.

Round the house were some fine trees and some wide and very green lawns, as in England. In the autumn, the Roosevelts hunted with the hounds; in the winter they spent long hours in the library around the log fire. On Sunday they went piously to church, and they conducted themselves as, for three centuries, their Dutch and Flemish ancestors had not ceased to conduct themselves, — with geniality, good nature and good spirits.

In the vicinity of the Roosevelts there resided a number of wealthy neighbors, with whom they were on good terms but whose life they did not share. And this was undoubtedly one of the important factors in the career of Theodore Roosevelt and also in that of Franklin Roosevelt. Their world afforded them a number of advantages — social prestige, refinement, culture and agreeable intercourse — but they were never the prisoners of their world, because they did not altogether belong to it, they were not entirely satisfied with it. They did not quarrel with it, but they were able to detach themselves from it at a number of critical moments, and they preserved a freedom of action which some more opulent politicians were never able to acquire.

They enjoyed the advantage not only of the Roosevelt legend but of a freedom which the public little suspected.

Thanks to the legend, Franklin Roosevelt, from his childhood onwards, had only to make a movement, and the newspapers talked of it without any need for his intervention. Mr. Hoover had to work for twelve years in order to construct a machine for glorifying Mr. Hoover, and ended by constructing it so well that it made him a monstrosity. Mr. Roosevelt had no need to construct the machine; he merely had to guide it and protect it against itself; and that is why, during his presidential campaign, all his Press work exhibited that character of precision, refinement and polish which made Mr. Hoover's poor efforts seem grotesque.

Thanks to the Rooseveltian legend and atmosphere, Franklin Roosevelt associated with politicians from the outset, and he very soon learned that exercising authority is a habit like any other. His father was intimately acquainted with President Cleveland, to whom, according to the legend, he introduced his son at an early age. And the good folk affirm that Cleveland, with the melancholy appropriate to the occasion, laid his hand on the child's fair head and said to the father: "I wish this child every good fortune in the world, and, among them, one of the greatest good fortunes of all: that he may never be President of the United States."

It was a memorable scene, but, as a matter of fact, Cleveland was mistaken; not to exercise authority would not have been a pleasure to Franklin Roosevelt, for he had the physical gift of command, and the *milieu* in which he lived cultivated this gift to such good purpose that, whereas the most trifling decisions tortured his predecessors, Messers. Harding, Coolidge and Hoover, he is able, amid the most catastrophic circumstances, to give orders of historic importance and to enjoy a good night's sleep afterwards.

He has always lived among those actors who are dubbed politician, from an early age he has been a politician himself, and he has learned not to blink beneath the glare of the footlights. Mr. Harding had dim-sighted eyes, which the dazzling light of the stage prevented from seeing anything whatever; Mr. Coolidge kept his eyes cautiously half-closed, and though they could see fairly well into corners, they were never able to discern the horizon. Mr. Hoover had a congenital blink, which the strong light of glory had aggravated to a morbid degree. He only saw in spasms, and his Presidency was one long spasm, in which he ceased to see anything clearly. Franklin Roosevelt, with his large, kind eyes, looks wherever he pleases, and as he knows that he has a smile capable of provoking an immediate smile on the faces of his hearers, he looks straight at them. It is not certain that he does it out of candor, for the head of a State is not pledged to candor, but it is clear that he does it from a sense of freedom. Now, of all the great forces which a chief may possess, his freedom in relation to things and men, and in relation even to his subordinates (who form, whatever the public may think, the most irksome constraint to which a leader is subject) is one of the most precious.

The opinion of great folk and small folk alike holds no terrors for him. Any one who has lived for a long time beneath the eye of the public learns to appreciate the vanity of this pleasure and the frivolity both of censure and of approbation. Opinion is a formidable but a fugitive, feminine and febrile force. No great man can do without it, but any man who depends upon its unfailing support is doomed to speedy catastrophe. Public opinion is one of those influential and dangerous friends with whom one must know how to quarrel in order to keep their respect and one's own liberty of action. One must understand it sufficiently to realize that its favor does not bring any very stable gifts, that its anger does not inflict any very dangerous punishments, and that its displeasure does not imply any very serious loss. One must understand it enough to grasp that, among all the dangers of public life, the most serious is not disfavor, neglect, or a temporary exasperation of public opinion, but false and clumsy praise which gains a hold on the public mind and distorts the true and living image of the hero.

For instance, Mr. Hoover, as a man, although he has no charm, has great qualities which might have earned him the esteem of his contemporaries if a stupid and lying legend had not tried to make him into a strong man, a man of iron. He later found himself imprisoned in this iron statue, which he had constructed for his own apotheosis, but which did not suit him at all and ended by crushing him.

Mr. Roosevelt was more at his ease with public opinion and he always managed to disengage himself from inaccurate and oversimplified legends and false praises; he remained at once illustrious and variable, supple and very much alive. He did not allow his panegyrists to build up for him a great, soulless legend, and he con-

stantly and fearlessly rectified, modified and elucidated
what was being said about him. He was able to do this,
for he was in the rare and fortunate position of being
a member of the Roosevelt family, a cousin of Theodore,
of Alice Longworth and of Theodore, Junior; and so
he could be sure that, whatever he did and however he
treated public opinion, it would never forget him.

It is the thought of being forgotten that holds the
greatest terrors for a public man, who, like a lover, can
bear anything — even hatred — from the object of his
devotion, but for whom silence is the portent and the
beginning of the end. Mr. Harding, Mr. Coolidge and
Mr. Hoover were obsessed by this ever-present threat of
the irremediable oblivion into which the specific gravity
of their personality would normally have plunged them,
if they once ceased to satisfy the party or the public.
This danger does not exist for Franklin Roosevelt; he is
a Roosevelt, and, no matter what he does, he will die
and he will be buried on the front page of the newspapers.

It would be idle to maintain that he is not a patrician.
Doubtless America does not possess a nobility, but she
does possess an aristocracy. By his name, his blood, his
family and the circle in which he moves, Franklin
Roosevelt belongs to this aristocracy. He belongs to it
also in virtue of his youth.

It is difficult to talk to the French about the American
youth and to make them understand the rôle played by
youth in the life both of the individual and of society
in the United States. For a Frenchman, youth is a stern,
interesting, not very agreeable time, in which man pre-

pares himself for life and works hard in order to become whatever he wants to be. During his youth, man is not yet a man; he is nothing, in fact, save a tense will and a hope. Hence, there is something austere and harsh in the youth of France. For them youth is an introduction to the book of life, whose first chapter begins after the period of examinations, when one has obtained one's diplomas, embarked on a career and begun to think about getting married.

For the American, youth is a part of life, and the most brilliant, the most significant and the most human part. In this climate, where everything develops swiftly and vehemently, the young man and the young woman have a certain brilliance which is lacking in the youth of France, and the invitations to enjoyment which are addressed to them are in marked contrast with the invitations to work and effort which French civilization addresses to its young people.

Every American is proud of his youth, and all America is proud of that youth which sheds its luster over the continent, the towns, the country, the race and every human being. Youth is not an introduction to a coming existence; it is life itself, and it is the summit of life. The young American does not fill his youth with preparations for future work but with the immediate accomplishment of actions which afford him pleasure and with the enjoyment of creatures and things; he uses it to give a complete and brilliant notion of himself. In his youth he attains a fullness of living which he will probably never experience again, for family life, work, the fatigue of business and the monotony of the office will brutalize him, limit him and confine him in a

narrow prison. His youth, on the other hand, affords him
the opportunity of living his own life in all its daring,
fullness and variety; everything that he aspires to do will
be approved and admired, everything that he undertakes
will have the support of his elders. All America showers
prizes upon youth, and any one who can take advantage
of this has won the game of life in advance. The football
player who has covered himself with glory at his college
and at the same time covered his college with glory, the
racer who has beaten the record, the swimmer who has
won a cup for his university, the baseball captain who
has led his team to victory: all these, on the day on
which they receive their diplomas, can be sure that the
old pupils of the college, the university or the school
will find some post for them, which will be advantageous
and lucrative in proportion to the success or the glory
which they have harvested as young students.

This is so striking and so general a fact in the United
States that it suffices to explain the invasion of the
schools, colleges and universities by millions of young
men and young women, who have little interest in
ideas, in the arts or in the sciences, little desire for excessive refinement and little inclination for intellectual
labor. But they are eager to taste the joy of life and not
to miss their chance, and they go to college in order to
gain *immediate* happiness and to win the success in sport,
the worldly distinction, and the reputation of being a
handsome fellow or a good comrade, which will forthwith insure them a good position in life.

If there is no nobility in the United States, there is
an aristocracy, and the various social classes are very
apparent to a trained eye. The American who has studied

at a college or a university is in quite a different social class from the poor boy whose means have not allowed him to get beyond the high school. A graduate of Harvard, Yale, Princeton, Dartmouth and the universities of the East in general is in quite a different rank from a graduate of the great state universities in the West, where the fees are nominal and access is afforded to all and sundry. In the United States, in fact, the college and the university are not content, as in France, for instance, with giving an intellectual education and a scientific, literary, artistic or linguistic training. The college shapes the young man for social life, moral life and religious life, and at the same time it is supposed to give him some instruction and prepare him for a career.

Each university has its point of view, its principles and its atmosphere; each of them addresses itself to a particular social stratum and confers upon its students not only a certain philosophy but also a certain hall mark of social distinction or of democratic simplicity. Now, of all the universities, the most brilliant, the most intelligent, the one whose traditions go back farthest and which, during the nineteenth century, underwent the most harmonious and systematic development, is Harvard University, in New England, near Boston, founded in 1636 by the Puritans.

The youth of Franklin Roosevelt was spent at his home, then at Groton, then at Harvard, then at Columbia.

He was strong, he had a robust and athletic young body, and he had a keen and swift intelligence. He had grown up in a circle where people read books, talked and engaged in free discussion. His father and his

brother,[2] who was twenty years older than himself, had
been his daily companions. He had hunted with the
hounds, he had sailed with his father, he had fished with
his brother. He had listened in silence to the conversations of the gentlemen in his father's library. In the
summer he had dreamed as he lay stretched full length
on the warm boards of the yacht. In the autumn, he
had explored on foot and on horseback the plains and
valleys of the Hudson, when the foliage was changing
color and all the trees of America seemed to be burst-
ing into flame. Compared with the little children of
the cities, reduced to life in the city, compared with
the little children of the country, reduced to life in
the fields, Franklin Roosevelt was a man acquainted with
all the shades and contrasts of that rainbow which is
real life. He had strength and he also had a good start.

He felt himself so strong, he was so conscious that he
had made a good start, that he had wanted at first to
do without his fellow men. His childhood dream was to
be a sailor and he confided this ambition to his father.
But Mr. Roosevelt was a business man, and the Roosevelt
family was a good old *bourgeois* family of the old-time
American variety. He decided that Franklin should pursue the ordinary routine followed by young men of his
circle who mean to go into business: he should go to
a good school, then to a good university; he should there
make friends, form connections, acquire some general
knowledge and a good reputation, and he should lead,
like all the Roosevelts of the past, a worthy and comfortable life, the life of a New York business man,
crowned by a tranquil maturity or old age at Hyde

[2] This son died when Franklin Roosevelt was still a child.

Park, on the estate which had for a century been the home of the Roosevelts. Such were the ideas of James Roosevelt, Franklin's father, and, as the Roosevelt family was an old-fashioned family, such was the young man's destiny.

He was sent to Groton. Groton is in 1933 a very smart school, perhaps the smartest in the United States, and its pupils are recruited among the sons of millionaires; but in 1896 it was simply a good school to which good and well-bred people sent their children, in order that they might be educated by good professors. Franklin Roosevelt was sent there at a time when he was longing to sail the seas and was smarting beneath the disappointment of a thwarted ambition. But, even at this age, he was not one of those who get at cross purposes with life. He was a good swimmer and he knew, then as now, that in life no less than on the water, in order to float and to swim well, one's body must be able to adapt itself to the form of the wave which bears it. In order to console himself for his loss of the sea and solitude, Franklin Roosevelt turned his attention to men; they interested him and he delighted in their companionship.

At Groton he was what American boys call "a good mixer." He worked, he engaged in sport, he was to be seen wherever he ought to be seen, he took part in all the things that a child of his age ought to take part in — running, rowing, football, baseball, singing — and even study, since it is an understood thing that in every school there is a certain amount of study. But, over and above that, he studied men and associated with them. Even at that date he had an instinct for social relationships; he spoke well and at length, he discussed politics and he possessed that twofold gift which alone makes an agreeable talker: he had as many ideas as were needed to fill up all the silences of life, and he was sufficiently detached from his ideas not to press them unduly or to let them be obstacles to friendship.

The result was that he was elected a member of the school team of orators. For every institution in the New World has a team for systematic debate, just as it has its football team and its tennis team. Franklin Roosevelt was a great success as a debater, and he excelled in political discussion, for he was already interested in public life. As a schoolboy he pleaded for a strong American fleet and against the occupation of the Philippines. (As though fate were amusing herself by making him play with the facts and ideas which would later be his instruments of work!)

After Groton he entered Harvard, which was then at the zenith of its glory. Young Roosevelt could attend the lectures of William James and Josiah Royce on philosophy, of A. Lawrence Lowell on political economy, and of C. E. Norton and Briggs on literature. Harvard, with its eager curiosity and its interest in Europe, had an international charm which blended oddly with its puritan atmosphere.

There Franklin Roosevelt continued his academic career, but this time he won a success which was to set him on the first rung of fame's ladder. The Harvard students publish a daily journal which is called the *Crimson* (after the Harvard color), in which they discuss among themselves the affairs of the college. This journal, which is edited seriously and carefully, runs the risk of being tedious if it is too serious, and insignificant if it is not. It also runs the danger of displeasing the professors if it is indiscreet, and displeasing the students if it is too discreet. In short, it presents all the difficulties which a daily newspaper always presents, and, in addition, it has to cope with some special problems of its own, since it is a journal published at the meeting-point of youth and manhood.

Franklin Roosevelt was at first reporter and was afterwards elected editor in chief of this journal, which was at that time languishing in a disastrous respectability. Immediately upon his appointment, he took it in hand. And he transformed it. He set to work to put life into it, and, at the risk of displeasing the Faculty, he fearlessly attacked the obsolete methods at that time practised by the university administration. At the risk of irritating his comrades, he told them the truth quite frankly, and one day, when the Harvard football team had duly beaten that of Maine, which is a far smaller and less famous university, he did not attempt to conceal his scorn. Whilst all were celebrating the victory, he declared to them in black and white that it was far from creditable and that the team had, in fact, been very indifferent. The article made a great sensation.

Thanks to a just balance between the censure he bestowed on the professors and the students respectively, both forgave him; so greatly does man delight to hear his neighbor criticized. Thanks to a wise equilibrium between good breeding and audacity, young Roosevelt was a successful chief editor, and he roused his journal from its torpor. He himself became famous in the college because of his success, and, when he left Harvard, he was already a personage.

Young as this personage was, he was not to be despised. Boston and Harvard were at that time the intellectual center of the United States and also one of the most important economic centers. The ex-students of Harvard, among whom Theodore Roosevelt was one of the most brilliant luminaries, formed a very influential social freemasonry. Franklin Roosevelt added to the prestige of his family the prestige of his university.

He added to it the experience of Columbia, the university to which he went to study law. Columbia is the largest university in the immense city of New York. Perched on a hill near the Hudson, it opens its doors to the urban population of this metropolis, which contains the largest Jewish population in the world, as well as a crowd of the most heterogeneous racial elements. Whereas Harvard is the citadel of the white, fair, Anglo-Saxon and puritan America, Columbia is one of those melting-pots in which international ideas are molded, in which races are fused, and in which the acute intelligence of the Jewish race delights to shine.

At Columbia, Franklin Roosevelt found that medley of ideas, types and points of view which render New York at once so fascinating and so fatiguing. Whereas Harvard, after its fashion which may be called puritan and might be called pagan, preserves a monastic atmosphere and remains detached from the things of this world, Columbia, the faithful servant of New York, does not allow earthly considerations to be forgotten. It contains more than one radical, in it may be heard more than one heterodox opinion, and in it is proclaimed more than one daring principle. And there, no doubt, the mind of Franklin Roosevelt, always interested in anything new and anything alive, gained, while diligently studying the law, an intimate knowledge of all the forms of audacity, revolt and radicalism.

Thus the young man ended his childhood life with a knowledge of good and evil.

He ended it as a young man of good family ought to end it in the United States. He had succeeded perfectly. He had conformed to type, and he had been able to preserve the liveliness of his intuitions. He was a Roosevelt, a graduate of Harvard and Columbia, and he possessed a vast and serene ambition. Everything was going well.

Everything went well. He married his cousin, Eleanor Roosevelt, and, at the wedding, the two branches of the family, the Democrats and the Republicans, met and mixed. Theodore Roosevelt led his niece to the altar, Franklin led her to his home. Their household was all that the novelists, for the most part, describe so badly and that the biographers would do better to skim over very lightly.

Everything went well. They had six children but one died in infancy. Anna, James, Elliott, Franklin Delano, Junior, and John gave them no cause for anything but joy and pride. They were good parents, they had good children, and everything was going as it should.

Franklin Roosevelt was prospering in his profession. In 1907, he became a member of the firm of Carter, Ledyard and Milburn. In America the legal profession is very lucrative and highly respected. It creates a great many worldly ties, it may give rise to valuable business friendships, it may lead to political life and sometimes it ends in diplomacy. Franklin Roosevelt had no need for anxiety.

Everything happened as it ought. In 1910 the Democrats were very much worried by a number of recent political scandals; as a last resort and without any great hopes they invited young Roosevelt to stand as candidate for the New York Senate. There was no likelihood that a conservative and rural population, which had been unswervingly loyal to the Republican cause since the War of Secession, would change its mind, but the Democratic Party could not forego the formality of putting up a candidate. It was out of kindness that they invited the young lawyer to stand; it was zest for the game, love of difficulty, and a secret instinct that prompted him to accept the invitation.

All went well. He was young, daring, vivacious and handsome. He emulated the frank and vigorous eloquence of his cousin Theodore, he denounced the corrupters and the corrupt in politics, and this pleased. Finally, he was a Roosevelt, and the good Republican countryfolk, who had heard about the great Republican President, Theodore Roosevelt, felt drawn to this other Roosevelt. After all, he belonged to the same family. Whether it was personal charm or *quid pro quo* no one will ever know, but Franklin Roosevelt, Democrat, was elected by 15,800 votes against 14,400 in a district which had always elected Republicans and where this party ordinarily had a majority of some 3,000.

In the Senate of New York State he was a great success; he was independent, intelligent, honest and adroit. At the Democratic Convention of 1912 he was still more successful; he was one of those who pushed Wilson's candidacy and who shared the honors of his hard-won and unexpected victory. As a reward, he was appointed Assistant Secretary of the Navy, which position he held from 1913 to 1920.

There too all went well. His chief was a worthy individual, whose surname was Daniels and who rejoiced in the Christian name of Josephus. Mr. Daniels was an excellent journalist, who came from a small town in the South, was well acquainted with public opinion in his district and estimated the psychology of his fellow men at its true value. He was not credited with much knowledge of boats, but Franklin Roosevelt was at his side and often ruled at the Navy Board in his stead. In 1917 he was ready and he succeeded in transporting the great American army to Europe, in protecting it from submarines and in blockading the latter in their turn. All went well, and it was no light work.

In 1920 Franklin Roosevelt was the perfect and consummate type of the American patrician. He had been a good student, a good athlete, a good lawyer, a good husband, a good father, an excellent politician and a skillful and energetic Secretary. He had even given proof of his initiative and his courage when he inspected the American naval forces in European waters during the war. In the navy he was respected, in his home he was adored. His blue eyes, beneath the blue sky of America and faced with the blue horizon of a rich, simple and distinguished life, reflected only happiness.

The peace brought a discordant note. Wilson fell ill, and his work was criticized. The League of Nations, his cherished offspring, was attacked. All the idealism which had rallied his disciples to his side was turned to ridicule, and no one was there to defend him. Franklin

Roosevelt did his best. At thirty-eight years of age he accepted the overwhelming task of candidate for the Vice Presidency of the United States. Cox, whom the party was putting up for the Presidency, was a worthy individual who deserved esteem and sympathy but whom the country did not know and would never know. There was no means and no reason for success. Franklin Roosevelt and Cox suffered an overwhelming defeat, as was only to be expected.

People murmured that this young man had been wrong to let himself be thrust forward like this at the wrong moment. It was bad taste. It was also bad taste to be a Democrat. And it was an error of judgment to have the misfortune to get beaten when all were abandoning themselves to the joy of peace, the pleasures of prosperity and the gayety of optimism.

In order to take a rest, he spent the summer in the North. It was a hot, sultry August, and one day, when he was picnicking with the children, they heard the alarm signal appealing for help against a forest fire. They made their way to the spot and all that afternoon they trampled among smoking embers and flaming shrubs. At length, towards evening, overheated and exhausted, they returned to their camping ground and made haste to plunge into the cool waters of the lake.

The children laughed, splashed one another, and could not be induced to leave the water. Franklin Roosevelt, for his part, came out of it hurriedly, for he was shivering and he felt ill. He stretched himself in an armchair and gradually he had the impression that life was ebbing from his limbs. A doctor, who was hastily summoned, could make nothing of it. Another was sent for, and then a third, and they discovered that Franklin Roosevelt had had an attack of infantile paralysis.

He was thirty-nine years of age, and every one took it for granted that his career was ended. He said: "It is humiliating, at the prime of life, to be floored by an infant's disease." Then he told his doctors that he meant to overcome the wretched thing. For a month he fought against it without intermission. He could not be moved and his only strength was in his eyes and in his will. When he was a little better, he was moved to New York, and his condition was summed up as follows: he would never recover the use of his legs, but, with a great deal of courage, skill and luck, he might manage to live a not unbearable invalid life.

All the newspapers, the country and the doctors looked upon him as done for. They pitied him, for in America, pity is more natural than jealousy, but they soon forgot him, for in the United States suffering is not fashionable and at that time it was less so than ever. It was Franklin Roosevelt himself who decided to go on living. He begged the doctors to do their utmost to restore to him the use of his limbs and he started to take up life again.

He returned to his office. He accepted the presidency of the Boy Scouts of his district, and he did a great deal for them. He did not lose touch with politics. He began to ride on horseback again, although his legs were still paralyzed. And everywhere he sought advice and remedies which might help him to fight against his disease.

George Peabody, of New York, had heard of an old

spa in the South—Warm Springs, Georgia—a small, little-known place but recommended for rheumatism; it was said that victims of infantile paralysis had found their strength revive there. Franklin Roosevelt went to Warm Springs and made it his headquarters. He set himself to swim in the pool of warm water indefatigably for hours on end, in order to exercise his arms and his trunk, which were as strong as ever, and in order to bring back life to his legs, which were now helpless. By this means he succeeded, little by little, in restoring their power of movement.

He vanquished his disease. He did not kill it; but it did not kill him. It did not vanquish him, and he vanquished it. Since 1921 Franklin Rosevelt has been a disabled man, and he lives with his disablement, but his life is not bound to his disablement; his disablement is not the center nor yet the limit of his life. Thanks to Warm Springs, he is still a robust man. Thanks to his iron belt and the jointed iron supports which he wears inside his trousers, he can stand upright and he can walk. He can make a speech standing upright, with his face to the audience. Before rising from his seat, he manipulates his iron legs beneath the table, he stretches them, he plants them on the floor, then, leaning his arms on the table, he raises himself with a single movement and appears like a laughing giant above the faces of the crowd. When one looks at him, his smile and his strength check compassion, just as they stifle any questions.

One day, in Georgia, during his presidential campaign, he was making a speech, standing erect, and as he was speaking of a difficult point, he stamped on the platform and leaned forward. Suddenly, to every one's horror, he lost his balance, swayed and fell head foremost into the crowd. People rushed forward to pick him up, he was carried back on to the platform, and there, raising himself erect once more, he resumed his speech at the point where he had left it, without explanation or hesitation. The audience of one accord gave him a tremendous ovation.

That day people realized that if his disease inhabited him and would doubtless inhabit him to the day of his death, he did not inhabit it, for he had allotted his disease only a small space, a narrow chamber, in which he kept it confined and whence it could not escape. In the face of a disease, men obey their deepest instinct: some nurse their disease, others nurse themselves; some nurse their body, others their mind, others their destiny. Some exploit the disease for the purpose of enriching themselves with its exotic, phosphorescent glamour; others exploit the fight against disease in order to gain more strength; others again have sufficient silence, disdain and vitality to seek no advantage from disease and simply shut it away like some useless object.

For Proust every moment of suffering and disease becomes a fever of creation; for Roosevelt disease is merely a trivial and tedious formality, like blowing one's nose or shaking hands with tiresome people; and between the two here is Pascal, to whom disease reveals from time to time some of the hidden resources of the human heart.

Franklin Roosevelt has taken pride in asking nothing of disease. He refuses facile sympathy and the commonplace pity which it is prepared to offer. To a young journalist who wanted to become emotional, he said once: "No sentimentality about that business; do you understand?" And, during the whole of his campaign, he refused to allow his friends to make capital of it. He spoke of it only twice, and then merely to prove that it did not prevent him from acting. He has mastered the brute, and he keeps it in a cage, tamed and vanquished.

None the less, it has given him something.

Franklin Roosevelt, at thirty-eight years of age, was a child of victory, of ease and of the fashionable world. His life had been open to every good fortune, and as none had shunned him, he had not turned his back on any. To this ease, this breeding, and this alluring good fortune he owed a part of his popularity. At thirty-eight years of age he was not very different from those Republican politicians, his comrades from Harvard, Columbia, the Club and New York, who built up political wisdom on prosperity and virtue on happiness.

From 1920 to 1930 all his class and all his group speculated on happiness, luck and on the machine for extracting happiness from luck and virtue from happiness. From 1920 to 1930, if he had continued to be the pre-war Franklin Roosevelt, would he have been able to extricate himself from that torrent of optimism which was sweeping America off her feet? Disease made it impossible for Franklin Roosevelt to be like other people. It introduced into his calculations and into his perception of reality that element which was always absent from the calculations of the Republican Party, because it was absent from the perception of its leaders: the possibility of misfortune, the fatality of pain. Believe in prosperity, said the Republican leaders, and it will exist. "The crisis," declared the admirable Mrs. Gann to the assembled farmers, "is a vicious state of mind." The Republicans, in the face of discontent, poverty and famine, employed the method dear to children's nurses who, when their charges are sick in the train or on board ship, shake them and shout in their ear: "Come, don't be silly, it's all fancy."

Because they had dined too generously, because they played golf too well, because their motor cars were too luxurious and their digestions too good, because their lives were too successful and their domestics too well-trained, it had become impossible for the Republican leaders to understand that America could suffer crises and difficulties and that a normal man could be discontented. Only a Communist, a degenerate or a drunkard could doubt the goodness of the world, the prosperity of America and the wisdom of the Republican Party.

Disease robbed Franklin Roosevelt of this illusion and this dream. Al Smith and he were the only two popular orators, the only two men, whose voice rang true in the ear of the crowd, for they alone, amid the Republicans who were denying the reality of misfortune and the Communists who were exalting imaginary misfortunes, spoke soberly and sincerely of the real sufferings which they knew and understood.

Franklin Roosevelt was a pioneer: he spoke openly of adversity and misfortune at a time when they were not fashionable in America, when they were denied any place in human life. But he had learned that adversity and misfortune have their place in every normal existence, and he knew what place ought to be assigned them. He was ready for the catastrophe well before the rest, and he knew the way to master catastrophes.

That is why, in 1932, his language seemed to the American people so calm, so wise and so sound. He did not anywhere excite those waves of enthusiasm which Theodore Roosevelt had once excited; he did not even move the crowds as Mr. Hoover, in his speech at Des Moines, succeeded in doing; but a graver, deeper and more decent sentiment was propagated wherever he went. People were conscious that between him and circumstances there existed a harmony which did not depend alone on his intelligence or his good will but also on his destiny and on the secret which the gods had revealed to his inmost self in August, 1921.

From the outset of his career, Franklin Roosevelt was a wise and adroit politician. He had, in fact, the sort of skill which consists in not being afraid of people or things, but, on the contrary, of inclining instinctively towards attack, where there is cause and opportunity for attack. As a patrician and as a Harvard graduate, he had a taste for liberty, independence and individualism. He entered politics at a time when they were dominated by a small number of political dictators, who held their districts by means of strongly organized clans. These bands had few scruples and little sense of shame, but no one dared oppose them. Franklin Roosevelt was one of the first to do it, and he brought to the task so supple a courage that he was able at once to succeed and to make himself respected and forgiven.

All the same, it was a dangerous game for a young politician. He had the sense to realize this, to withdraw in time from local politics and to transfer himself to Washington, where, for seven years, he was an excellent Assistant Secretary of the Navy. A great many praiseworthy details are recounted concerning him, and it would be pleasant and profitable to reproduce them here, if they had not the disadvantage of being official praises drawn from official documents. The savings which Roosevelt effected on purchases, the kindnesses which he lavished on his military and civil subordinates, the orderliness which he introduced into the offices, the liberality which he showed in disregarding the political opinions of his subordinates — all these proofs of wisdom will be easy to describe later, when he has ceased to be President of the United States; for the moment they belong to the domain of political commonplaces. True as they are, they are too useful to his candidature to be taken very seriously.

Franklin Roosevelt was a good Assistant Secretary of the Navy, and, in order to prove this fact, it is sufficient to say that the Republicans, once they came into power, could find nothing with which to reproach him and were forced to hold their tongues. His perfect honesty, his love of work and his gift for leadership were conspicuous at Washington from 1913 to 1920. He pleased every one. In his simple home, his wife and he entertained in charming style, and their most distinguished colleagues, the pick of Washington society, took pleasure in visiting them. Franklin Roosevelt had succeeded.

However, he was not yet mature. His wisdom was not yet infallible. At that time he made a mistake which created some sensation in 1919 and 1920 and which it is worth while to relate here. Among the associates of Mr. Wilson, there were three men who enjoyed the admiration of the Press, who were considered as distinguished minds and for whom a brilliant future was predicted: they were Franklin Lane, Secretary of the Interior, an amiable, attractive and philosophic personality, the young Franklin Roosevelt, and Mr. Hoover, the engineer. These three men met frequently, and they believed themselves to have in common a number of rather vague tendencies and liberal or even idealistic views.

Franklin Roosevelt believed this so firmly that he conceived a great plan. Mr. Wilson's reign was then in its period of decline. Minds and hearts were turning away from the sick leader; the League of Nations was beaten from the field, and the ranks were thinning around the President, whom the Republican conservatives covered with abuse and on whom the radicals and Socialists of the *New Republic* and of *The Nation* lavished their insults. Franklin Roosevelt, dreaming of the future, said to himself that only a noble personality endowed with a great prestige and the gift of command could stem this current, and, casting his eyes around him, he saw only his friend, Mr. Herbert Hoover, the great philanthropist, the organizer of the Franco-Belgian relief scheme. . . . He spoke of it to his colleagues and he drew up a vast plan. All the Progressives of the Democratic Party were to agree together to push Mr. Hoover's candidacy at the 1920 convention and finally, in 1924 at latest, to get him accepted by the party as candidate for the Presidency. Franklin Roosevelt clung to his idea and he took some trouble to make it known.

But one day, when he was dining in town, an amiable woman, the daughter of Senator Lodge, the great Republican leader of Massachusetts, revealed something which suddenly opened his eyes. She confided to him that Mr. Hoover was a Republican and that he had said so to Mr. Lodge and to the other Republican Senators. She was perfectly sincere and her information was correct. Franklin Roosevelt had to yield to the evidence. He regretted the necessity, but there was nothing to be done; such was destiny.

And that is why Mr. Hoover was not the Democratic candidate for the Presidency in 1924, that is why he was the Republican candidate in 1928, when he was thrust to the fore by the Progressive elements of the Republican Party. It is also the reason why, in 1928 he beat Governor Smith, Democrat, and why in 1932 he was beaten by Franklin Roosevelt, Democrat, who, since 1920, had learned a few truths which he had not known then and which Mr. Hoover never knew.

In 1921, Franklin Roosevelt found himself deprived of his health, of the companionship of his fellows and of a number of illusions. He had to learn over again a great many things, to rediscover a great many people and to restock his life with friendships.

His great discovery was Governor Smith and the art of governing without a majority.

Franklin Roosevelt is a patrician, and in America it is still possible to be a patrician and to engage in politics, but, with the advent of the crisis, it became difficult. Franklin Roosevelt would doubtless have been involved in the disfavor of his circle, if he had not had the good fortune to meet Alfred Emanuel Smith and to make friends with him.

Mr. Smith is an Irishman, and as a boy he sold newspapers in the streets of New York. He has the rich and drawling brogue of the less educated Irish, and he will never seem distinguished to the Anglo-Saxon aristocracy. Al Smith is a man of the people; he loves and understands the people and knows its qualities, its defects and its foibles. In politics he has a keener flair for public opinion than any other man, and he knows better than any other man how to satisfy it without soiling his hands or losing his self-respect. Al Smith, by his virtues, his failings and his gifts, is the perfect complement of Frank Roosevelt; he is as perfect a type of the Catholic and plebeian Irishman as Franklin Roosevelt is of the Protestant and distinguished Anglo-Saxon.

The two men had once known and respected each other, although they were pursuing different paths. Mr. Smith had not revolted against the Tammany organization, which Roosevelt was attacking; he was content to obey it with discretion and to temper his loyalty in relation to this Irish political club by a scrupulous honesty in relation to the public. By different, less brilliant, less striking, but equally effective methods, he was aiming at the same result as Mr. Roosevelt: to free himself from local dictators, to free the masses from these demagogic exploiters and to build up in the State of New York a strong and clean Democratic group.

By their combined efforts the two men succeeded. In 1918, 1920, 1922, 1924, 1926 and 1928, Franklin Roosevelt generously supported Mr. Smith, who, in his turn, had Mr. Roosevelt proposed and accepted as candidate for the post of Governor of the State of New York in 1928, thus setting him back in the saddle for the first time since the beginning of his illness.

In 1918 it was Roosevelt who got Smith proposed

and selected as Democratic candidate for the post of Governor of New York, to which Smith was elected in the autumn. In 1924 it was Roosevelt who put forward Smith's name as candidate for the Presidency and who fought for him at the Democratic Convention, though without being able to get him accepted on account of the opposition of McAdoo and of the other dry, Protestant and Anglo-Saxon Democrats. In 1928 it was Roosevelt again who proposed Smith, and who this time got him accepted, in the teeth of the same obtuse and implacable faction. Smith was not elected, but it was not Roosevelt's fault that he was not, for Roosevelt employed all his strength, his resources and his energies in the interests of his friend.

Smith was beaten. But Roosevelt had not wasted his time nor his efforts. The small folk of the towns, the Irish and the Jews, thought of him henceforth as Al Smith's friend; they no longer saw in him the Harvard graduate, the sportsman who had hunted the fox from the age of twelve, nor even the brilliant New York lawyer but the judicious and democratic statesman, who had been able to recognize one of their number as possessing one of the best brains in America and had dared to say so publicly, at the risk of shocking and infuriating the members of his own class. Thus when, in the course of his campaign of 1932, Roosevelt pronounced his famous phrase about "the forgotten man," which the Republican Party treated with so much scorn, these words, instead of appearing ridiculous, rang true. Franklin Roosevelt had proved publicly that he dared to recognize superiority wherever it was to be found. The compromising services which he had rendered

Smith ten years before were one of the surest guarantees
of his election.

From 1920 to 1930 Mr. Roosevelt was under a cloud
of misfortune and difficulty. While the country was
growing rich and prosperous, he was fighting to reconquer inch by inch the freedom of his body, and, in the
State of New York, a Republican majority. Now the
State of New York, because of its electoral laws and
of the contrast between the cities, which were crammed
with Democratic Irish, and the country, which was inhabited by isolated and cross-grained Anglo-Saxon
farmers, ordinarily gives a large majority of votes to
the Democratic candidates for the post of governor
and that of lieutenant governor, whilst it returns a
majority of Republicans to the State legislature. Under
these conditions, the governor almost always has to
contend against a ruthless, hostile and compact parliamentary majority.

This was Mr. Roosevelt's experience from 1928 to
1932, at a time when the beginning of the great economic depression and its subsequent development
rendered the administration of a thickly populated industrial district both a delicate and a dangerous matter.
The Republicans, representing the farms, opposed every
obstacle they could to the measures and laws which
might have made it possible to improve the situation
of the towns.

For four years Roosevelt was able to grapple with
this problem without succumbing either to anger or to
lethargy, and he was able to get things done. He was
not content merely to cling to his office; he governed,

and for this purpose he made use both of the Press and of public opinion. Thanks to these, he intimidated the Republicans and led them step by step in the direction in which they did not want to go but in which he intended to drag them. It was done with the skill and care of an artist. As long as it was possible to be conciliatory, Roosevelt was conciliatory, but, when the critical hour arrived, he spoke firmly and he unloosed the thunder of his Press. The Republicans treated him as a demagogue, but, as they wanted to be reëlected, they were forced in their turn to accept or to annul the measures which he had advised.

In 1928 he had been elected by a majority of 25,000, whilst the State gave Hoover a majority of 103,000 over Smith. He himself had received 40,000 votes more than Smith. In 1930 he was elected by the formidable majority of 725,000. Now at that time the crisis had already been in progress two years. And when he had governed the State of New York another two years, he received from his electors a majority of about 600,000 over Mr. Hoover.

This evidence is sufficient to prove the political acumen of Franklin Roosevelt.

With his election to the Presidency of the United States, his political goal was reached. He ceased to represent a party; he had become a sovereign, and he knew it.

He was better able to do so than any other man, for, throughout his life and throughout his political career, his instinct had been to raise himself above parties and to free himself from their narrow rules without ceasing to take account of realities.

Franklin Roosevelt, helped forward by the Roosevelt legend, assisted by his youth, revealed to the country by his work as Assistant Secretary of the Navy, made acquainted with man's inmost needs by suffering and misfortune, inured to government by four years of conflict and of difficult administration, acceded to power with the good wishes of the upper classes, who recognized him as one of their number, with the affection of the masses and of the unfortunate, who felt that he was near to themselves, and with that confidence in his star, which his struggle against and victory over misfortune had rendered impregnable.

Up to 1920 his smile had been that of a Harvard student who has won without any effort all the races for which he has entered. After 1920 his smile was that of a man who has striven unceasingly to win — and who has won.

CHAPTER II

MR. ROOSEVELT AND HIS BRAIN TRUST

WHEN Franklin Roosevelt took over the power, his personality attracted forthwith the sympathy of the whole country, and even the Republicans paid him homage. However, he excited little curiosity, for, after all, people had the impression that they knew him already. For thirty years the Roosevelts have figured on the front pages of the newspapers, and for twenty years Franklin Roosevelt had played his part in the political life of New York and Washington; and since his fifty speeches delivered from September to November, 1932, he had ceased to be an enigma.

He attracted sympathy, but the curiosity was all concentrated upon his "Brain Trust", as it was termed. This Brain Trust was a group of professors, intellectuals and business men who, since the winter of 1931–1932, had served him as advisers and general staff. These discreet — and even, according to some people, mediocre and obscure — individuals had until recently led a studious life in colleges, for the most part small colleges; destiny did not seem to have designed them for a national notoriety, yet suddenly they found themselves pursued by journalists in quest of news, photographers in quest of famous faces, little girls in quest of autographs, and old ladies in quest of lions.

The foolish and the wise alike turned towards the Brain Trust: the foolish because they always turn the way the wind is blowing and because their secret demon always whispers to them which way it is blowing; the wise because, according to universal opinion, Mr. Roosevelt had a supple character which would be molded by his advisers. Franklin Roosevelt is not one of those men who appeal to solitude and silence for answers to the problems of life and politics. His chief interest has always been man, and the opinion of men has always haunted his mind. He has always wanted to help them, and he has always been able to do it in a way they liked. Never has any enemy succeeded in isolating him. His great strength as a politician is that he is a leader whom contact with his fellows neither frightens nor fatigues. On the contrary, he feels the better for their company, and gathers instruction from their gestures and their words without being either bored or irritated, and he knows how to make use of them without letting himself be trammelled by them. At the various junctures of his life, he has contrived to adjust his contacts with humanity simply and successfully, so that he was always informed, supported and defended, without ever being dominated by his environment.

As early as 1931, in anticipation of his new functions, he had organized a sort of privy council, which aided him in the maneuvers and speeches of his campaign and went to Washington with him when he took up his residence there. This body is the so-called Brain Trust, which is commissioned by the President to keep him in touch with the world, to inform him concerning public opinion, and to draft for him plans of action, laws, messages and campaigns. It is a private telephone wire linking him with the outside world and with ideas.

Few men on this earth are more isolated than a President of the United States, and this is the fault of the French, or at any rate of one of the most illustrious of their race, Monsieur le Baron de Montesquieu.

For the guarding of his person a President of the United States possesses the most vigilant of jailers; in order to chastise him he has the most patient and untiring of enemies. And both live quite close to him, in the next-door house; both, during the four years — or the eight years — that a President of the United States is in office, never cease to gaze over the railings of the White House in order to spy upon the President's every gesture, every act, every letter, every word, and even his ideas and intentions.

The jailer is the United States Supreme Court; the intimate enemy is the United States Congress, which the Constitution of the United States installed in front of and by the side of the President, in order to safeguard the United States against despotism and the whims of a single man. Drafted in 1787, the Federal Constitution of the United States is the product of minds which were obsessed by the example of England and only knew England as interpreted by Monsieur de Montesquieu.

This exceedingly witty and exceedingly aristocratic Frenchman, who discovered in foggy England all sorts of precise forms which had never existed in that country, subjected the strange agglomeration of customs known as the English Constitution to a stern and logical analysis, and he decided that the ideal government is one in which the liberty of the citizen is protected by an exact division of the powers between three quite distinct groups — the judiciary, the executive and the legislative. The legislative makes the laws but does not apply them, the executive executes them without making them, and the judiciary criticizes them and superintends their application and those responsible for their application. The legislative and the executive are under the supervision and the rod of the judiciary; the executive is under the tutelage of the legislative. And thus everything is perfect in the most perfect of worlds.

Or, rather, everything would be perfect, if men themselves were perfect, if they knew how to differ without quarreling and how to debate in a spirit of mutual understanding. The balance of the three powers would be excellent if balance were possible and if human passions allowed a human authority to consist of three distinct, rival and divergent elements. For thirty years the whole world has been suffering from the maladies caused by this too optimistic view of human nature. All over the world, between 1780 and 1830, people tried to establish the three famous powers and their balance, and wherever they succeeded, the result was a more or less complete impotence of the Government. The majority of parliaments do not manage to achieve a stable majority, but they always end by forming blocs which prevent the executive from acting usefully and promptly. The executive, in its turn, succeeds, as a rule, not in accomplishing the overwhelming duties of its office, which the legislative does not allow it to discharge, but in rendering the laws voted by its parliament both futile and inoperative.

236 AMERICA FINDS HERSELF AGAIN

Thus the system of the three powers culminates in a harmony which is the harmony of nothingness.

Unfortunately for the United States, their Constitution was discussed, drafted, voted and ratified at a moment when the theory of the three powers was still in its youth and had all the charm and glamour of youth, and when, moreover, it still presented a clear and definite aspect. In the United States the framers of the Constitution were therefore obliged to adhere to it on all points, and they succeeded, for the country was still plastic, ready to lend itself to innovations and madly in love with constitutions.

To tell the truth, the framers of the Constitution of 1787 were neither fools nor fantasts and they believed that their three powers were capable of functioning. For this purpose all that was required was that each of the three powers, and all of them together, should be in the hands of a sufficiently restricted and sufficiently homogeneous group of men, whose union must, moreover, be sufficiently cemented by common interests. Doubtless this had been Montesquieu's idea of the President, for Montesquieu was a parliamentarian and an aristocrat who, at the beginning of the eighteenth century, can hardly have imagined that the people would be called upon to vote frequently, regularly and *en masse*. Montesquieu, like Washington and the other godfathers of the American Constitution, had dreamed of an authority divided into three but controlled by a homogeneous aristocracy.

From 1790 to 1800 the American Federalists tried to put this system into practice, and their two great men, Washington and Hamilton, tried to consolidate the power in the hands of this governing group, whose unity and harmony had insured for the Government strength, self-confidence and efficiency. Unfortunately America, because she was exposed to the stream of European immigration and allured by the virgin territories in the West, contained within herself a number of heterogeneous elements and the most ambitious and conflicting desires. It was impossible to stabilize her; for this it would have been necessary to adopt an altogether different attitude, to renounce the conquest of the West and to treat America as a cut-and-dried European country. No one had the courage or the desire to do this. And, since the immigrants were allowed to stream in, since American territory was extended in all directions, it was also necessary to enlarge the governing class, to make place for newcomers and to suffer the formation of various groups.

By degrees, but persistently and inevitably, a distinction arose between the three powers, and each of them came to represent a different element of the American population, social life and civilization. The Presidency, to which only individuals known to the whole nation could be elected, was ordinarily the appanage of the upper classes of society, who either occupied it directly or else suffered or dictated its occupation by one of their satellites. Around the Presidency the higher officials, the ambassadors and most of the generals were also drawn from that landowning or commercial, industrial or financial higher *bourgeoisie,* which forms the upper class in the American towns and countryside.

The United States Supreme Court, whose judges are selected by the President, is recruited from a similar but narrower circle, that of the lawyers. They are sprung from the same class, but from the more intellectual and methodical element of this class. They have more weight, more authority, fewer economic cares and less good nature.

The legislative, on the contrary, is drawn from every region and every social class in America. Some of the Congressmen have Indian blood in their veins, occasionally one is a Negro. Among them are Jews, Italians, Greeks and Slavs. The legislative is no longer the domain of the Anglo-Saxon and of good society; it is the sphere in which the various ethnic groups share the influence among themselves and where the more modest of the *bourgeoisie* exercise their sway.

The present executive in America is interested in ideas, anxious about world problems, secretly sympathetic towards Europe and vaguely attracted by the glory of a great rôle. The legislative has little use for ideas; it is occasionally stirred by sentiments, but only for a short space of time, and it is still near to the soil of the fields and the floor of the shops whence it comes. It bears in mind the multitudinous small interests of the small folk or small groups. It feels an instinctive aversion for Europe, a lively distaste for any brilliant adventure and an invincible suspicion of every intellectual or ideological scheme.

Since 1800 Congress has represented the local and provincial small *bourgeoisie*, the Presidency has represented the big national *bourgeoisie* and the Supreme Court has represented the serious lawyers. Since 1790 these three powers have been quarreling and pulling in different directions, according to the vicissitudes of politics, with an inexhaustible patience which has often exhausted the patience of the country and cost the United States very dear; for the Constitution was drafted with so much care as to make it very easy for Congress to reduce the President to impotence and very easy for the President to let Congress talk into the void.

Only Presidents blessed with a very delicate political intuition and persistent luck have been able to avoid conflicts with Congress and the solitude which these entailed. But even they never managed to be on terms of mutual trust and frank intimacy with Congress. An adroit President avoids too frequent contacts with Congress; he keeps it busy, does not ask too much from it, does not give it too much, and, in short, treats it as strict and enlightened parents treat a rather difficult child. He knows that he cannot depend on its unfailing aid in governing the country, for Congress has its electoral interests, which are distinct from those of the President. Doubtless the parties could have obviated and ought to have obviated this evil; they ought to have created stable majorities and have secured an active collaboration between the Republican President, the Republican Senators and the Republican members of the House of Representatives.

This did sometimes happen, but not often and never for very long. The Democratic Party is composed of very various elements, and is only united during the short period preceding the presidential elections: that is to say, four months every four years. The rest of the time, the Irish Democrats of the East are quite unable to agree with the Baptist and Presbyterian Democrats of the South and the Lutheran and freethinking Democrats of the Middle States. Congress reflects their local quarrels and its impotence renders the President impotent. The Republicans were for a long time more fortunate, for their party was strongly organized and represented the industrialists and traders of the whole country at a time when even the farmers regarded themselves as industrialists and traders. But very soon the clash of interests between agriculturalists and industrialists, manufacturers and bankers, became so acute that it shattered the unity of the Republican Party. In 1912, Theodore Roosevelt, by creating the Progressive Party, which recruited its principal adherents from the West and Middle West of the United States, where the agricultural element predominates and there are a great many Scandinavians, had revealed this divergence of tendencies within the party, which until then had been homogeneous and appeared to become so once more in 1926. In reality, from 1920 to 1932, all the Republican Presidents had to contend against the systematic hostility of the agrarian bloc and of the representatives from the West, who objected to the rôle played by the Wall Street bankers and the great industrialists of the East. Congress, led by professional politicians devoted to local interests and groups, made war on the President and his friends, the great national and international *bourgeoisie.*

Deprived of the collaboration of the legislative and without much contact with the judiciary, the President of the United States lacks the support and counsel which he needs in order to fill the rôle imposed upon him by the Constitution. It is difficult for him to speak to the country over the heads of Congress, and it is almost impossible for him to obtain information concerning the needs, intentions and desires of the masses apart from Congress. He is obliged to seek outside those advisers which the members of the national assemblies fail to supply.

For twenty years, one after another, the Presidents have tried to surround themselves with a general staff. Wilson, with his intellectual and ideological tendencies, had journalists, professors and lawyers. But, on the whole, he was not averse to solitude, and out of weariness, he ended by contenting himself with solitude, a fact which caused him very serious annoyances towards the end of his career. Harding, who was an amiable and very modest man, not devoid of good sense, tried to make up for his own defects by the high quality of his associates. He gathered around him as Cabinet ministers the "best minds" — as they were then called — of Congress and of the country: Hughes, the great New York lawyer, was his Secretary of State; Mellon, the biggest banker of Pittsburgh, was his Secretary of Treasury; Hoover, the most illustrious philanthropist and organizer of the age, was his Secretary of Commerce; and at every opportunity he appealed to the *élite* of the nation for information and advice. But he was not very successful. The Senate frowned on his "best minds", the country made fun of them, and he himself was very much hampered by them, for they had weight, importance and readymade ideas, which could not be put into practice without irritating Congress and which could not be relegated to the scrap heap without irritating their illustrious authors. Gradually, behind his "best minds", Harding collected his little group of old friends, in whom some people claimed to see the "worst minds", and who, in the opinion of many, were the real holders of power in 1921–1922. The attempt had been a failure.

Coolidge was too crafty, too wise and too well versed in politics to burden himself with troublesome personalities so near to himself and in such high office. He too, however, needed some support outside Congress, which resented his stiffness and lack of cordiality. This was the time when the country, intoxicated by its prosperity, was repeating, in unison with its chambers of commerce, its commercial universities and its business training schools: "We want more business in government and less government in business." In order to please the nation, therefore, Coolidge encouraged the "experts." As soon as a problem presented itself, he invited a few famous and influential persons to Washington, in order that they might discuss the matter with him and submit their point of view. As he was an excellent listener, he thereby acquired some highly interesting information. But these experts could not agree with one another, their opinions were fragmentary and conflicting, and Congress, which was just a little jealous of them, ended by disregarding their advice and getting back to the point from which it started. And, after all, it mattered very little, since everything was going well, and the machine was advancing by its own momentum.

Mr. Hoover, after he came to Washington, had quite realized this difficulty. He had seen Wilson punished for failing to surround himself with a sufficiently large number of advisers; he had seen Harding crushed by the exacting demands of his "best minds", and he had seen Coolidge bewildered by the discordant recommendations of his experts. He himself, confronted with a Senate and a House of Representatives who bore him a grudge for not being a politician, had decided to surround himself with wise and useful but neither cumbersome nor capricious counsellors. When a difficult, burning and dangerous question presented itself, he immediately formed a fairly large, fairly stable and very enlightened commission, drawn from the pick of the nation; and he gave it all the time and the money required in order to make a detailed report. This report was never more than a recommendation and it did not bind the President to anything, any more than it bound Congress. None the less, it had an effect on public opinion and it foreshadowed an action.

But he was unlucky. His commissions increased and multiplied. They published huge, boring and sterile reports, which the public did not read and of which the comic papers made fun. Mr. Hoover himself, engrossed with the tasks imposed upon him by Congress and with the pressing problems of every day, was unable to follow with sufficient care the labors of his commissions and to draw logical conclusions from them. It was all fruitless chatter which ended by irritating public opinion, and by exasperating against the President even those whom he had just consulted. The method seemed a good method, but it was, in fact, worse than those employed by his immediate predecessors.

All these efforts, fumblings, vexations and failures show clearly the difficulty experienced by a President of the United States, when he wants to seek aid and counsel.

President Roosevelt was determined to overcome this difficulty.

That was why he formed his "Brain Trust."

He had no need, like Mr. Harding, to make himself respected.

He had no need, like Mr. Coolidge, of people whose chatter should fill up the silences.

Nor had he any need of commissions to discover the method or dodge appropriate to the situation, for he did not believe in dodges.

But he did need to multiply his contacts with reality and to define his conception of reality, in order that he might never be outflanked by circumstances and that he might always understand them; for, since his illness, he knew that there exists a reality outside the scope of man's will, which man rarely perceives, but to which he must adapt himself if he is not to perish. Congress, by dint of reading and discussing the letters of its electors, lives in a perpetual dream, from which each Senator or representative only emerges on the day when he is defeated at the polls and returns to private life.

Franklin Roosevelt knew that it is possible to understand life clearly and to define it precisely. He knew also, after his illness, that men rarely have the time to stop in order to touch, take hold of and understand reality. As a sick man, he had come to understand man's tragic destiny: as long as man is free, active and robust, as long as he has the strength and the means to move about, so as to look things in the face, discover them and feel them, he fails to do so and is not even very interested in this intimate knowledge of reality.

But the moment he is a prisoner of his body and of a place, he is seized with a frantic craving for reality, for the whole of reality; his activity, freed from the alluring and exhausting incidents which encumber the existence of ordinary men, gives him no respite until he has understood and perceived the vast expanse of reality around him.

Franklin Roosevelt was one of that rather limited number of human beings for whom life is a real event and not a dream. Now, suddenly, in the midst of his existence, destiny had deprived him of a part of his body and at the same time endowed him with a more exacting intelligence; he had to give all his senses the activity which they suddenly lacked and to satisfy all the demands which suddenly beset him.

That is why, during the winter of 1931–1932, to the astonishment of everybody, he began surrounding himself with college professors.

In no country has education more prestige than in the United States. Everything is taught there, and every subject, useful or superfluous, profound or frivolous, scientific or cabalistic, finds a professor, students and a public. But there is no country where the professor enjoys less prestige. For many decades the selection of recruits from the universities for the teaching profession was effected automatically: certain of the students wanted to go into business, others were destined for an academic career. The former were bold, active, intelligent and ambitious; the latter were deficient in executive talent and self-confidence and generally mediocre. This was not an absolute rule, but it was a general rule.

There is a story of how once, when Theodore Roosevelt received the famous negro teacher, Booker Washington, at the White House, he invited a few whites to meet him. One of these white guests was very much embarrassed. He belonged to a Southern family and he did not like the idea of lunching with a man of color, but, as the invitation came from the White House, he could not refuse it. None the less, he could not bring himself to treat Booker Washington as an equal.

"I can't call him sir," he said to his wife, "and since the President has invited me to be his fellow guest I can't call him George" (this being the generic name given by the whites to their negro domestics). "What am I to do?" he asked his wife.

The latter was a woman of resource and she answered at length: "Call him Professor." And in this way the problem was solved.

Since the time of President Wilson the prestige of college and university professors has not increased, for his reign did not leave a pleasant memory in commercial and industrial circles. The American is proud and detests not being able to understand. Now the mass of the American population, having received only a rather brief elementary education, fails to understand the professor and his theories, the more so since the American professor is far more specialized than in Europe and inclined, like every specialist, to employ an unintelligible jargon, which to him seems science and to the public seems double Dutch.

But the less the professor enjoys the public affection and esteem, the more is he feared. He seems a sort of magician, and even if he has never been able to do much for himself, for he is badly paid, it is always feared and generally believed that his favorable or unfavorable influence is very far-reaching.

Thus America suffers from a sort of professorial mania.

And certainly Wilson did nothing to cure this mania. "After promising us peace," people said, "he drags us into a war." He upset industry, which had from 1914 to 1917 been very prosperous, and he was obliged by circumstances to subject the railways to federal control — a step which greatly displeased the railways and left a bad impression on the public. Nor could people forgive Wilson for having taken to Europe with him a number of college professors instead of politicians and business men. They blamed this irregularity for all the defects of the Treaty of Versailles.

From 1918 to 1932, the Republican Party had been very careful not to push the professors to the fore. They were suspected of radicalism or even of socialism, and while people were content to let them occupy the well-paid chairs at the national universities, they did not want them at Washington. It was the business man who was in vogue at this time, and the talk was all of the "captain of industry", who is exactly the opposite type to the professor. Whilst the college professor delivers lectures on things which he has never lived and of which he has no real knowledge, the captain of industry conquers life and rules men. From 1919 to 1929 America could conceive of no higher ideal than this.

When the crisis set in, people began to feel doubts about the captain of industry; when the crisis was thoroughly established and had deprived all the business men of their income, their means of livelihood and their security, whereas the college professor was still tranquilly giving his lectures and motoring to his university in his little car, the prestige of the captain of industry declined while that of the professor rose. Instances began to occur of intelligent and ambitious young men adopting this once despised profession.

It was then that Franklin Roosevelt formed his "Brain Trust."

Whatever the newspapers may think and say about it, this Trust ought not to be regarded as a council of augurs.

Mr. Roosevelt had always liked to surround himself with live people and to hear the advice of those who enjoyed his confidence. From 1921 to 1932, all through his illness, Mrs. Roosevelt and Louis Howe, Mr. Roosevelt's private secretary, guarded him from contact with the outside world and enabled him to live. They were in reality his first "Brain Trust", and Roosevelt owed more to them than to any other human beings.

But in 1932 he needed something different. He had to revive his knowledge of the rising generations and of the facts and theories which he had been unable to observe from his bedroom. If he was to perform the duties of his presidential office with the earnestness and energy befitting a Roosevelt, it was essential that he should make himself conversant with all the eddies of opinion, all the tendencies and all the possibilities which went to make up the United States of that day.

Raymond Moley was the instrument selected by him for this purpose.

Raymond Moley was at that time a professor at Columbia University, and he lectured to the young ladies at Barnard College, who entertained for him such sentiments of lively admiration as are entertained by the young women students of large colleges all over the world.

Professor Moley is of French descent, and, although he is the chief member of the Brain Trust, he is an absent-minded, modest and cautious man. He has a huge, honest nose in a huge round face, and nice plump cheeks. His mouth is small, pinched and inexpressive. His eyes are rather large and very straight; they have no pretension to depth, but they do not blink; they do not seek to fascinate, and, though they are not furtive, they prefer to avoid abrupt meetings. He further possesses a beautiful, deep, rather drawling voice, which relates fairly well, replies very well, and fills the silences with an agreeable resonance.

There was nothing very glorious or remarkable about the beginning of Professor Moley's career: he taught in various colleges in the Middle West and he made a fairly long stay in the Western Reserve University, at Cleveland, where he specialized in social economics and, particularly, in the branch of that science known as criminology. Although Mr. Moley is one of the most honest and normal of men, without any apparent aptitude for this department of human knowledge, he was very successful in it and he became a famous criminologist. He had too much moderation or tact to claim the title of first criminologist in the universe or even in America, but he was the first criminologist at Cleveland, and in the Middle West his name was pretty well known.

Possibly in a city like Chicago, where crime is more brilliant and abundant, he would have gone farther, but this did not really worry him and, with the modest but sufficient crimes which Cleveland afforded him, he compiled excellent statistics, excellent theories and excellent books, and at the same time acquired an excellent reputation.

This reputation reached the ears of Governor Roosevelt. They met, and this peaceable professor, agreeable, serious and well-informed, without arrogance, pretensions or false modesty, this honest man, with his open but not uneasy mind, pleased the Governor. During his electoral campaign, Mr. Moley became his assistant secretary. He never left his side, he prepared his speeches and made fair copies of addresses, letters and articles. He helped Mr. Roosevelt to clarify his ideas and to collect the information which he needed in order to reply to the questions which were put to him. The work was not overwhelming, for Mr. Roosevelt felt that his success was insured; he knew that Mr. Hoover was beaten, and he did not want to put himself to too much trouble for the public. He did not therefore demand from Mr. Moley any very complicated intellectual acrobatics, but he was satisfied with the work accomplished by his secretary.

Once the battle was won, Mr. Roosevelt began to have a very much greater need of Mr. Moley. Instead of the labor — which was, after all, not very arduous for a college professor — of composing coherent and amiable speeches, and of replying to incoherent and acrimonious questions, it was a matter of grappling with innumerable, mysterious and transient facts. But Mr. Roosevelt

had recognized the qualities of his confidant, and he
kept Mr. Moley. When Mr. Roosevelt went to see Mr.
Hoover, he took Mr. Moley with him, and while Mr.
Hoover was trying to persuade Mr. Roosevelt to assist
him in solving the debts problem, Mr. Roosevelt re-
peatedly turned to Mr. Moley to ask his opinion and advice. These interruptions made Mr. Hoover very nervous, very agitated and, finally, very annoyed. But Mr.
Roosevelt, though all the time perfectly courteous and
suave, was determined, before replying to his predecessor, to verify the accuracy of the facts which he cited
and the justice of the arguments he employed. It was a
painful interview for Mr. Hoover, who got nothing out
of it, and it was one of the most important moments
in the career of Mr. Moley, who contrived to assist Mr.
Roosevelt not to compromise himself before entering
upon his office.

From that time until his resignation to take up the
editorship of a magazine, Mr. Moley remained the President's daily confidant. Every afternoon he went to the
White House. He drafted a great many letters and official communications; he brought schemes and suggestions, documents and statistics; he collected every day
plans of action, and theories, petitions and reports. Mr.
Moley had two great qualities: he could speak as much
as Mr. Roosevelt wanted when they were together; he
knew how to hold his tongue as far as was desirable when
he was not in the President's company. He does not
appear to have had any other ambition save that of
pleasing his chief nor any other pride save that of being
useful; and he is devoted to his twin sons, whose portraits
occupied a conspicuous place in his office.

Mr. Moley was regarded as the head of the Brain Trust, but behind him was a whole staff of professors and young technicians, who fed Mr. Moley with ideas, in order that Mr. Moley might, in his turn, feed President Roosevelt. Thus only after being twice filtered — by the professorial wisdom of Mr. Moley and by the political experience and intelligence of Mr. Roosevelt — were these ideas put into practice.

They frequently emanated from the man who is looked upon as the most brilliant intellectual luminary of the Brain Trust, Professor Rexford G. Tugwell, who also comes from Columbia University and is famous for his works on political economy. Whereas Mr. Moley exhibits an urbane modesty, without any definite technique, Professor Tugwell is a specialist. He is in less close contact with the President, but he seems to exert a more forceful influence upon him. His two books, "Industry's Coming of Age" (1927) and "American Economic Life" (1932), are lacking neither in boldness nor precision.

Mr. Tugwell is not a Bolshevist, but he has not a blind faith in modern capitalism and he is quite prepared to ask from the rich what the poor need. He accepts science and industry as a fatality, whose advent may be regarded with a joy more or less intense but whose sovereignty it would be vain to deny. He merely seeks in his books the means of rendering them endurable and of compelling them to contribute to the happiness of humanity instead of allowing them to propagate themselves like the plagues of Egypt.

In one of his works [1] he declared:

[1] "American Economic Life and the Means of Its Improvement."

Our political democracy offers a startling contrast to the autocracy in industry, and it seems unthinkable that the two can exist permanently side by side, and presumably functioning together, in the same social system. Our governmental agencies have acted during the last decade as though their theory were frankly plutocratic. They have done everything to strengthen and protect those who are already strong and well protected and have done very little to guard from still greater injury and degradation those groups who already torment us with our past neglect. This situation, a democracy with pretensions to some ideals of justice must remedy. And the time for action is far past due.

More recently, but before Mr. Roosevelt's accession to power, he wrote with a more categorical audacity:

If we lack purchasing power we lack everything. Possessing it, we have everything we value in prosperity values. It cannot be brought into being by magic, as many people seem to believe. But neither is its creation so mysterious as to be beyond possibility. In such a situation there is just one thing to do: Take incomes from where they are and place them where we need them. Practically, this means extreme income taxation and distribution by Government to consumers who will spend for goods, start the productive processes again and gradually restore their earning power. The energy and ingenuity which have been expended on our financial institutions ought to be turned towards the repairing of a nationally damaged purchasing power — not to confidence, but actual power to buy.

Thus for six years Tugwell had been announcing and predicting in his books what was later to become Mr. Roosevelt's creed, once the wisdom of Mr. Moley had infused into it those reservations, subtleties, postpone-

ments and adaptation to present circumstances which
are the most striking feature of all the laws put forward by the Democratic administration of Franklin
Roosevelt. Moreover, Tugwell's influence is balanced,
controlled and compensated by the influence of the
other members of the Brain Trust.

Whereas Raymond Moley was Assistant Secretary
of State, Rexford Guy Tugwell is attached to the Department of Agriculture, and August Berle, another
ex-professor at Columbia University, is at the "R.F.C.",
or Reconstruction Finance Corporation. In the Department of State, there has been installed a personage
who was thought to have permanently vanished from
the scene, namely, William Christian Bullitt, who was
at one time a picturesque member of the Department
of State and then quitted it abruptly. He is a member
of a wealthy Philadelphia family, and in Philadelphia
he was educated. During the war he took part in Ford's
peace crusade and was one of those who embarked on
the famous ark. Then he made a stay behind the German
lines. This experience gave him a claim to enter the Department of State and to accompany President Wilson
to Paris in 1918. A little later, in February, 1919, he was
dispatched to Russia, in order to negotiate a peace with
the Bolsheviks. He believed himself to have succeeded,
and he returned to Paris with a treaty already drawn
up. President Wilson and Lloyd George, however, threw
his plan in the waste-paper basket, and he never forgave
them. In May, 1919, he handed in his resignation; in
September he made a deposition before a committee
of the Senate and heaped denunciations upon President
Wilson, the Treaty of Versailles and European diplo-

macy. He thereby supplied the Republican Senators with weapons against Wilson and so incurred the censure of his old Democratic friends. But the years passed. After a marriage, a divorce, a number of travels, a few books, a little of Moscow, London, Berlin and Vienna, and a great deal of Paris, he returned to the United States. There he assisted the cause of Mr. Roosevelt, who rewarded him by giving him a vague but important post in the Department of State, where he represents the Brain Trust and works in collaboration with the Secretary of State himself. Mr. Bullitt is still young, but he is very bald. He terrifies the dowagers, the serious Senators and the more cautious of Mr. Roosevelt's friends, and he fascinates the ambitious.

By the side of this strange career and this reckless and bizarre intelligence, James Paul Warburg presents a strange contrast. He is the son of the famous German-American banker, Paul Warburg, and he himself was born in Germany thirty-six years ago; then he studied at Harvard and worked in the banking business at Boston and New York. He has the accurate, swift and supple intelligence of the best type of Jew, and this and his profound discretion have enabled him to render eminent services to Mr. Roosevelt. He was entrusted more particularly with the question of the war debts, and he evolved the plan of a settlement with England in addition to many others.

We ought also to mention Mr. L. W. Douglas, who is in charge of the budget and manages it very well; Charles William Taussig, an industrialist and sugar refiner who accompanied Mr. Roosevelt during his campaign; Mordecai Ezekiel, who passes for a sort of magician; and a whole group of professors, young and old, illustrious or simply distinguished, who are to be met at Washington and of whom the most outstanding is undoubtedly Mr. Sprague, who was repatriated from London in order that he might be entrusted with the stabilization of the dollar and the rehabilitation of the currency.

There are no very definite limits to this Brain Trust, and sometimes, in the sarcastic newspapers and in the crowd, one hears jests about the President's intellectuals. The following anecdote, for instance, is told:

"One day, when there was a fog in New York harbor, a boat which was bringing from Europe six hundred European statesmen to confer with the President collided with a boat which contained six hundred intellectuals, who were on their way to Washington, where they were going to advise the President. The two boats sank in the harbor. What do you think happened? The next day the six hundred statesmen were found floating on the proposals which they had brought, for these were hollow, and the six hundred intellectuals were keeping themselves from drowning by clinging to the theories which they had brought, for they too were hollow."

Mr. Roosevelt's Brain Trust is not eyed with favor by the whole country. The members of Congress are uneasy at the scope given to individuals without political qualifications or experience. When Mr. Bullitt was nominated, the Senate protested vehemently, and thrusts, insinuations, or downright attacks are frequent.

It is declared that not one of the members of the Brain Trust is possessed of more than mediocre ability. And this is not altogether untrue. None of the members

of this group ocupied a leading position in the profession in which he was previously engaged. They are all
intelligent, adroit and experienced men, but they are
not luminaries of the first rank. Professor Moley himself
is not the type of those university professors whom his
colleagues would pronounce unimpeachable. The Brain
Trust does not suffer comparison with Mr. Hardings's
"best minds", nor even with Mr. Coolidge's experts, nor
yet with Mr. Hoover's futile but brilliant committees.
The Brain Trust is, first and foremost, a working tool,
and Mr. Roosevelt's considers that the most important
quality in a working tool is that it should be manageable.
He has excluded from his staff all with too pronounced
personalities and too brilliant careers. He is determined
to preserve his freedom of action, and this, indeed, is
his best chance of success; he is determined to escape
the tutelage which celebrities would, with the best will
in the world, have imposed upon him; and he chose,
deliberately or instinctively, men who could help him
without being a burden to him, and concerning whom it
would always be absurd to say that they had been able
to lead him. They serve the President as living diction-
aries, who are not content to answer life's question coldly
but can make them live. And among these men Mr.
Moley was not the chief expert; he was simply the most
level-headed and the most detached from his own solutions and the solutions of his colleagues.

The only man of whom it might, perhaps, be said
that he is a sort of keeper of the President's conscience
is Felix Frankfurter, a professor at the Harvard School
of Law, an extremely brilliant and daring mind, in
whom Mr. Roosevelt reposes great confidence and whose

opinions are always heard with deference at the White House. It is said to have been Mr. Frankfurter who decided the President, when he was greatly hesitating, to go through with the investigation of the Morgan firm. Of all the President's advisers, Professor Frankfurter is the most virile and he is also the one most rarely seen at Washington. His masculine intelligence charms and stimulates all that is feminine in Mr. Roosevelt's political adroitness.

Thus, with a dexterity unique in the history of the United States, President Roosevelt has contrived to surround himself with men who enable him to extend his personality beyond the narrow limits of a human being and to make contact with worlds and circles with which it would be impossible for one man to become acquainted in a whole lifetime; and all the while he has remained master of his movement and the sole confidant of his thoughts. His "Trust" has not been responsible for a single indiscretion since he has been in power nor yet for a single serious false step.

Throughout his political career, Mr. Roosevelt has taken great care not to make a mistake and not to compromise his career. He has always contrived to break off a connection in time. He left the local politics of the State of New York in 1913, when he had played the rôle which he could fill usefully; he ceased to be Assistant Secretary of the Navy in 1920, when the period of work and great efforts was over. He never lingered in a blind alley. Among American politicians, Franklin Roosevelt is perhaps the only case of a leader who has never had to eat his words.

He owes this to his instinct for public opinion and to his knowledge of the Press. He owes it to his close friendships with journalists and to the mutual understanding which he has been able to arrive at with them. It was certainly not chance that his stanchest supporter between 1921 and 1930 in his battle against disease and discouragement was a journalist, Louis Howe. Whilst the doctors were declaring that his active life was ended and that it was impossible for a man to reconquer his body, muscle by muscle, Louis Howe had no doubts of Franklin Roosevelt and stayed by his side to help him with his task. He succeeded.

For some time another journalist has played an important part in the life of Franklin Roosevelt.

At the beginning of the year 1932, Walter Lippmann was not favorably disposed towards Franklin Roosevelt.

Mr. Lippmann is a New York Jew, educated at Harvard, who for twenty years has been writing in the advanced newspapers and reviews. He occupied a leading position on the *New Republic*. The articles which he published in the *New York World*, of which he was the chief editor, subsequently attracted much attention, and when he joined the staff of the *New York Herald Tribune*, it was an event.

Lippmann has an accurate, rapid and cultivated mind, with a very quick grasp of things and of people; he has the intuitive mobility of his race, but he also has a courage and a perseverance which have made him a leader of opinion. He has a taste for reality, whereas many Jews have a preference for the potential and the emotional. America has left her mark on his supple nature, and Walter Lippmann is admirably adapted to the New York atmosphere, where the human spirit is avid of novelty, interested in ideas and theories, but chiefly engrossed with facts and, above all, very ready to be impressed by strength.

When, during the winter of 1931–1932, people began to speak of Franklin Roosevelt's candidacy, Mr. Lippman was influenced by the views and statements current in the city. He knew that among men of the world, intellectuals and business men, there was a strong distrust of Franklin Roosevelt's character. He had heard their views, and, since it is impossible not to be affected by one's environment, he treated Franklin Roosevelt rather disdainfully. He was too preoccupied with solid reality and with actual forces to be interested in a man whose outstanding qualities appeared to be suppleness, dexterity, and elusiveness. At first, he attacked Franklin Roosevelt's candidacy.

He had by this time left the *New Republic,* which had gone over to Communism and was proclaiming the impending victory of the proletariat from the roofs of New York and in the elegant drawing-rooms of fair ladies. He had left the *World,* which had ceased publication, and he had joined the staff of the *New York Herald Tribune,* the principal organ of the conservative and distinguished fraction of the Republican Party. There is no Republican orthodoxy more pure than that of the *Herald Tribune,* and there was something decidedly picturesque in the entry of Walter Lippmann into this *milieu,* in which he had never before been encountered. The *Herald Tribune* fought honestly on behalf of Mr. Hoover, although he did not excite its unmixed enthusiasm; but Republican honesty and loyalty to tradition made it a duty to support him. Mr. Lippman wrote every weekday an article which appeared under the general title "To-day and To-morrow", and in which he commented on the events of the day with intelligence, acumen and a prudent pessimism.

It was a rude shock to the faithful readers of the *Herald Tribune* when, one fine morning, they discovered in their newspaper a eulogy of Mr. Roosevelt and saw that it was signed by Walter Lippmann. They were puzzled at first, but they were forced to believe the evidence of their eyes when this article was followed by other articles and Mr. Lippmann embarked on a regular campaign in favor of Governor Roosevelt. A few old readers protested, a few convinced Republicans stopped taking the paper, but as Mr. Lippmann's articles appeared simultaneously with Mr. Hoover's clumsy speeches, which were beginning to alarm the whole of the middle classes, and also with Mr. Roosevelt's prudent and guarded orations, a good many of the readers of the *Herald Tribune* ended by coming over to Mr. Lippmann's opinion and following his lead. This was no small gain to Roosevelt, for Lippmann's articles not only appeared daily in the *New York Herald Tribune,* but were also reprinted in a large number of Republican newspapers, great and small, throughout the country. Thus, thanks to Walter Lippmann, in the last and most critical stage of the electoral campaign, Mr. Roosevelt was able to press his offensive and his arguments to the very heart of the most convinced Republican circles and into the most remote corners of the Union.

The November elections proved to Mr. Lippmann

that he had been right in backing Mr. Roosevelt and to his readers that they had been right in following the great journalist. From that time, Mr. Lippmann, impelled by his enthusiasm and guided by his flair, has never deserted Mr. Roosevelt's camp.

He is in good company, with some old comrades on the *New Republic,* such as Rex Tugwell, with some old college and university friends, and with liberal and radical intellectuals who, instead of turning towards Communism and martyrdom, decided to exercise a practical and positive influence in a country which was evidently not ripe for Communism. A large number of the most conspicuous members of the Brain Trust are Mr. Lippmann's friends, and it is easy for him to collaborate with them. His rôle is not, like theirs, to bring the President a daily résumé of his suggestions and plans. A brilliant journalist and publicist could not confine himself to the fruitful, but silent and modest activity of all these satellites who form a sort of Graduate School of Arts and Sciences around President Roosevelt. Mr. Lippmann, by reason both of his talents and of his reputation, had not the necessary qualities or aptitudes to be an active member of the Brain Trust. He needed both more and less, but, above all, he needed freedom to express himself.

He has therefore occupied, outside Mr. Roosevelt's intimate circle, and without any definite tie with this circle, the position of benevolent advocate and voluntary guide. Between the President and the country he establishes a communication very advantageous for the Government, whose actions he generously defends, and very agreeable to the public, which is thus better equipped to understand the intentions and the reticences of the Adiministration.

In the period of crisis which lasted from Mr. Roosevelt's accession to power until the first of June, Mr. Lippmann acted as sheep dog. He rallied opinion around the President and his programme, he did the President a service by keeping the mind of the public occupied, and he did the public a service by telling it about the things which interested it. When Congress began to evince a desire for inflation and the President felt that this solution would soon become inevitable, Walter Lippmann wrote several articles proving the advantages of inflation in a country where deflation had gone too far, where money had gained too high a value and where raw materials, manufactured articles and agrarian products had consequently too low a value. When Mr. Roosevelt made his decision, when the dollar deserted the gold standard and a wave of protest was sweeping over a dumbfounded, disconcerted and discontented world, when murmurs of censure came from England, and even in America more than one person was heard to mutter, "It is a national disgrace!", Walter Lippmann did in the newspapers what Franklin Roosevelt was doing over the radio. He explained to the people that the American inflation was not a disgrace or a robbery, since all that was being aimed at was to bring back the dollar to the value it had in 1926, which appeared not only to be its normal value but the value best suited to the country and calculated to insure the happiest equilibrium between the interests of production and those of consumption. When through the anxious and impatient country, the rumor spread that the President would content himself with talking of and promising inflation but would not put it into practice, Walter Lippmann published in the *Herald Tribune*, on May 23rd, an article in which he recommended the putting into immediate execution of the programme of financial expansion, and the next day, on May 24th, all the newspapers announced that the Federal Reserve Bank was taking the first measures towards inflation.

It matters little whether Mr. Roosevelt and Mr. Lippmann are in direct communication, or whether Mr. Lippmann is content to keep himself well informed and to follow carefully the steps taken by the President. Here the journalist's rôle is to give public opinion the impression that he is in agreement with the President, that public opinion is in agreement with the President, and that the President himself is pursuing a coherent programme, which is developing in accordance with a logical rhythm and is directed towards a definite goal.

In fact, a consummate wisdom has dictated the organization of this whole Brain Trust. Closely surrounded by his discreet and modest professors and his mysterious and unapproachable experts, served in the country by brilliant journalists, to whom he does not confide too many secrets, the President advances by daring and carefully regulated stages. All the time he has his eye on circumstances and unceasingly he watches the faces of the public and the expression of individuals. For the rest, every one is free to approach him, on condition that no one stays too near him.

Franklin Roosevelt is the most eclectic and the most courteous of Presidents. So far as the burden of power allows him, he receives and sees visitors. He talks with them and welcomes them cordially. Every day he sees the enormous correspondence which the post brings him, and he tries to master its contents. He does not disdain this stream of letters and this mass of anonymous and often puerile advice. Towards foreigners too he is studiously frank and affable, and one of his first steps after his election was to see Mr. MacDonald and Monsieur Herriot, to whom he sent a personal invitation.

He has friends in all the different groups, and, over and above his professors, his journalists and his political confidants, he has made room for the business men. One of the Democrats who gave the most generous and devoted support to the party and Mr. Roosevelt during the electoral campaign was the New York Jewish financier, Mr. Bernard Baruch, who had already played the rôle of adviser to Mr. Wilson and was one of the few celebrities who did not forsake him. When Mr. Roosevelt took office, the post of ambassador in London or Paris was suggested for Mr. Baruch, but the latter is a man devoid of vanity and he values his liberty. He refused to accept any post and preferred to remain in the wings as a discreet adviser, not too near, and by no means desirous of being involved in complications, but none the less anxious to exert a beneficent influence. Further, among all the offices which the President has at his disposal, an important and delicate one was reserved for a friend of Mr. Baruch, Mr. Hugh Johnson, who was put at the head of the work of industrial reconstruction. Mr. Roosevelt does not forget his old friends in the Democratic Party.

He displayed the same courtesy and generosity towards Colonel House, who was for a time the faithful and indispensable friend of President Wilson. Colonel House, who was a Texas banker, and as such became a colonel, occupied in Mr. Wilson's administration the strange position of an adviser who alone knows how to soothe and tame a dangerous master. As such, he enjoyed a peculiar prestige and, although he had not received any technical training for diplomacy, although his interests and his culture were entirely American, Anglo-Saxon and Southern, he toured Europe during the war on those famous missions which so perturbed the European chancelleries and by degrees induced Mr. Wilson to throw in his lot with the Allies. Colonel House further accompanied Mr. Wilson on his journey to Paris and took part at his side in the negotiations which preceded and prepared the Treaty of Versailles. At this time he found himself in disagreement with his illustrious friend, whose mind was becoming more and more set and dogmatic, whereas that of the Colonel was becoming more and more supple and better able to adapt itself to the contingencies of life.

Their intimacy suddenly gave place to an estrangement which lasted until President Wilson's death, but which did not prevent the Colonel from remaining faithful to his memory, nor the Republicans from heaping their sarcasms upon Colonel House and President Wilson alike, nor the Democrats from preserving a just and profound respect for this honest man who, in the most troublous and feverish hours, had worked quietly and peaceably, without ever abandoning his serenity, in order to bring to a just and reasonable conclusion the most sanguinary and brutal conflict the world has ever experienced.

For a number of years, Colonel House lived in New York in tranquil obscurity, surrounded by the friendship of all with whom he came in contact and only anxious to publish those of his papers which might interest the public. Public life was ended for him, and he had no intention of returning to it.

Consequently, people were surprised and touched when one of President Roosevelt's first steps was to pay his respects to Colonel House and to let it be known that they had had some intimate and serious conversations together. This was not a mere chance. Just as, through his Brain Trust, Mr. Roosevelt wanted to keep in touch with the audacious younger generation of the United States and to utilize for the benefit of the nation and himself such imagination as the reformers might possess, similarly he wanted to make it clear that, in acting thus, he was following a tradition of the Democratic Party and a discipline of his youth, and that he was conforming with the precedent of Mr. Wilson. True, the last years of Mr. Wilson's Presidency had left a disagreeable impression on most American minds and the memory of the ideologist President, in spite of the years which have elapsed, has not recovered the popularity which his person enjoyed in 1914 to 1917; but the group of his disciples and admirers is beginning to increase once more, and, among the Democrats, he is becoming one of the fixed stars in the firmament for the party theoreticians.

Franklin Roosevelt was faithful to the memory of his first great patron but he could not regard President Wilson as a prophet and the time of blind obedience was past. Yet, among the ideas and forces which Mr. Roosevelt wants to utilize, in order to rouse the American people from its torpor and give it the impression of greatness, is the Wilsonian tradition. It mitigates the audacity of the Brain Trust, which might otherwise rather shock the traditional Democrat.

Franklin Roosevelt has chosen his associates well, and, as always happens when the sun is rising, every face and every enthusiasm is turned towards him.

He has contrived not to repulse any one, and his Brain Trust has not served as a barrage to protect him from the public but simply as an instrument for controlling and extending his relations with the outside world.

However, when one comes to think, one group is almost completely excluded from the President's circle of intimates — big finance and the big banks. Whereas Mr. Harding, Mr. Coolidge and Mr. Hoover were reputed to refer invariably, as a last resource, to their Wall Street advisers and not to take any serious decision without having received at any rate the tacit approbation of the magnates of American finance, it is generally affirmed that Mr. Roosevelt acts without ever consulting Wall Street. It is said that on the day when he decided to abandon the gold standard for the dollar, the New York bankers had received no warning and learned the news at the same time as the rest of the world.

Mr. Roosevelt, a man of the upper New York society, a patrician of the biggest banking city in the world and a distinguished lawyer, had innumerable ties, at once regular and intimate, normal and solid, with the big New York banks. But his illness loosened these ties, and his great ordeal created between himself and the upper *bourgeoisie,* who were abandoning themselves to an orgy of happiness, a conflict of tendencies which cannot be denied. After all, the only dangerous enemy encountered by President Roosevelt in the course of his career was Wall Street, and the only critical moment in this career, in which good fortune, ill fortune and will power seem to have worked together to produce a perfect curve, was that hour when, from New York and Wall Street, from all those places where Franklin Roosevelt was well known, there emanated rumors — perfidious, adroit and precise, like all treachery — which very nearly ruined Roosevelt's chances. . . .

The hit below the belt which the upper *bourgeoisie* tried to deal him was parried by a few insignificant professors. Public opinion, which his enemies had hoped to exploit for his defeat, supported him against his accusers.

And Roosevelt, profiting by this lesson, and henceforth more suspicious of his own class than of any other group, surrounded himself with a bodyguard of professors, who are always on the alert. They keep watch, they observe public opinion and they supply him promptly with all the tools, ideas, opinions, facts and theories which he needs for his struggle.

The Brain Trust is an insurance against unpopularity, against sterility and against the upper classes of society.

CHAPTER III

ROOSEVELT AND CONGRESS OR THE ART OF TAMING ASSEMBLIES

IF he is well and happily married, a President of the United States encounters no more difficult problem than that of his relations with Congress. When the majority of Congress belongs to the same party as himself, he has to find some means of satisfying it, and this is not easy, for parliamentarians are fairly modest people, but they have to keep their promises to their electors, and, in every country, the promises of parliamentarians to their electors are a form of lyrical poetry which has very little relation with reality. It is not easy to discover a method of transforming these optimistic sallies into facts capable of satisfying the voters. Here the imagination and the skill of the President have to grapple with a problem worthy of the greatest minds and the greatest efforts.

If the opposition party is in the majority, the President has to conciliate it, and this is doubtless rather easier, for it is, as a rule, less difficult to satisfy one's enemies than one's friends. This general maxim is applicable everywhere, and in the United States no less than in Patagonia; but the parties in the United States have this peculiarity: that though in the Republican

Party and in the Democratic Party there is no guarantee
of stable unity, a certain instinctive loyalty will always
dispose a Republican member to hate a Democratic
President, even if he really likes and esteems him; while
a Democratic member will always scorn and despise a
Republican President, even if he admires and respects
him from the bottom of his heart. One of the essential
qualities of democracy is to give hatred a tinge of idealism and to exalt insincerity into a form of loyalty. Thus
the poor President of the United States is condemned,
no matter what happens, to live among friends whose
eyes will always be filled with reproach, or among enemies whose whole being will express a sympathy per-
meated with disdainful and disapproving pity.

However, if he is clever, he may get results, for the
problem is not a simple one, and, therefore, it is capable
of a solution. It is only the very definite and explicit
questions which admit of no reply. Once one is faced
with a complex situation, it is possible to maneuver and
to feel some hope.

Congress, as a group and as a bloc, can never feel
any sympathy for the President. Congress is housed at
the top of a hill, in a rather handsome building of classi-
cal design, with a rather handsome dome, surrounded
with rather handsome gardens and constructed partly
of marble and partly of stone. Congress dominates the
City of Washington and could hardly escape the illusion
that it dominates the United States, whilst down below,
amid its green gardens and surrounded by its white
railings, the White House conveys the impression of a
private estate. Everything is homely at the White House;
everything is imposing at Congress.

Washington is a charming city. It was very well designed by a Frenchman, of the name of L'Enfant, who
had great talents and an execrable character. He planned
broad avenues, fine straight roads, very green parks and
shady little squares; the roads intersect at right angles,
and the avenues and streets together form a beautiful
and effective ellipse. Washington is an imperial city
built by an eccentric royalist Frenchman for an infant
republic. And it has to be admitted that the soul of
Washington is not the President and his attractive White
House, but Congress and its huge classic edifice with
dome and cupola, its vast buildings designed to house
the offices of the members, and its spacious library.

At Washington the President seems rather like the
president of a college. He is there to manage the house
and to keep it in order and good condition, so that his
charges shall be contented and amused. Turbulent Congress, like a band of unruly children, with its explosions,
its whims and its fancies, is the real sovereign of Washington. Great or small, the President is a man who has
arrived, who will stay awhile and who will pass on,
taking his life with him and retaining from his exalted
office an enhanced personal prestige which he will always enjoy. The member of Congress, on the other
hand, is born into a new life when he enters Washington
and he dies when he leaves Washington. He will not
preserve his halo, as the President will do; whatever
happens, he will not remain a national and international
figure; he will not preserve in his drawing-room the
presents of the kings and of the municipalities of this
world. Once returned to his district, he will have to
obtain forgiveness for his notoriety, and very soon he

will disappear, swallowed up in the vast mass of the people. He knows this, and he devours jealously, greedily and gluttonously, the few years or the few months which he spends at Washington.

In his soul a battle is waged which renders him anxious and uneasy. He is and he remains an honest fellow come from some part or other of the United States. That is true of all, but it is more tragically true of those who come from very far. Those who come from near by return to their homes, and Washington is no more than a stay in the country. Those who come from afar have to make a home for themselves in Washington; the city becomes a sort of second country to them; and they have to evolve a second personality. They are Mr. Smith of Utah and Senator Smith of Washington. Now this is not the same thing, for Mr. Smith of Utah may never have had any occasion to possess a dinner jacket or to be able to eat asparagus in the Paris fashion, whereas Senator Smith of Washington cannot dine in town without a dinner jacket and without having mastered the use of those redoubtable asparagus tongs.

Moreover, if Mr. Smith of Utah could lead a solitary existence at Washington, he would not suffer so much, but he is immediately besieged by complex desires and aspirations which torture his will. Congress has a certain *esprit de corps,* which, even if it does not imply a daily intimacy between all its members, does establish between them a certain community of thoughts, of manners and of points of view. This is very satisfactory and quite simple. Unfortunately, however, Washington is also the Capital of the United States, and it contains all the embassies with their staffs, and the most charming and hospitable old ladies with the best chefs in America. The poor member of Congress is thus constrained to live in an elegant world of which his native district may have given him no inkling. He was once a local politician; he is henceforth a professional and national politician, and if he wants to amuse himself, if he has a wife and wants to please her, he must also become a man of the world.

Every member of Congress contains within his heart these three tendencies which he succeeds in dissimulating or does not shrink from revealing, according to his greater or less strength of character; and they give rise to inward conflicts. Rarely does he succeed in establishing a perfect harmony between his sentiments, his desires, his profession and his habits. Furthermore, the atmosphere of Washington, which ought to be utterly peaceful and replete with urbanity, good nature and ease, is, on the contrary, rather strained and subject to explosions of temper. People who play this game of worldliness, for which they are usually ill prepared, with excessive care, devotion and absorption, are the more hungry for respect and approval, since, even in political questions other than local problems, they feel themselves at a loss and have great difficulty in concealing their bewilderment. Such men are always on the alert; they are like rabbits, not ferocious but ready, should any unwonted incident occur, to jostle against anything in their path in order to get back quickly into their holes.

Thus the atmosphere of Washington is an atmosphere of fear. Every one tries not to make false moves, or, if

he makes one, to cover it up hastily by a dignified gesture. Throughout the year, one might be witnessing a
competition in decorum, good manners and reticences
organized for adults. Doubtless it is the same in every
capital, but it is less conspicuous in Berlin, London,
Paris or Rome, for these capitals are also very large
cities where the life of the representatives and of the
officials passes unobserved amid the hubbub of business,
the tumult of a feverish activity and the various passions which agitate the souls of men.

At Washington the suave and monotonous activity of
parliamentary life and the regular routine of administrative life are shut off from the clamor of the outside
world. Each man is abandoned to his anxieties and his
fears. This exotic collection of human beings of all
races and all regions, who have come from all the ends
of America and whose ancestors came from all the ends
of the world, has been assembled by chance, or the
whim of their voters, on the shores of the Potomac;
and they hardly dare to indulge in any other dream save
that of remaining in or returning to Washington. Everything depends on that and everything comes back to
that. The decision of the elector, every two years, every
four years or every six years, according as one is a
member of the House of Representatives, President or
Senator, dictates the fashion of one's existence, and it is
impossible to forget it.

Thus, outweighing every minor care and every tran-
sitory preoccupation, there reigns over Washington, as
over every capital in the universe, this great obsession
and this great fear: "How to be reëlected?" The same
fear, though in varying shapes and degrees, haunts the

member of the House of Representatives, who has to make haste to display his knowledge, his wisdom and his energy during the two years of his mandate; the Senator, who can indulge a few whims and allow himself a little latitude in his six years; and the President, who must not lose a minute of his first four years if he wants to spend another four at the White House, but who, during his second mandate, can take things easily and give free play to his propensities to heroism or indolence, idealism or grandeur. Thus the representatives always try to play a cautious game, the Senators prefer to have recourse to audacity, and the Presidents, as a general rule, begin by prudence and zeal and end by audacity.

This obsession with the craving for reëlection is an instinct common to all — and to all parliamentarians in all countries — but one which unfortunately, so far from bringing them together, is a cause of mutual estrangement.

As it is not possible on this earth that things should always go well, and as it is not conceivable that a parliamentary representative should be able to keep all the promises he has made, the member of Congress, whether he be representative or Senator, has to find an alibi; he must be able to point his finger at a culprit and denounce him to his voters. If he means to escape the reproach of indolence, negligence and lack of vigilance, the representative's first care must be to find a scapegoat whom he can sacrifice to his constituency. Even if he is very skillful and very influential, even if he has obtained for almost all his protégés almost all the posts which they desired, even if all the persons with whom he has had to deal have reason to commend him, he must still appease the group, which is worked upon by bitter passions and will recriminate and complain unceasingly.

The representatives and the Senators are in search of victims. The President too is in search of them. And, in this City of Washington, where, apart from a few journalists and a few amiable hostesses, there is hardly any one save Congress and the President, the President and Congress almost always end by meeting, and Congress generally ends by selecting the President as predestined victim, whilst the President selects Congress for the same purpose. These selections are so natural that, even if the President and Congress did not make them, the journalists would make them in their stead. This is a tradition to which all are accustomed and it is a theme which the Washington correspondents of the big American newspapers exploit untiringly.

Some Presidents, such as Wilson or Hoover, are the victims of their Congress; others turn the tables on their Congress and, like Coolidge, end by intimidating it. Between the President and Congress it is a contest both of skill and of authority. Against a President who is supported by an enthusiastic public opinion, Congress can do nothing; against a Congress supported by the people, the President is powerless.

President Wilson was crushed without being able to defend himself, for he had the country against him. President Coolidge ended by reigning in peace, for the American public loved his taciturnity. But such clear and simple cases are very rare. More often, Congress and the President can count on neither a general popular sympathy nor on hostility. They please some; they displease others. They receive the support of some social forces and are attacked by others. Sooner or later they are forced to take part in the great conflict which divides the American people, and it is then that they stake their future.

The United States are not inhabited by a people with clearly marked classes and well-defined social and political doctrines. The American is capable of adapting himself very rapidly to a more refined mode of life, but, on the other hand, he can be contented with a very simple existence. He never anchors himself in any social rank. He is prepared to admit any theory, provided its application is not too complicated and it gives good results; even the great parties have hardly any fixed and inherited doctrines but only rather vague tendencies, and they have never hesitated to change their attitude whenever necessary. After having been dry, the Republican Party has become frankly half-wet. The Democratic Party, which formerly advocated a low tariff, now alludes to this question only with great reserve and without insistence. It has, in fact, forsaken its old attitude. All this is merely a question of opportunity, strategy and circumstances.

There does, however, exist in America a definite opposition which divides the inhabitants of the United States into two irreconcilable camps. It traces its origin to the first years of the American Republic, but it did not assume a serious character until after the beginning of the nineteenth century.

From 1780 onwards, there were the Americans who wanted to call a halt and the Americans who wanted to continue advancing.

The former said: "If we don't stop and settle down, this country will never be habitable and civilized."

The latter said: "We came here because we wanted to be free to move about, and if we don't move about, if we don't advance, we might just as well stay in Europe."

It was the second group who won the day. They trailed the flag and the frontier of the United States from the Allegheny Mountains, where they were settled in 1783, to the Gulf of Mexico and the coast of the Pacific. They dictated the policy of the country and they steered the course of its civilization, but, as the years rolled by, the group of those who wanted more stability, more fixity and more systematic organization increased in numbers, in power and in effectiveness. It was composed mainly of the inhabitants of the coast and of the eastern regions of the United States, where existence assumed a rhythm similar to that of Europe, and where the notions of economy, method and distribution were very much the same as in the Old World.

To the West of the Alleghenies, on the other hand, a multitude of Americans remained nomads. It was a matter not merely of those unstable and discontented elements which, in any society, float about vaguely and are unable to settle down in any fixed abode, but of a whole vast mass of Americans; in fact, of all the agriculturalists of the Middle West and West. It is difficult to define them, for they are not peasants like the agriculturalists of Europe, and the term "farmers" applied to them in the United States is incorrect and ambiguous. They are men who cultivate the soil, but whose labor on it is like the labor of a town workman. They are not peasants, but rural workmen; they are not farmers or even landowners but nomadic exploiters. In our old countries agriculture is sedentary. A man settles in a place, he attaches himself to a soil and a locality, and his whole family live there. They are anchored there and they will remain there for generations. This place will be bound to their family indissolubly and there will be no change save the slow increase of the ancestral domain.

In America, on the contrary, the true tradition in agriculture was to be constantly on the move and to occupy a fresh piece of land with each new generation.

The emigrant arrived with a great stock of courage, ambition and daring. He got together a little money, he bought tools and implements, and he set off in search of new land. The nation distributed this land and it could be had almost for the asking. The emigrant tramped on until he reached a vacant site which pleased him and he then attacked this untouched soil. If he had to hew down the virgin forest, he began by acting as woodcutter; then he cleared the ground and the new land gave him magnificent crops from which he profited during his lifetime. Later, when the time came for his children to earn their living, they in turn set off, leaving behind them their father's farm, which was by this time in the midst of a civilized district and already less productive, for the lands, which had not been given any manure and had been impoverished by years of intensive, uniform and careless cultivation, no longer yielded the same harvests. The children pushed on and settled down a little way off. The parents remained behind, and gradually, instead of remaining farmers, they became shopkeepers, for in these districts industry advanced rapidly in the wake of agriculture, and the soil exhausted by maize, tobacco or wheat was found to contain petroleum, iron or natural gas.

The life of these families was perpetual movement, perpetual advance, full of the joy of discovery, of space traversed and mastered and of young and virgin land, offering to the newcomer the best of itself.

This went on until the end of the nineteenth century. This shifting population had elbow room until that date. About 1890, however, the Government made its last distribution of lands. For the last time, the settlers could be seen drawn up in line, waiting until the revolver shot gave the signal for them to start towards the place where the first comer had the right to occupy the soil. From this date the Government had no more good lands to distribute; the Pacific had been reached, and only here and there were a few uncultivated plots which human ingenuity might have succeeded in turning to account, but not without work, outlay and method.

None the less, the farmers retained their craving for space and movement, and they also retained their wasteful and capricious habits. They did not want to be peasants, and as it was becoming more and more difficult for them to be nomads, they were discontented. For the last twenty years the politics of the central and western States of the Union have been tinged with bitterness and rancor. By dint of perpetual advancing, the nomad farmer of the United States has reached the end and has had to stop. By dint of successive triumphs, he is defeated, and he must either resign himself to adopting the old customs of Europe, or he must invent new methods and build up a new civilization. The American farmer is in no sense a radical or a revolutionary; he is not, like the French socialist peasant, haunted by the idea of the class struggle and social jealousy; he does not bother much about political formulas or even economic nostrums, but he does not want to be brought to a halt, and he does not want to be forced to work like a peasant. He is indignant at the suggestion that he must adopt the methods and civilization of the East.

For some time, this conflict between East and West, between the sedentary American of the European type, and the American who emulates the migratory habits of his Indian predecessors, has dominated the debates of Congress; but as long as the inhabitants of the West could advance into vacant territory, they did not complain unduly. Now they are prisoners, and this confinement chafes them and makes life difficult for them. They are straitened and they grumble. Their representatives in Congress are constantly voicing protests and complaints. People have sometimes expressed surprise at the position occupied by Senator Borah, who is not a very cultured or clear-headed individual, not a very skillful leader or yet an exceptionally gifted political tactician. But Senator Borah has a flair for public opinion, and he has a good knowledge of the western plains. He is filled with the irritation which prevails in these regions, and it is responsible for his outbursts, protests, exclamations and whole attitude, which so delight a section of the United States and everywhere give the impression of sincere conviction and splendid vigor.

None the less, there is a fierce conflict between Senator Borah and the politicians of the East and, in a recent discussion, which had nothing to do with agriculture, ex-Governor Smith, a typical example of the stable small *bourgeoisie* of the United States, called Mr. Borah "a great Idaho potato" (Idaho being a State in the West which produces gigantic — and delicious — potatoes). In the opinion of the population of the East, the people of the West are hysterical folk whom nothing and nobody could satisfy and who refuse to grasp the necessities of the present hour. In the opinion of the people of the West, the Eastern centers are dominated by an obtuse, backward, egotistical and foolish clique, which has no understanding of the modern epoch.

The conflict has become more acute since the lands in the West have become impoverished, since Canada, the Argentine and Soviet Russia have improved their methods of cultivation and have succeeded in supplanting the United States in the exportation of cereals, and since America, by raising her industrial tariffs, has provoked reprisals which have closed France, England, Germany and most of the large countries against agricultural exports from the United States. Since 1920, Congress, dominated by the Republican elements of the East, has passed and maintained customs tariffs which were designed to protect American industry but took very little account of agriculture. Industry has not reaped all the advantage which had been hoped, for it too needed to export, and it has been excluded from many of its markets by customs reprisals. Even its home market has gradually deteriorated, since first the farmers, then the speculators, and finally, in 1928, 1929 and

1930, the great mass of the capitalists have been hit by the economic depression and the financial crisis.

The East had wanted to protect its industries at no matter what cost. It succeeded only in aggravating and prolonging the crisis. On all sides there were protests. The farmers, formerly the most active and extravagant of all the clients of industry, were unable to sell their cotton, their wheat, their tobacco, their maize, etc., and consequently had no money with which to buy. Big finance too was no longer purchasing; its balance sheets recorded only losses, not profits.

The policy of the Republican Party was bankrupt. Disgusted with Europe in consequence of the war, the Republicans had wanted America to keep herself to herself. Conscious that a new era was dawning, they had tried to stabilize the home market and to teach the Americans to be self-sufficing and to be content to live quietly and peaceably within their own frontiers.

The result was an immense bankruptcy. The foreign markets were barred; the home market was impoverished and congested. At the elections the Republican Party had no other programme to submit save the policy of immobility, whilst, this time, the Democrats announced that they were determined to effect rapid and important changes in every domain. Roosevelt went and said so, in all the Western States, and although he did not explain very clearly what these changes were to be, he said enough to attract and win over the mass of the agriculturalists. In the East, moreover, the confusion and destitution were fairly serious, and Mr. Hoover's personality had been so disliked that the country was prepared to welcome changes and thus

a formidable majority voted in favor of Roosevelt and
his programme.

The election of November, 1932, was unprecedented.
Roosevelt was elected by approximately 22,521,000
votes, as against 15,957,000 for Mr. Hoover.

In 1928, Mr. Hoover had obtained 21,400,000 votes,
as against 15,000,000 for Mr. Smith.

In 1924, Mr. Coolidge had had 15,725,000 votes, as
against 8,386,000 for Mr. Davis, Democrat.

And in 1912, Mr. Wilson, Democrat, had been elected
by 6,286,000 votes, as against 4,126,000 for Theodore
Roosevelt, Progressive, and 3,484,000 for Mr. Taft,
Republican.

As compared with the other elections, that of Mr.
Roosevelt is a plebiscite.

It is so from every point of view, for the country, at
the same time that it returned the Democratic candidate to the White House, returned to the Senate and the
House of Representatives a Democratic majority such as
had never been seen before in the history of the United
States.

In the Congress of 1931–1932, the Republicans had
48 seats in the Senate, the Democrats 47 and Farmer-
Labor 1. In the Congress elected in the autumn of
1932, the Democratic gains were so considerable that
henceforth they had 59 seats in the Senate, while the
Republicans had only 36 and Farmer-Labor 1.

In the House of Representatives, which in 1932 contained 220 Democrats, 210 Republicans and 1 Farmer-
Labor member, the Democrats now number 313, as
against 117 Republicans and 5 Farmer-Labor.

These figures do not adequately express the extent and completeness of the Democratic success. Ordinarily, in the United States, one of the most important factors is the geographical element. The Democrats can always count on the sympathy of the South, whereas in the West and the Northeast the Republicans can be sure of a loyal body of supporters. Now in 1932 there was not a single region which did not manifest its approbation of Mr. Roosevelt and its estrangement from the person and policy of Mr. Hoover.

For the first time in the history of the United States, all the States of the West, without exception, returned a majority for the Democratic candidate. And the upshot was that Mr. Hoover had a majority in only six States (four of which were of little importance) : Connecticut, New Hampshire, Maine, Vermont, Delaware and Pennsylvania. It should further be added that in each of these States — not even excepting Pennsylvania, where hitherto loyalty to the Republican Party had been a sacrosanct tradition — Mr. Hoover's majorities were small and well below the expectations of his supporters.

While in national politics the Democrats were carrying everything before them, in local politics too they were winning the confidence of the voters. A large number of elections of governors of States took place on the same day as the presidential election and they furnished occasion for remarkable popular manifestations in favor of the Democrats. It was a new man, a new party, a new programme and a new *régime* of which America was thus recording her approval.

This result was important in itself, and it was rendered

more striking by the disappearance of the two great forces which had quarreled for the ascendancy in preceding Congresses. One of these, known as the Republican Old Guard, was composed of Senators who had grown old in harness, who were familiar with all the inner workings of parliamentary life and who were first and foremost politicians. Their attitude in the face of national and international problems was conservative, uncompromising and inflexible. They had urged on Harding, respected Coolidge, dominated Hoover, and they had tried to escape the ruin which was threatening their party in 1932. But they were the worst hit; their group was practically wiped out.

Opposite them had formed a group variously named and not so clearly defined, but whose tendencies and doctrines had sufficient unity to make it seem the embryo of a party. Its members were the "insurgents" of the Republican Party, such as Senator Norris, Johnson (of California) and the famous Magnus Johnson, who saw fit to milk cows in order to prove to his colleagues that he was good for something. Mr. Borah too figured in this group and Mr. La Follette.

Now, this group was decimated. The sons of Senator La Follette were turned out of the posts which they had occupied; Messrs. Norris and Johnson left the Republican Party and threw in their lot with the Democratic Party and President Roosevelt. Senator Borah, though he grumbled at Mr. Hoover and criticized his attitude in almost every respect, refused to forsake him definitely, and remained in the Republican Party, which memories of Theodore Roosevelt and his old antipathy for the Democrats made him loath to quit. But though

Mr. Borah remained in the Senate, he had forfeited the high position and influence which he had once possessed in that body. He had been chairman of the Senate Foreign Relations Committee and, as such, he had been able to exercise a constant and redoubtable influence over the Government, for his criticisms were always acute and sometimes judicious; and occasionally it even happened that he was right. With the advent of a Democratic majority to the Senate, Mr. Borah, Republican, found himself deprived of the chairmanship of the Foreign Relations Committee.

The whole atmosphere of the Senate was changed. The quarrels between these two blocs and these two tendencies had occupied most of the parliamentary sessions since 1920; they seemed to be the magnetic pole of the Senate and there was no escaping them. They entailed great waste of time, energy and wisdom, but these oratorical jousts were believed to be as inevitable and indispensable as they were vain.

Now in 1932, at the same time that he obtained for himself and his party an unmistakable plebiscite, Mr. Roosevelt had the good fortune to witness the disappearance from the scene of these two groups, whose obstinate and monotonous quarrel might have greatly embarrassed him.

This made it easier to arrive at an understanding with Congress.

The group in power was homogeneous.

However, as every one knows, political life allows of such miracles of ingenuity that even in a group in which the big public fails to discern any precise difference of opinion, doctrine or attitude, there constantly occur squabbles, splits and disagreements. Even in Russia, Trotsky quarreled with Stalin, and although the world never succeeded in fathoming the cause of this rivalry, it was, none the less, very serious. Mr. Roosevelt, in November, 1932, had every reason for apprehension regarding his Congress.

In March, 1933, the situation was different. A sudden, violent and overwhelming fear had seized upon the members who had been elected on the strength of handsome and generous promises, when they began to grasp the situation in the United States: a budget deficit, a growing economic crisis, growing unemployment, an increasing number of crimes and the whole world upside down. This was enough to disturb the best-balanced minds.

In fact, the United States were faced with the most serious catastrophe they had ever known, for it was at once the most personal to themselves and the most universal. It affected all and it affected them in what they valued most, — in their most intimate existence. The homes of a great many Americans were threatened. The debt-laden farmers were going to be turned out of their farms and reduced to begging in the streets. After three years of economic and financial crisis, the moment had arrived when the reserves of the individuals were exhausted, and those of the banks and of the State were in like case; every one's credit was ruined, all the settlements postponed by temporary arrangements were now falling due, and a formidable explosion could not fail to occur.

All were frozen with terror. Congress more than any other body or any other individual, for the members knew that their voters would blame them for a situation which they had no means of remedying. For once, the fear of Congress was so profound and sincere that it forgot its ordinary tactics, which consist in teasing the President and putting him in the wrong in order to whitewash themselves in the eyes of the people. The moment was too serious; the only thing left standing in America was the President, and it was impossible to attack him, for to do so would have been to attack oneself and to accept overwhelming responsibilities.

Franklin Roosevelt's greatest political triumph was, undoubtedly, that he grasped this situation swiftly and saw how to turn it to account. Congress was too frightened and too feverish to be capable of prudent deliberations and of difficult decisions. The Senators had neither the requisite time nor the ease of mind to vote more than a few measures, as simple as possible. And their terror made them dread any decision.

It was then that Franklin Roosevelt invented those dictatorial laws which conferred upon him, for a specified period, a special and very great power over the army, the navy, the agriculturists, the industrialists and the national currency. These laws had been carefully prepared and they covered a considerable field. It was evident that they constituted the President a dictator.

Congress did not protest. It realized that by conferring upon Franklin Roosevelt absolute powers at the most serious moment of the crisis, it was ridding itself of an overwhelming responsibility and further creating a precedent which might be useful and agreeable. When the President refused to grant the demands of the ex-combatants, when he set himself at the head of the movement for repealing prohibition, Congress, with a feeling of mingled trepidation and admiration, retreated farther and farther into the background.

It was then that Mr. Roosevelt selected the opportunity to be more and more charming to Congress. Mr. Roosevelt has delightful manners; his beautiful, grave and well-pitched voice and his graceful, simple but dignified gestures are extraordinarily attractive and convincing. Even on the radio he speaks graciously; even before the microphone he is still a man of the world. He decided that, in order to enable the public and the country to understand the trend of events and the rôle which he proposed to play, it was necessary that he should from time to time deliver a little speech over the radio.

He began by praising Congress. He described the amiable and fruitful collaboration of Congress, the cordial atmosphere which prevailed at Washington and the advantage which circumstances so propitious represented for himself and for the country. He did not dwell upon this subject too long, but all that he said was carefully chosen and subtly emphasized. The public was impressed and Congress was touched.

Congress was all the more gratified by this attention since it was not merely an utterance from the President's lips but corresponded with his general attitude. Although he was surrounded by his professorial advisers, the President never lost sight of Congress, and he followed with unfailing interest every event that occurred there and every incident that was brought to his notice. No sooner did a whim make itself known than the President took note of it. He studiously avoided all disputes with Congress, and, in order to guard against being obliged to fight, he took upon himself to propose the measures which Congress wanted to put forward.

Mr. Roosevelt was never more adroit than on the occasion of the inflation.

He himself was not very favorable to inflation and, with his innate good sense, he wanted to spare the country the dangers and difficulties which inevitably result from a big inflation, however carefully guided, watched and organized. In all his speeches, therefore, he had referred sympathetically to the position of the debtors and of the insolvent farmers, but he had also talked of a sound and honest currency, and this had led the defenders of the gold dollar to believe that they could count on the President.

However, in the Senate, under the influence of the members from the West and from the silver-mining districts, the inflationist agitation assumed wider proportions every day. In January, 1933, a vote had shown that there were eighteen inflationist Senators; in the middle of April another similar vote showed that this time there were thirty-three inflationists. Their strength had almost doubled, and it was time to take account of it. Mr. Roosevelt was the more convinced of this, since business was not recovering, and the crisis and closing of the banks, and the failure of a large section of them to reopen immediately, were further emphasizing the disadvantages of deflation, rendering the circulation of money still more meager and aggravating the general stagnation.

Mr. Roosevelt did not hesitate. He summoned to his office the leader of the inflationist group, Mr. Thomas, of Oklahoma, and told him that he was on his side and that they could come to an understanding on condition that the operation was carefully conducted. He begged Mr. Thomas to link his proposal for inflation with the far-reaching agrarian law which Mr. Tugwell was preparing and which conferred immense powers upon the President, including the power to manipulate the currency. If Congress voted this law, he, for his part, was ready to declare the embargo on the country's gold, that is to say, the end of the gold standard for the American currency. They came to an agreement and both were content. Mr. Thomas was by this means attaining more rapidly the end he had in view, and he and his colleagues were avoiding a large part of the responsibility and the difficulties of the operation, since the President had taken them upon himself. At the same time, the President acquired a new and special power, and he transformed into a new means of action, of which he had the control, what might have been a difficulty in his path, if Congress had passed measures prescribing inflation. He was consolidating the union of the country and of Congress behind him, and he was sweeping along the whole nation in a common enthusiasm.

This incident is an admirable illustration of Mr. Roosevelt's method of dealing with Congress: he never refuses to satisfy the aspirations of Congress, when they are explicit and when Congress furnishes him the means of satisfying them. Thanks to his staff of intellectual workers, he always has in readiness a formula which transforms into a precise and flexible programme the vague intentions of Congress, but, in the course of this transformation, it sometimes happens that the execution of the measure entirely escapes Congress and is left to the President. All this is perfectly constitutional, but it was a new education given by Mr. Roosevelt to a Congress spoiled by the last three American Presidents. His predecessors had given up trying to do what Congress wanted; they watched it making mistakes and invading and trampling their domain without any other sentiment save pleasure at seeing a troublesome person trouble their neighbor as well as themselves. The respect for Congress displayed by Mr. Roosevelt prevents him from allowing it to depart from its rôle and lay itself open to abuse.

And since every human being, no matter how well-intentioned, has his weakness and his human side, Mr. Roosevelt takes care to keep Congress in suspense by another means.

At the outset of his administration, every President of the United States has at his disposal a fairly large number of posts for distribution among all the States of the Union. It is a delicate but agreeable task, for it wins you the favor of a number of influential personages and the gratitude of a number of small folk. As a rule, in order to assert their authority, to please their friends and to accomplish promptly a delicate task, the Presidents do not lose any time and they hasten to fill these posts, great and small. They are then besieged by Senators and representatives, for every one of these parliamentarians considers that the President is bound to consult him in regard to the posts in his district or State.

Mr. Roosevelt, unlike his predecessors, has shown no haste in making his appointments. He is ready to discuss them with Senators and representatives, he is open to all suggestions, but at Washington people say that he is not hurrying himself in the matter. He has so much work, he has so many important affairs in hand, he has so many anxieties of every sort! This is no cause for ill will; on the contrary, it proves that he is anxious to be thorough and scrupulous, even in small matters. But meanwhile the Senators and the representatives are in suspense, and they turn smiling faces towards Mr. Roosevelt, who smiles too, as is right and fitting.

All the collaboration between the President and the Senate is accompanied by smiles, and it seems like a dream when one compares it with the preceding era. But Mr. Hoover never mastered the art of smiling; smiling was contrary to Mr. Coolidge's principles; and Mr. Harding was too worried to be able to smile with much conviction towards the end of his life.

Wiles and smiles and dexterous use of a handkerchief are useful in politics, for politics is an art and the method of practising this art greatly influences the success or failure of the enterprise which one has in hand. But these enterprises must be judicious, or the art of politics will be mere juggling. Many politicians dupe themselves and only use their skill to mask their utter inertia.

Mr. Roosevelt knows how to employ his dexterity, for he has a firm and straightforward will to guide him.

When he sets Congress and himself on a certain route, he marches straight to the end, and he is careful not to make false starts. The country has many worries, and Mr. Roosevelt has decided to spare it all those which can possibly be relegated to the background. Mr. Roosevelt wants to treat the country kindly and he thrusts to the fore the things that are pleasant to discuss, to vote upon and to get done.

The country is sick of prohibition. No one wants it any longer. Apart from the Salvation Army and a few groups of obdurate churchmen, every one loathes prohibition. But the machinery which has to be put in motion in order to eliminate the Eighteenth Amendment from the Constitution is unwieldy and complicated. It is necessary for Congress to vote the repeal of this Amendment and for the President to approve it and to submit this vote of Congress for ratification by the States. Only after the voting by three quarters of the States of motions approving this change of the Constitution, will the people of the United States be able to drink in perfect freedom and contentment. But this, it appears, will be speedily accomplished.

Mr. Roosevelt knows that prohibition is a subject of conversation dear to Americans; he knows that it is not now really a very important matter and is one on which the unanimity of all the best minds of the nation is already secured. Although, therefore, prohibition is already in its death agonies and hardly needs a finishing stroke, Mr. Roosevelt has not allowed it to stagnate, but has made it the subject of speeches and of repeated attack.

In order to get things going, he persuaded Congress to vote a law which allows the manufacture and sale of beer containing 3.2 per cent. of alcohol. This is not a nectar, but it is at any rate a better drink than lemon or orange juice, even when flavored with pineapple and peppermint. Moreover, this beer is heavily taxed and consequently a source of revenue, and this gave the nation courage to support the rigors of the summer.

But it is not sufficient, for this beer is, after all, very indifferent. Therefore, at the moment when he is proposing a series of new taxes of every kind and to suit every taste, but all a little bitter to swallow, this elegant and artful President has just declared that, if the repeal of the Eighteenth Amendment were voted expeditiously and if the sale of wine, beer and other liquors were made possible in the United States, this would put resources in the hands of the Government which would enable it to abolish the new taxes. He therefore advises his good people to bring pressure to bear on their state governments and not to let the matter rest.

By this procedure he will probably expedite the repeal of prohibition by several months, and he will keep the minds of the people engrossed with visions and dreams more agreeable to contemplate than the depression, the new taxes, the agrarian situation, recognition of Soviet Russia and other problems of the hour.

It is well that prohibition should thus be buried and rapidly conducted to its tomb by a man of brains. It has lingered on too long in American politics, where it occupied a place out of all proportion to its real merits and importance. It has cost the Government, the people and the churches of the United States very dear, but it has cost the human spirit still dearer, for it belongs to that species of errors of the human mind, the folly of which is so flagrant that it is impossible to speak for or against it without to some extent sharing in this folly. A eulogy of alcohol is as grotesque in its way as a diatribe against it. To hear a convinced old lady explaining to an audience that it is impossible to grasp the beauty of life without five per cent. beer, is as distressing as to contemplate an assembly absorbed in the discourse of another lady, no less convinced, who is demonstrating the necessity for every American wife to be able to concoct fruit-juice beverages if she wants to go to heaven, for this is the only means of preventing husbands from dreaming of forbidden alcohol by night and from drinking it by day. The humiliating farce of prohibition is ending, thanks to President Roosevelt, in a witty and well-bred jest.

When the President sees that he will not be able to carry Congress and the country with him in a certain direction, he has the prudence to turn back. He is a man of no little wit, and he cannot fail to realize that the inter-Allied debts will never be paid. Many Americans less intelligent than himself have realized it and said it. And certain passages of his published speeches prove that this is so.

But he also knows public opinion, and he knows that it is quite inflexible on this point. It persists in the attitude which it adopted four years ago and which President Coolidge illustrated by a little witticism. His companions were talking about war debts, and some one asked him his opinion. He replied at last: "They hired the money, didn't they?"

The inter-Allied debts have become, like prohibition, though in a different way, an obsession of the American people. It is no longer a question of a material and practical but of a moral problem, and, as such, it unfortunately excites the passions of the populace.

The thing began badly. The Allied nations signed documents which were quite in order, and they signed them as if they had the firm intention of paying. And in an undertone people were saying to them: "You certainly don't imagine that you'll ever be made to pay back all that money!" This was what was being said by numerous semi-official personages and murmured by numerous official personages. But after all, it was mere friendly chatter, vague and cordial conversation at the corner of a table over a glass of champagne. There was perfect mutual understanding.

When the moment for payment arrived, the Europeans had forgotten the papers they had signed, but they remembered the friendly conversations, whereas the Americans had forgotten the random remarks made by some of their number, but they had a very clear recollection of the documents they had in their drawer.

They demanded payments and fresh signatures, but they added: "Of course, if it bothers you, we can come to an agreement later." With less enthusiasm, the Europeans signed, paid, and listened to these amiable words. When their hard times came, they turned to the Americans and asked for a new agreement, but this time they were told that the times were hard for everybody and that it was impossible to grant their request.

Such was the origin of the present confusion and the little seed from which there germinated so great an evil. The whole question would never have become as envenomed as it actually is, if grave blunders had not been committed on both sides.

One of the obsessions of the American, and one of the most estimable among them, is his determination to preserve his self-respect. He is sometimes vain, but he is always proud, and if he expresses it clumsily, his pride is none the less deep. Now, in regard to this question of debts, some honest folk, impelled by a sincere rather than enlightened zeal, began to tell the Americans that the insistence upon repayment of the war debts was a wicked action, unworthy of a true gentleman. The American was very much perturbed by these remarks, for he does not mind being made conscious of his clumsiness or his lack of elegance or his ignorance on such-and-such a point, but he clings to his morality as he clings to his life. The American could not bear hearing his generosity and his morality attacked in connection with the war debts. Just as the German is particularly indignant with the article in the Treaty of Versailles which compels him to admit responsibility for the war, so the American protests without ceasing that debts have always been debts and that there is no reason to abolish them by a stroke of the pen. He maintains that there is nothing immoral in insisting on their payment; on the contrary, he declares that it is his duty to insist upon it, if only to prove to the world the sacred character of international obligations. He reads in his newspapers and reviews that he is right in holding this view, and he also reads it in his conscience. From that moment he is embarked on a crusade.

As, however, the French and the English, for their part, read in their conscience that to pay these sums would be to sanction an unjust action, the result is a deadlock: the governments are powerless to negotiate, and it seems as if the only logical solution would be a moratorium which would enable the people to forget the

squabble and would be followed by an amicable, stealthy
and rapid settlement of the problem between the re-
spective countries.

President Roosevelt has reflected upon and talked
about this subject, but he has refused to commit himself towards Congress and the country. He knows that
Congress will follow him on every subject and in every
domain, and he knows that the letters with which all
the members of Congress are inundated enjoin them not
to abandon the path along which he is leading them.
But he also knows that, in regard to this burning subject of debts, the letters of the voters do not urge the
representatives to patience, forbearance and conciliation.

Therefore President Roosevelt lets the time slip by.
He lets June 15th arrive without any action. He does
not ask Congress for plenary powers to settle this business, and doubtless he knows that Congress is not inclined to give them to him.

It almost seems as if he were waiting for the moment
when a fresh refusal to pay on the part of the European peoples would enable him to say to Congress: "You
see now! Perhaps if you had let me negotiate, we might
have been able to reap some advantage, whereas now
both the money and the opportunity are lost." Perhaps
this is what he is thinking. The wisdom of which he has
always given proof and his knowledge of human nature
encourage this belief, but his silence conceals his inmost
thoughts, and his speeches contain only expressions
adapted to the current of American popular sentiment. The President saw that, on this subject, the mind
of the people was not ready, and he deliberately refused
to commit either himself or Congress.

There are other problems less simple than the inter-Allied debts and prohibition.

When he took over his office, the President found himself between the partisans of inflation and those of deflation, between the defenders of the gold standard and the advocates of a depreciated currency. The majority of his party was favorable to the gold standard, but the minority which was hostile to it was active and on the verge of desperation.

The President began by trying to find a way of sparing Congress and the country this dangerous adventure. Then he concluded with Mr. Thomas, Senator from Oklahoma, the bargain to which we referred above, and he made the decision which will continue to rank as the most important of his administration.

It seems strange that America, the richest country in the world, to whom every one owes money, and who makes enormous sums by her trade in gold and silver, should lightly — indeed gayly — resign herself to throwing her currency overboard, as has been done perforce and amid lamentations by all the European peoples since 1919. How is it that this great and proud nation does not realize the loss of prestige which this sacrifice necessarily entails and the confusion into which all the world markets are plunged as a result of the abandonment of the gold standard by the United States? For twenty years the dollar was the standard currency, which served as a common measure and as the basis for most transactions. This was natural, and it rendered the depreciations of the other currencies less tiresome, for the dollar always afforded a means of accurate reckoning.

But now that both dollar and sterling are fluctuating,

no other currency can any longer be guaranteed perfect stability; the whole monetary system is in a perpetual state of oscillation and transformation. There is no longer any norm or rule or stability; long-term contracts are becoming impossible to execute or to sign; and at the very moment when the whole world is in greatest need of certainty, it is greeted with the most discouraging and distracting piece of news which has come on the market since 1920.

The Americans know all that, but if one talks to them about it, they shrug their shoulders and say, "Yes, but all that together is better than a revolution in our country. The dollar was killing our farmers and two thirds of our industry."

In fact, the President found himself under the necessity of suspending the gold guarantee of the dollar in order to try to make life possible for all that agricultural and once nomadic America, which is now existing in a state of paralysis on farms which have not been paid for, which are burdened with mortgages and which have already deteriorated. These poor wretches are perishing of hunger and discouragement. A wave of fury has invaded these regions and incited the inhabitants to attack a judge who had ordered the sale of a farm the mortgages on which were due for settlement. But, even when there is no risk of personal violence, the misery is so profound that it is becoming dangerous, and a terrible crisis is threatening the country. It is a physical and moral disease.

While the industrialist was taking advantage of the prosperous post-war years to sell to the whole of Europe, to purchase a plant, to build himself a fine house and to travel in the Old World, the American farmer was already having difficulties. They began to appear immediately after the end of the war, and in 1928 the situation of the whole central region of the United States was already very bad. But conditions became intolerable only when the small local banks, whose loans and accommodation had made life possible for the farmers, collapsed one after the other beneath the too heavy burden both of the farmers' demands and of the slump on the market.

In fact, whilst the farmers were suffering in the postwar period and the industrialists were flourishing, the bankers and financiers too were having some very good years. They were speculating, and, as a result of the general rise of shares, bonds and securities of all sorts, they were amassing wealth. In all the American towns, one may see sumptuous buildings which were erected between 1920 and 1930 and which testify to the importance of the wave of prosperity in financial circles.

The farmer reaped no advantage either from the prosperity or the speculation. What he had to buy cost him more and more; and for what he had to sell he received less and less every month. When the crisis began, the farmer, who had already been suffering for several years, was hit no less hard than those who had for ten years been piling up riches. The prices of his products dropped still lower.

He had lost on the boom; he lost on the slump. He ended by seeing red.

It was he who decided Mr. Roosevelt to try inflation. It is impossible to abandon a third of the United States to destitution; it is impossible to consign all the farms in the country to bankruptcy. And how could these unfortunates be helped save by decreasing the value of what they had to pay and raising the price of what they had to sell? By diminishing the value of the dollar, Mr. Roosevelt made it much easier for the farmers to pay their debts and to clear off their mortgages, while at the same time the price of agricultural products automatically rose.

Nomadic America and all those agricultural adventurers who had for two centuries kept alive in the United States a spirit of audacity, vigor and courage were in danger of perishing. In order to save them, the President demanded from the rest of the nation the sacrifice which should put the farmers on their feet again. This initial sacrifice of the capitalists and salaried employees of the East will, it is hoped, enable the farmers to make a fresh start, to buy and to sell, and so to restore to American political and financial economy its old vitality. This will be to the advantage of all.

This famous measure, which has caused such excitement and perturbation in Europe, is really a settlement between stable America and nomadic America. It is an effort to restore the balance between the two and to compensate by a financial migration for the migrations which geography and politics no longer permit. It is not the result of a financial necessity, like the French inflation, or of an economic crisis, like the English and the German inflations; it is the outcome of a social conflict of long standing. It is a surgical operation necessary to save the life of the pioneers of old America.

A European will exclaim: "You are destroying your prestige, you are destroying a part of your wealth, you are robbing yourselves of a part of your resources, and you are breaking one of the best tools you ever created: It is a sort of suicide!"

This is quite true. The American is slaying his dollar god. And the spectacle of the American wrestling with his dollar, which does not want to fall or depreciate, which resists and clings to its value and its old honesty, is at once tragic and comic. The American Government and the American banks seem to have difficulty in drowning their dollar, which is struggling and trying to keep afloat.

By killing their old traditional dollar, the Americans are despoiling themselves of a part of their wealth. They are not merely destroying a symbol; they are ruining a part of their power; they are wiping out a part of the debts owed to them by foreign countries and a part of their own assets. And this is very baffling to Europeans.

But, in truth, what the Americans are doing and what Mr. Roosevelt is doing for them is quite in the tradition of this country, where waste of things was one of the methods employed for saving human energy. The American has a craving to act; he has such a craving to move about that sometimes he does not seem to recognize clearly the difference between action and mere movement. He craves fatigue and effort, and in 1932 he suffered less from the lack of things than from the glut of things. The suicide of the dollar is a symbol and a fact. The Americans need to destroy a certain number of the objects they have made, for they have made too many; they had made such a large number that they were no longer able to utilize them all, and this grieved them; but, above all, they had made so many that they no longer had the right or the excuse to make any more, and at length, doomed to inactivity and mere enjoyment, instead of action and creation, to idleness instead of labor, they could not endure this state of things. They preferred to break up a part of the objects they had made, to squander a part of their wealth, and to give men once more the opportunity of work, and a reason for bestirring and exhausting themselves.

The death of the dollar god is an *auto-da-fé!*

It is a revolt of the human being against his things.

And this act, which Europe fails to understand, is the pact which binds together with a secret and indissoluble tie the President, Congress and the people.

For the first time America is one nation, said a journalist.

For the first time America has realized that she preferred her activity to her happiness, her wealth, her greatness and her glory.

CHAPTER IV

ROOSEVELT AND THE AMERICAN PEOPLE

THE task undertaken by Mr. Roosevelt is stupendous. It exceeds the powers of one man, even if he were a genius and even if he were spurred on by fear of disaster or hope of an apotheosis.

President Roosevelt cannot succeed without the sympathy and collaboration of the American people; his officials, his ambassadors, his Congress and his judges will not be able to execute his programme unless the will of the people coöperates in it and unless the hopes of the nation infect those who are wavering.

In 1932 it was possible to doubt whether Mr. Roosevelt was one of those men who can sway the crowd. In New York rumor credited him with more charm and tact than strength of character and will. As Governor of the State of New York, people said, he had given proof of suppleness but not of virility. The people were attracted towards him, but his character was still wrapped in uncertainty.

It became more distinct after March, 1932, when the attacks from Wall Street had brought him the prestige of persecution and had enlightened the people concerning the attitude of his adversaries. In politics it is doubtful whether our friends help us much, but our enemies are always useful. They define and emphasize our attitude and procure us from the outset the aid and sympathy of their opponents. A wise man once said that, in order to secure all the collaboration one needs in politics, one has no need of friends but only of well-chosen enemies.

Mr. Roosevelt's enemies rallied around him the great masses of the people. He contrived to utilize this reflux, his general staff contrived to transform it into a regular torrent, and already in September, Franklin Roosevelt possessed the good will and the confidence of the American masses. He did not electrify them as his cousin Theodore had once done, but he exercised over them a profound, serious and touching empire. He had stirred the inmost depths of the people's conscience.

This was apparent in March. He acceded to power amid catastrophe and ruin. But, thanks to him, there was no panic; it was a period of difficulty and trial but not of confusion. All the banks in the country were shut and the economic activity of the whole nation was at a standstill. Yet instead of feeling that uneasiness and distress which had weighed on the country for three years, all the citizens remained calm, and the aggravation of the crisis kindled in them a sort of hope.

This was still more apparent in April. One afternoon the astonished world learned of the death of the dollar god. Mr. Roosevelt had summoned the journalists and had announced to them that henceforth the Government of the United States would cease to support the dollar and that it was about to put an embargo on gold. The dollar ceased to be the supreme law to which all the contracts of the entire world were referred. In Europe there was general consternation, and a recrudescence of the crisis was expected, for this step seemed equivalent to an admission by the richest country in the world that it could not fight against the depression. It was a new element of disorder in a world already suffering from quartan fever, hay fever and, in fact, every fever, terror, delirium and ague liable to afflict a patient at the very height of his crisis.

In America, on the contrary, Mr. Roosevelt's proclamation excited immediate and general enthusiasm. The people in the streets congratulated each other, the Senate was all smiles, the shopkeepers and hotel proprietors sent addresses to the President, and even the bankers, even Wall Street, once stealthily hostile to the President, announced through the medium of Mr. Morgan, the most discreet, taciturn and reserved of its magnates, that the news was a swallow heralding the spring. Mr. Roosevelt on this occasion attracted more than the sympathy and trust of the country; he became a veritable dictator supported by the affection and enthusiasm of the masses.

The most spiteful natures, the groups most prone to criticism, the newspapers and reviews which practise discontent with consummate tenacity and method, even the radicals and Communists, were forced to abandon themselves to the torrent of popular approval. They were forced to recognize that, this time, a man had succeeded in understanding the people and making himself understood by them; a man outside every notion of class or party was taking his stand in the midst of the American masses as a guide and as a father. Franklin Roosevelt had shown and had made the people realize that his famous formula exhorting them to remember "the forgotten man", at which some had been inclined to laugh, was not a mere phrase invented for the purpose of an electoral campaign but reflected a determination aided by an instinct. Franklin Roosevelt is one of those who, without detracting from their own personality, can establish contact with the crowd.

The radicals praised him on this account and looked upon him as one of themselves. But it would be a mistake to imagine that he is a radical. Franklin Roosevelt, a patrician, a faithful member of the Episcopal Church, an Anglo-Saxon by race, attitude and taste, brought up among the best society of the Eastern States, a pupil of Groton and a graduate of Harvard and Columbia, is not a Lenin or a Trotsky of the New World, any more than he is a Kerensky. If he understands the people and tries to please the people, it is not because he means to offer it a holocaust of the already ancient civilization of the United States, of which he himself is one of the most finished products. When the people turn towards him with such enthusiasm, it is not because they are expecting him to provide them with an orgy of revolution and disorder.

The American people is in no sense radical or even Communist. It is composed, on the contrary, of emigrants who left old Europe because it no longer afforded them the possibility of work and wealth. They came to the United States because they were suffering and, above all, because they were individualists and they wanted to become proprietors and capitalists. These instincts have persisted in them, as was evident in 1700, in 1776, in 1830, in 1848, in 1900 and throughout the whole course of American history. The elections of 1932 did not symbolize any triumph of radical ideas. Certainly in the universities a few restless young Jews, a few sons of millionaires, and a few sons of Protestant pastors in quest of new allegiances and a new creed, have grouped themselves into communist cells, but the American Federation of Labor is foremost in demanding that diplomatic relations with Russia shall not be resumed. Radicalism in America is for the most part an offshoot of worldliness or the result of sexual troubles.

For the politician of the New World the radical problem does not exist. And for Mr. Roosevelt, it does not exist. In 1932 the workless and the ex-combatants in the Great War, who were without employment or resources, organized pilgrimages to Washington in order to complain of their condition to Mr. Hoover and Congress. They got a bad reception and the incident ended deplorably with a street battle in which the poor wretches were charged by the cavalry and brutally handled in order to drive them out of the city. At that time there was talk of an effervescence of radicalism, and people were uneasy at the spread of Communism and fancied themselves on the eve of a Red revolution.

In 1933 the unemployed and the destitute ex-combatants decided to make another demonstration in Washington. They were even more poverty-stricken and embittered than in 1932. Processions, banners, trumpets, speeches and tracts began once more, just as in the previous year. But this time Mr. Roosevelt, like a prudent and well-bred host, had prepared quarters for them and when they drew near to Washington they found, some six or seven miles distant from the city, a fine large camp already prepared for their accommodation. Some days later they sent a delegation to Mr. Roosevelt, who greeted them with a pleasant smile, made them a friendly little speech, and questioned them concerning their wishes. The men were photographed in his company, holding American flags. Then Mr. Roosevelt told them that, if they so desired, he would procure them work in the reforestation camps which were being organized. A large number of the men replied that they would be glad to go and work at the reforestation of the United States, while others, who were not at all anxious for work, decamped as discreetly as possible but not without evoking the boos of their companions. In the barracks which Mr. Roosevelt had had prepared for ten thousand persons about twenty-five hundred took up their quarters. This great radical demonstration had ended in an absurd fiasco.

No, neither Mr. Roosevelt nor his partisans, who at this moment comprise the whole American people, are adherents of the radical creed. Neither to him nor to them do the measures which he proposes to employ represent articles of faith or even infallible remedies. It is simply a case of getting something done. Mr. Roosevelt and the American people would not say in 1933, as the Government and American public opinion were still saying in 1932, We are merely seeking a road to prosperity. This formula is out of date; prosperity no longer excites either enthusiasm or confidence! But the American people want to live, and the remedies which Mr. Roosevelt is employing at this moment have as their aim — both in his eyes and in the eyes of the people — to make labor in the United States once more universal and productive.

It is the craving for action which has rallied America to the complex, ambitious and audacious programme of the Roosevelt Administration. But once the goal has been reached, once vitality has been restored to this great body which to-day lies inert, the measures will be abandoned or relegated to the background. Mr. Roosevelt never tires of saying to the journalists when he receives them: "The powers conferred on me are *powers*, not orders; they do not represent an imperative mandate." He has the power to decree inflation, to devalorize and to revalorize the dollar, to control agriculture, to compel the farmers to limit their crops and their sales and to force the industrialists to renounce competition in order to maintain a certain stability and a certain regularity in the market. He could, in fact, go as far as Stalin and destroy private trade if he exercised to the letter the instructions which he has prepared and which Congress has voted. But he will not do it, or at any rate he hopes not to do it, for his sole aim is to employ these collective means for the purpose of stimulating individual life, not of suppressing or supplanting it.

He is so far from being an enemy of capitalism that, in the bill relative to the reorganization of industry, he has inserted a paragraph which renders possible once more those trusts which his cousin, Theodore Roosevelt, had once proscribed. And, for the purpose of applying this vast and audacious law, he has selected a man who was in the army, who played a patriotic and military rôle during the Great War and who is an intimate friend of Bernard Baruch, the great financier, namely, Hugh Johnson. Lenin, Trotsky and even Kerensky would have been shocked at such a choice. Just as they would have been shocked to hear Franklin Roosevelt, on the day of his installation as President of the United States, invoke the name of God and pray for divine guidance in his overwhelming task.

"Do not let us confuse aims and methods," he himself said in one of his speeches. Anything that may seem socialistic or communistic in his measures is really only there in the character of a remedy worth trying, to be laid aside once it has produced the desired effect or failed to produce any effect.

It would be easy to understand such an attitude if this were not a juncture in American history when the people of the United States are turning towards Franklin Roosevelt and demanding two monumental and apparently contradictory reforms.

All that part of the nation which once belonged to the shifting masses of agriculturists who colonized the Mississippi Valley, is still dreaming of migration, liberty, change and daring activity; it has a surplus of strength, restlessness and will power waiting to be expended. It needs danger and novelty. And the President is quite conscious that it must be supplied with these, if a moral rupture of the Union, which might later give rise to political difficulties, is to be avoided.

But the other section of the United States, the section which colonized the coasts and settled there and which forms the civic and social framework of the country, is demanding that the nation should be organized, stabilized and centralized. It is no more reactionary or conservative than the other section is radical; it does not ask for any abandonment of democratic principles, although it does not deem them as a rule very

fruitful, but it asks, above all and without delay, that
the economic and political structure of the nation shall
be modernized and made more solid and more practical.

Any one who has traveled in the United States and
tried to study there the problems of municipal administration, public and private law, interstate commerce,
maintenance of the roads and public instruction, has
very soon realized that this immense country is in truth
a mosaic of small communities living side by side and
bound together by common customs, which are often
sufficient to enable them to collaborate, sometimes powerless to insure veritable coöperation and sometimes even
liable to give rise to conflicts. Louisiana employs the
code Napoléon, whereas all the other States have derived
their laws from England. Each Supreme Court of each
State has its own way of interpreting English precedents,
and therefore the decisions which it makes create in
course of time a usage which is binding in that particular State.

For three centuries America has been improvising an
immense empire. She has built it hurriedly, boldly, successfully and with a genuine feeling for the grandiose,
but she has never had time to fit together the different
pieces. Her empire and her civilization have grown up
in obedience to sudden impulses, just as the twigs of a
fir tree grow in the spring, straight ahead, without
troubling about the rest of the tree; and now America
finds herself embarked in diverse directions with re-
sultant waste of her resources, her strength and her intelligence. The problems are becoming so complicated
that the human mind is distracted by them. The network of towns and of country districts is such a mosaic

of police organizations that criminals are rarely cap-
tured, even if they be monsters abhorred by the whole
country, like those who killed the Lindbergh baby. The
schools and the universities are so numerous and so
varied that it is impossible to know the meaning and the
value of a doctor's degree: it may belong to a rich industrialist who has never learned a word of history, literature or science but has made a donation of one hundred thousand dollars to the university; or to a student
who has succeeded in outstripping in knowledge all the
Oriental scholars in Europe; or to the college janitor
who, by way of amusing himself in his spare time, has
attended one or two courses of lectures every term for
ten years. These contrasts and this waste are perfectly
healthy and natural in a young country, overflowing
with wealth and more concerned to goad its citizens
to action than to turn its human and industrial material
to the best account, but once it is necessary to consider
husbanding the resources which are becoming indispensable to the country, a new policy must be adopted.

Now the East of the United States is beginning to
realize the danger of extravagance. Whole regions where
natural gas once abounded are now devoid of it. Land
which was once excellent and did not need any manure
now requires costly fertilizers. Forests have been destroyed in so barbarous a fashion throughout the national territory that it has become necessary to purchase
wood-pulp from Canada and to replant trees in all the
Northwest regions. The United States is no longer
what it was up to the middle of the nineteenth century, a sort of wild garden where thousands of fruits
and millions of flowers flourished at random and the

children were let loose to gather and eat to their heart's
content. The flowers are spoiled, the fruits are becoming
rare, and a gardener is needed to put things in order.

Franklin Roosevelt has realized this, and he means to
be the gardener. But he means also to be the prophet
of action. What renders these laws of agrarian rehabilitation and industrial revival, which the Washington Government has just prepared, so complex, subtle and almost
unintelligible to the foreigner, is the twofold aspect of
the question: the necessity of restoring order to the dis-
orderly activities of a young country which still thinks
of itself as a child, and the obligation upon the Government to administer a fresh stimulus to the creative
forces of the western and central States, whose discouragement and destitution were threatening all America
with catastrophe.

The Government wants to give at once a vigorous
drive, like those explosions of energy which marked
the great political epochs of the United States and produced their great moments of economic expansion, and
to regulate strictly the course of the national life, so
as to abolish waste, contradictions, vain repetitions and
phrase-mongering.

Roosevelt can succeed in this only if the whole population follows him.

He is going to offer the farmers an easy way of paying off their mortgages and making a fresh start. It is
further essential that the farmers should know how to
take advantage of the assistance thus rendered them,
and set to work again patiently and efficiently. The
great weakness of American agriculture was that it was

too industrial. The farmer did not live on his farm as the farmer does in France, Italy and Germany. The American farmer was a manufacturer of wheat or maize or cotton who, with the aid of machinery and the soil, produced a merchandise which he afterwards sold. He lived on the financial profits of his industry, not on his labor itself. Whatever the economic amelioration of the United States, in an America which has lost its foreign markets for agrarian exports, there can be no security or prosperity for the farmer unless he learns to live *on* the soil rather than *from* the soil.

It would not be sufficient for Roosevelt to give the farmers money and tools; he must give them a method and get them to work steadily and systematically. It is a case of a moral reform as well as an economic and political reform. But he ought to be able to bring it to a happy issue if Congress continues its friendly collaboration or leaves him free to do the work, for he is extricating the poor farmers from a desperate situation, he is conducting for their benefit a bold and dangerous operation, and, lastly, he is restoring hope and happiness to their lives. For them he must be a sort of god to whom they will render blind obedience.

He will need too the other social element of the United States, the stable element, the people of the East; for they form the existing and, undoubtedly, the necessary framework of American civilization and political life. It is they who, by their language, their religion, their struggles against the French, their victories over the English and the Mexicans, their triumph over the Indians and their repression of the revolt of 1860, made the United States their territory and their civilization.

It is they who are the most fruitful elements in this brutal world; it is they who, since 1630, have given the country its strength, its continuity and its meaning.

The abandonment of the gold standard will hit them, for the Anglo-Saxons, the financiers, the *bourgeoisie*, the shopkeepers in the towns and, more particularly, in the towns in the East, are those who saved money, who worked in order to create reserves and who, on the whole, in spite of many vicissitudes, succeeded. Though there are Jewish financiers in the United States, the Anglo-Saxons of the Northeast of the United States also have a flair for money, economics and finance. Boston and New York, the two great financial metropolises of America, are governed by these offshoots of Puritan stocks. Mr. Morgan, Mr. Lamont, Mr. Mellon, Mr. Young, and Mr. Wiggin are Anglo-Saxon. Mr. Gary, the founder and chairman of the United States Steel Company, the biggest enterprise in the United States, was also an Anglo-Saxon. They further constitute the great economic power and the true social strength of the country. Any reformer who tried to dispense with them or to attack them would be committing a grave error. It will be of no use for him to call himself a liberal, a radical, a philosopher or a Christian; he will end by breaking his head against a wall of cold and stubborn hostility.

Mr. Roosevelt has made a good begininng. Several of the most important posts in his Cabinet are occupied by members of this group. When he decided to renounce the gold standard, Mr. Morgan, the great Anglo-Saxon banker of New York, and Mr. Traylor, the great Anglo-Saxon banker of Chicago, published letters approving this step. The members of the *bourgeoisie* remember that he is a Roosevelt and they appreciate his distinction, his personal charm, his courage, his love of work and his efforts to bring about fruitful reforms. Even the inflation, which will injure them by reducing the value of their savings, did not excite their indignation; they shared in the general enthusiasm with a good measure of cordiality and without grumbling. This Anglo-Saxon group in America possesses a very just sense of reality and of the present and at the same time a certain apathy which prevents it from committing such rash mistakes as might be committed by groups more intelligent and highly strung. They have not offered any systematic resistance to the inflation, although, here and there, voices were raised in protest, like that of Senator Carter Glass; and any one who has studied carefully the American newspapers and, in particular, the curious section headed "Letters from Readers", will have observed between March and July, 1933, frequent notes, essays and regular articles sent by Americans, mostly Anglo-Saxon and *bourgeois,* protesting against the disgrace of this governmental decision, and demanding that the dollar should be stabilized as soon as possible, if America is to escape the reputation of a dishonest, deceitful and undignified country.

These, however, are mostly merely indignant outbursts emanating from sour-tempered old maids and idle old gentlemen who compose letters to send to the newspapers for lack of any more interesting occupation. But suddenly, if the Government made a false step, it might find itself faced with a bloc no less solid than silent. And then it would be too late, the game would be lost, the situation would be ruined. In May, 1933, when the Senate summoned Mr. Morgan in order to question him concerning his methods and obliged him to reveal the list of important and official personages to whom he had granted loans and the names of the bankers and public men to whom he did the favor of offering his issues at specially favorable rates, Anglo-Saxon public opinion began to be refractory.

These sessions took place in an extraordinary atmosphere. Washington, full of verdure, heat and turmoil, seemed alternately bathed in a moist radiance and in torrents of silver. The temperature in the streets was intolerable, indoors one could hardly breathe. Yet in the hall where Mr. Morgan was summoned to appear were crowded the most eminent personages, the most illustrious journalists and all the citizens of Washington most conversant with and interested in current affairs. And they all turned not towards the members of the Senate but towards Mr. Morgan. They had heard that he was not very intelligent. The newspapers had whispered it and people had come to amuse themselves at his expense.

Mr. Morgan detests speaking in public. He has a horror of notoriety, advertisement and discussion. He never allows himself to be photographed and he is the most modest and the most studiously unknown of all the great personages of this earth. However, he and all his partners came to Washington to reply to the questions of the Senate and of its legal adviser, Mr. Pecora; he had to submit to being photographed thirty times a day, and to being interviewed by all the journalists of all nationalities assembled at Washington. But, above all, he had to reply to the questions of Mr. Pecora, a worthy Italian, transplanted at an early age from the laughing shores of the Mediterranean to the frigid coasts of the Atlantic, but gifted with that eloquence which once glowed in Cicero and which now kindles Signor Mussolini.

Mr. Pecora proceeded to torture Mr. Morgan. His Italian rhetoric, his proletarian zeal, his political skill, were discharged upon the least voluble, the wealthiest and the most peaceable banker in the world.

Mr. Pecora wanted to prove that Mr. Morgan had not paid taxes for two years, and he proved it.

Mr. Pecora wanted to demonstrate that Mr. Morgan had immense power, and he demonstrated it. Half the great electrical companies in the country are directly or indirectly dependent on Mr. Morgan.

Mr. Pecora wanted to exhibit the affluence of Mr. Morgan amid the general destitution, and he succeeded: even the crisis had left the Morgan firm in so prosperous a state that it had made a nice little sum by trying to support the securities which were collapsing and none of the enterprises launched by Morgan on the New York market had gone bankrupt. The Morgan firm was colossal!

On hearing these revelations, the newspapers owned by Mr. Hearst and the Scripps-Howard Press bellowed with indignation. It seemed as if Mr. Morgan ought to be roasted alive or hanged on the spot.

Nothing of the sort: Mr. Morgan had not paid income tax because he had not any to pay, in accordance with the American law. Mr. Morgan, despite his losses and despite the crisis had remained very rich, because his investments had been very judicious; and he still controlled an enormous network of electrical companies, because that had seemed to him one of the sound American investments, in which he was right. In short, the investigation revealed Mr. Morgan to be a very worthy, capable and well-informed man.

It was not found possible to convict him of any offense. At length it was discovered that he had a list of favored clients, whom he allowed to enjoy various advantages, and, despite his protests, this list was ruthlessly published. Alas! On Mr. Morgan's list there figured numerous politicians of both parties, members of Congress, Mr. Roosevelt's Secretary of the Treasury, and his ambassador extraordinary in Europe, Mr. Norman Davis.

The public laughed and hissed. But it was difficult to know who was being hissed: Mr. Morgan or his envied friends in the Government? . . . All eyes were turned towards the hall of the Capitol, where Mr. Pecora was daily putting Mr. Morgan to the rack.

Now one day, in the torrid heat of the afternoon, when all were settling into their places for the evening session, a tall man, holding by the hand a female dwarf, entered the hall. He crossed it with a majestic stride, approached the platform on which Mr. Morgan was seated and greeted him politely. Then, lifting up the dwarf, he set her carefully on Mr. Morgan's knees. Mr. Morgan smiled at this minute female and amiably asked her a few questions. Why not? Doubtless the dwarf was an item in the investigation; Mr. Morgan had seen so much of the world that it was not surprising to him. The dwarf was more attractive and less absurd than Mr. Pecora, who was perpetually asking questions about things which everybody knew, expressing indignation at proceedings which were universally sanctioned and displaying an almost obscene indiscretion, by the side of which the timidity of the dwarf and the decorous behavior of her tall impresario presented an agreeable contrast. For the dwarf did not budge; she contented herself by smiling and politely replying to Mr. Morgan's questions.

The public gazed with gaping mouths and wide-open eyes. The Senators who composed the Commission were purple in the face. The journalists, the news photographers, while hurriedly taking pictures, were bubbling over with astonishment. Only Mr. Morgan gently patted the dwarf, as one fondles a toy animal to amuse a child.

Finally the Chairman of the Commission, seething with indignation, ordered the dwarf to be removed from Mr. Morgan's knees and forbade the newspapers to publish the photographs they had taken. He added that what had just happened was an insult.

The dwarf made her exit with a smile, the impresario withdrew with a bow, Mr. Morgan stretched himself with a sigh, and the public burst out laughing.

All the newspapers published photographs and ironic commentaries on the incident. And the final word was pronounced by a Senator who exclaimed: "This investigation is a circus turn!"

He was right and, thanks to the dwarf, it seemed as if the public and the whole country awoke to the fact. The investigation lingered on a few days and then adjourned. After which the newspapers announced that Mr. Morgan was a perfectly honest man.

Anglo-Saxon opinion does not derive any pleasure

from seeing the successful persecuted. The interrogation of Mr. Morgan produced a bad impression in the country. And the Government will risk losing a large part of its prestige if its enthusiastic partisans and its innovating friends continue to harry the great magnates of finance and industry.

The Anglo-Saxon East and the urban *bourgoisie* accept the sacrifices which Mr. Roosevelt is going to impose upon them in the interests of the common weal under the name of inflation. They are resigned to seeing a part of their fortune disappear and pass into other hands. They are ready for great and numerous sacrifices, for in the last years they have been afraid they might lose everything, and Roosevelt's personal prestige reassures them. But if once they became over-excited and irritated, the work undertaken by the President would become impossible. His bold plans, his experimental socialism, his temporary communism, can only succeed if they are supported by the *bourgeois,* possessing, Anglo-Saxon class.

America knows well that she is entering upon a new era and that she must destroy her ancient gods. She is ready for the sacrifice.

She is trusting herself to President Roosevelt as a patient trusts himself to the doctor. She has realized that the operation will be a painful one, and she is trying to laugh about it. The other day, during a discussion of the Chicago Exposition which is called "A Century of Progress", a wit remarked: "Yes, let us celebrate this last century and extol progress. Where were we poor wretches in 1833? There were none but Indians to kill each other on the shores of Lake Michigan, whereas now the 'bootleggers' have improved upon their methods. The dollar was still worth its weight in gold, whereas it is far from that now. In 1833 all the banks in the United States were open, whereas in 1933 we have succeeded in closing them all at one stroke. Long live progress!" But in their hearts the people of the United States realize that America is engaged on a work of moral and physical rehabilitation. They know that it is a case not of progress, as our good and pure ancestors understood the term, but of *an attempt at reaction.*

After the intoxication of ease, good fortune and expansion in all directions, the United States are entering upon a stern period when the people will have to appreciate more the pleasures of intelligence, discipline and selection.

It was not only Mr. Hoover or Wall Street or optimism of Mr. Ford's variety, but also mechanization and science that were defeated at the elections of 1932. The American public renounces from now onward the craven doctrine that everything that emerges from the brain of the scholar is good and that every scientific invention is a benefit to the human race. The great industrial, chemical and metallurgical companies are still allocating large sums for the investigation of new processes and the taking out of patents. But it is now no longer a question of transforming as soon as possible and as sensationally as possible all industrial methods, as was the dream of the last decades. It is a question, on the contrary, of regularizing and slowing down the progress of scientific work. It is realized now that an invention is at once creative and destructive, that it has a positive value and a negative action. At the present moment people are careful not to launch on the market the recently discovered scientific appliances which would enable them to supply the public with television apparatuses. And in every great laboratory there is an accumulation of ingenious, curious, powerful and explosive inventions, which are being concealed or buried, in order to protect poor human life, bewildered society and panic-stricken capital, and to preserve a little of that continuity without which life is a nightmare devoid of repose and reality.

American science and industry are trying to humanize their inventions and even the rhythm of their production. Mr. Roosevelt is trying to humanize and regulate the political and economic life of the United States and to render it more kindly and hospitable to man. He would like to revive in the American people their taste for things and for work without allowing them to become intoxicated by it as they were before. Like a wise, firm master, he is armed with a large whip which he cracks now and then, and he has a pair of stout reins which he holds tightly in his hands but, above all, he smiles.

This mastery and this smile are particularly evident to visitors who have access to the President.

Comfortably settled in an armchair, in which he seems almost recumbent, swinging his legs and nodding his head, Franklin Roosevelt looks at the crowd of sixty journalists confronting him in his office. Behind him his Secretary of State, Cordell Hull, is seated, listening in silence, much as a wise old pedagogue follows the lesson of a gifted pupil. A few stalwart young men — bodyguards, diplomats or detectives in plain clothes — are standing behind the President. They are the only persons for whom this delightful half hour is a source of anxiety, the only ones whose faces express tension and gravity.

All the others are laughing or smiling. Young and old, men and women, yellow and white, elegant or humble.

The President raises his head: "Is every one here?" he asks. Then the chatter begins. There is no order, no discipline; the journalists chirp out their questions like a flock of sparrows, and the President replies like a schoolboy, promptly and fluently if he knows his lesson, slowly if he is less well informed; and sometimes he raises his eyes, bursts out laughing and cries: "What a splendid question! How learned you are! I wish I knew the answer, — but I don't know it." And every one laughs. One can say anything to him and one can ask him anything.

His perfect manners protect him against familiarity, and familiarity protects him against indiscretion. One journalist cries boldly: "Mr. President, it is said that you are going to get rid of your Secretary of the Treasury because he once accepted favors from Mr. Morgan. Is that true?" The President looks as though he had not heard the question, and although it was shouted, he makes no reply. He prefers to address a young journalist who is asking him in a whisper what he thought of Monsieur Herriot. Mr. Roosevelt has fenced. The journalist has learned his lesson and he holds his tongue.

After a few minutes, the President begins to smile more broadly and he says to his questioners: "To-mor-

row, Saturday, I am going to have a rest. I am going
on the yacht with a few intimate friends, none but
intimate friends, just to have a rest. Let me see, there
will be Mr. and Mrs. Woodin and one or two more.
That's all." The company bursts out laughing. The
President does the same. The indiscreet journalist is
radiant.

Thus, for thirty or forty minutes, amid a bombard-
ment of questions and insinuations, the President pursues a curious dialogue with the country, receiving
through the journalists the questions which haunt the
minds of the crowd and furnishing them with replies,
ideas and formulas calculated to calm and reassure the
United States. The apparent hubbub is not an annoyance to him but a method; it enables him to adapt himself to people, to understand them without appearing
to do so, to listen to what he does not seem to have
heard, to reply to what he appears to disregard and to
adopt what he seems to reject.

That is Franklin Roosevelt's great strength: politics
is life to him. He shuns neither risk nor improvisation;
he recoils only from rigidity and system. He prefers
suppleness. From radicalism he takes its taste for the
life to come, from conservatism its taste for present life
and its respect for past life.

For his ideas are merely means of action. He always
guards his independence in relation to them. He is not
afraid of them.

Such is his great strength or his secret weakness.

EPILOGUE

ROOSEVELT RULES

THE greatest achievement of President Roosevelt, the one that has delighted, surprised and stirred the American nation more than any other single thing in the last thirty years and that has astounded the world, is that he has been willing and able to rule.

He was elected, he spoke admirably to the country, but many people before him have spoken well to the nations; he surmounted great difficulties and was strong enough to face the test, but many men, and even second-rate men, have been able to show greatness in times of stress. It is not so difficult to be a dictator and give orders when nobody else feels like taking any responsibility. But to take responsibilities, to guide people, to get them to understand, approve and obey every decision you take without ever bullying them or attempting to blind them, and at the same time make them really do what they should do — to rule them, in a word — is, in an era of newspapers, wireless, parliamentary excitement and economic crisis, the most difficult and brilliant feast that any Government can offer to its citizens.

President Roosevelt has succeeded in ruling the American nation without fear and without violence; he has succeeded in managing Congress without ever being overbearing or weak. He has received the backing and approval of the majority of the nation for a longer period than any other President in the recent history of the United States; and though Congress has granted him in fact the actual power of a dictator, he has politely avoided this honor and this danger; he has resolutely chosen to run the United States as President and to rule rather than to dictate.

For a hundred days he kept Congress at work. And for a hundred days he collaborated with Congress. During these hundred days he avoided all conflicts and all quarrels with both Houses. He had innumerable conferences with Congressional leaders and, far from ever adopting a contemptuous attitude towards Congress, he always treated it with the utmost courtesy. At no time did he proclaim the failure of parliamentary government. At no time did he make fun of parliamentary methods, and while newspapermen were daily comparing him with Signor Mussolini and Herr Hitler, he behaved in fact very much more like a French Premier, who never can make a move and never does make a move without having previously obtained the assent of his majority.

Roosevelt's friendliness towards Congress was not merely an attitude; it was a method. He aimed at establishing national unity and understanding and first he secured it in Washington by securing the governmental coöperation between President and Congress that had been so sadly lacking during the last five Presidencies. He knew that it was difficult and had to be handled carefully, so he was just as prudent as he was kind.

He avoided distributing jobs and patronage as long as Congress was in session. He felt very properly that the members of Congress were too much engrossed by the affairs of the nation to have time to give him advice about rewards for party workers and other friends, and he felt that he himself had no reason to hurry. Consequently, he took no decision whatever and postponed all the appointments except those that could not possibly be delayed; and owing to this, his relations with Congress were to the very end of the session tinged with a shade of expectancy which is the best part of young love.

But he went farther than being prudent and kind; he was deferential to Congress. Everybody knew that President Roosevelt was in favor of international agreements, a lowering of tariffs and a final settlement of the inter-Allied debts. But it was clear also that, on the subject of tariffs, Congress was sensitive, because the interests of so many of their backers were concerned in it, and that it was not inclined to make many concessions to America's late partners in the war. A dictator might have gone ahead, and President Roosevelt, then at the pinnacle of his huge popularity, might have carried the country, and with it Congress. He did not even try, and to the great surprise of the outside world he allowed the session to end without asking for any special power concerning either the revision of tariffs or the settlement of inter-Allied debts. He bowed before Congress.

Congress delegated to him great powers, of course, but only the powers to do things that Congress wanted to be done, and for only so long a period as Congress may choose to permit. Congress helped him to establish and confirm his authority, but not at the expense of parliamentary authority; in fact, Congress and President worked together to strengthen the power of both the executive and the legislative branches of Government. When they went back home, the representatives and the Senators of the United States felt clearly that their best asset for reëlection and the most illustrious chapter of their record was the work done with President Roosevelt and the work they had given him power to perform. They had entrusted him with the task of reorganizing banking and industry, of putting agriculture on its feet, and of keeping a balanced budget for the nation. And they had given him authorization to resort practically to any methods to achieve these aims, because they finally realized that he would never resort to any means that would anger the people or get Congress into trouble.

They could see at once that they were right in trusting him. He paid them a compliment that no European Parliament has received for a long time. As soon as Congress had ended its session, the President took his vacation. He went sailing along the northeastern coast of the United States. In Europe, as soon as Parliament is dismissed, President and Prime Minister breathe a deep sigh, sit at their tables, ring for the Ministers and say to them, "Now let's get to work." But Mr. Roosevelt showed Congress that his real work had been done, and done with Congress, and that now he could rest and relax. He was sailing his yacht and smiling. Nothing worried him much any more.

Not even the great World Economic Conference

in London, which was being convened and at which sixty-three nations were assembling to save the world from chaos and despair. This Conference had, in fact, received warm encouragement from the President. He had talked matters over with the English Prime Minister, MacDonald, and the French Premier, Herriot, so as to clear the ground; and for a time there was a persistent rumor that President Roosevelt wanted the Conference to be held in Washington. Nevertheless, he went sailing and he sent his delegates to London with instructions to report to him before signing any important document or taking any grave decision. And he himself was not going to take any rash step, as he had shown by abstaining from asking Congress for any special powers relative to tariffs or the refunding of debts.

In this he was doubly wise and astute. He knew that a diplomat who has few powers has always enough authority to get concessions from others, though he has not enough to grant them any. Consequently he is in the best possible position from a bargaining point of view. He knew also that the London Conference was not very likely to achieve great things or many things, and that there would be no advantage in becoming too much interested and too deeply involved in it. It was better to keep the mind of the American people interested in its rising prices, its reviving industry and its great fair in Chicago, than to try to stir up interest amongst them for a rather shapeless and over-talkative International Conference: from his yacht, while keeping close to the New England coast, he watched what was happening on the coasts of England, where hundreds of diplomats were then landing.

It was a pleasant month of June, a little hot, but very bright and very agreeable, especially for people who like sailing, swimming and all kinds of outdoor games. People were buying a great many motor cars throughout the United States and business was looking up. People were drinking beer and discussing the fall of the dollar, and as they were talking of it, prices gently rose; the Stock Exchange was buoyant, the farmers were rejoicing because their wheat and their pigs had at last recovered some value. It was a pleasant month of June followed by a very agreeable July, somewhat cooler, but distinctly prosperous-looking. For the first time for many months the country was cheerful and America was in a good mood. Franklin Roosevelt had taught her to smile again.

In London, after settling down, and going to a few teas, and shaking many hands and meeting innumerable photographers and newspapermen, the delegates started their work in earnest. They started talking. They knew that they could not do much more, but they expected to do a good deal of talking and eventually they felt confident that they would sign a few "formulas." A "formula" is a diplomatic text on which a good many nations have reached an agreement and which they publish solemnly; later on they have them discussed in their parliaments, and finally they edit little (or big) white, red, yellow or orange books concerning them. A "formula" ought to possess great literary precision and great political vagueness. It ought to be high-sounding but in fact to bind you to nothing. It has been the regular and chosen food of diplomatic and parliamentary life in Europe for the last decade. Diplomats are terribly avid of formulas, and parliaments are great consumers of them. In fact, nearly everybody likes them.

But this time Mr. Roosevelt was not anxious to subscribe to a formula. On the contrary, a formula was positively dangerous for his programme. He had just renounced the gold standard, without inflating or devaluating the dollar, which shows that he meant to use the possibility of inflation as a mental stimulus for the nation and wished to avoid, if possible, actual recourse to it. In London the delegates from the whole world were begging America to take a clear stand. "Do anything you want," they said in substance; "inflate or do not inflate, make silver your standard or come back to gold, but for pity's sake, say what you are going to do; sign a formula." They were terribly anxious to reach the ordinary and expected goal: a nice, clear yet hazy formula. But in fact that was the only thing the President could not do without spoiling his work at home, and it was the thing he was set upon not doing.

Consequently he said "No" to the world. And the world, the delegates who had gathered in London with great expectancy and who remembered his speeches of the spring, were quite shocked, but the American nation was delighted. Most of the newspapers extolled Mr. Roosevelt as a national hero, and declared that his letter of July 3d was "A second Declaration of Independence." Members of Congress were overjoyed. They felt in complete agreement with the President, and Mr. Borah went as far as to say so.

He had done exactly what his parliamentary majority

would have wished him to do, and probably more than they would have expected or asked him to do.

It was a very good climax to a very good summer.

The gesture was not pleasant to European diplomats, of course, or to European nations, but, in fact, it was unavoidable, and also it was much less negative than it seemed at first sight.

Out of the wreck of the London Conference, which could have been a dignified wreck, but could not help being a wreck, the President of the United States emerged with colors flying, and he turned into an asset for himself and his policy what would have been otherwise a serious drawback. He managed to retain the confidence of the country at a critical time and, as a matter of fact, he made possible an understanding at a later date between America and Europe. In June and July, 1933, President Roosevelt, with all his popularity, might have been strong enough to sign an agreement with Europe for the stabilization of currencies, but he was not yet in a position to carry with him the whole-hearted support of the nation, which was needed to make such an agreement valuable and effective. In discarding it, he proved to the people that he stood by them; they were delighted; now they trust him, and they will be much more ready to accept any subsequent international agreement with Europe suggested by him, because they have seen that they can trust him. Thus he sacrificed a present, which was not of much value, for a future which, let us hope, is more promising. He did not discard his principles and theories of international coöperation, but he refused to jeopardize them at an unfavorable moment.

But he did it in such a way that it sounded like a clarion, and it stirred up the whole American nation, because his greatest gift seems that he is able to do always and exclusively things that have a meaning for the American mind. This time he succeeded in rallying behind him many elements which had hitherto been rather cool to him — all the conservative, old-fashioned nationalists and isolationists, who suspected him of weakness towards Europe, and who were watching him with doubtful friendliness. They were astounded, delighted and won over by his letter of July 3, 1933.

It happened at the right time, when he needed them, when America needed more than ever national unity. Franklin Roosevelt was then beginning to work in earnest on his many-sided N.R.A. He was starting boldly the great enterprise by which he may stand or fall.

Everybody in America, everybody throughout the world, agrees that the greatest man on earth will be he who brings back prosperity to nations and good fortune to individuals. But this man had not yet been discovered. Most of the rulers either stay at home, trying to sleep and waiting to see if Fortune will be sensible enough to visit them in their dreams, as she is supposed to be apt to do, because she is a woman; or they run all over the world in search of the abode where Fortune is hiding. Franklin Roosevelt did not sleep and did not run; he acted.

It surprised some people, and they claimed at once that it was a revolution, an absolutely new thing in American history; as if action, rather than waiting, had not been the typical attribute of American life and philosophy as opposed to English life and philosophy and to European methods in general. Other people were alarmed at seeing the country of "rugged individualism" become suddenly the most centralized and sternly organized one. They probably forgot that in all great crises the first reaction of American citizens is to get together and organize the strongest and biggest machine they can think of. They did so in 1917, in their fight against Germany; they do it now in their war against depression. The great Roosevelt drive of 1933 is the revival of a tradition, it is not a strange invention.

The huge N.R.A., controlled by the outspoken General Johnson, is picturesque and striking. It makes a lot of noise and it upsets many people. It is not yet sure that it will upset many things. By establishing codes to limit commercial and industrial competition, to regulate and diminish hours of labor, to create new jobs and raise the salaries of employees, it seems a brand-new venture in the economic life of America, but it simply hastens a process of evolution that was inevitably coming. All over the world industry tends to organize and concentrate more and more: "cartels" in Europe, "trusts" in America, are not new things. By encouraging labor unions and gently pushing workmen into the ranks of the labor unions, the N.R.A. does nothing that most European governments have not done recently; and by imposing more or less forcibly on employers the duty and necessity of giving higher wages to employees, the N.R.A. and President Roosevelt simply *do* what President Hoover and even President Coolidge had always asked for and suggested, with more or less emphasis.

The only brand-new inventions of the N.R.A. are psychological. Business in the United States was an individual game and work was the great excitement of life. The N.R.A. is a tremendous effort to instill into the country the idea and the sense that business should be a national game — not necessarily a communistic one, but one in which the individual should never forget the interests of the nation. The N.R.A. does not make the remuneration of capital impossible, as some people claim, and it is clear that such was never the idea and intention of the President, but it obliges captains of industry to put the general interests of the country before profits and returns on investments. On the other hand, if it works well, it will make returns on investments a possibility and a reality, while the present crisis and method of waiting made them nonexistent and every day less likely. The N.R.A. is not an effort to destroy capital or capitalism, but a step towards establishing a psychology of "national capitalism" in place of an individualistic capitalism. And it is clear that the wish of the Government in Washington is to succeed in creating this atmosphere without resorting to state capitalism. As much as possible, General Johnson allows employers and employees to draft their own codes. He urges them to do so, but he tries to keep in the background as far as possible. And he does not take drastic measures against those who choose to keep out, as was seen in the case of Henry Ford, the champion of old-fashioned individualism.

The N.R.A. strives to spread the same spirit of national enthusiasm and coöperation amongst the masses; President Roosevelt's first great effort to help the unemployed, the "reforestation army" is not a socialistic experiment; the boys who work in the big forests of the North and Northwest do not work much harder than socialist workmen would do, but soldiers would not work much more, anyhow, and the spirit that is instilled into them is the spirit of fair play, discipline, optimism and social coöperation. They are kept busy, happy, healthy and eager.

In the discussion of codes and later in the enforcing of them, it was inevitable that the N.R.A. should give rise to some difficulties between organized employers and organized employees, but General Johnson tries to reduce these as much as possible. He was prompt to state emphatically that any anonymous letter and denunciation would be regarded as worthless by his administration; and he consistently labored to bring together the two sides. Many people fear that the strengthening of the employers on the one hand and of the labor unions on the other will breed industrial war and social difficulties all over the United States, but it is plain that the Administration believes that once the whole American nation has started to work again, employers and employees will be more interested in working than in fighting against each other. Franklin Roosevelt feels that the first thing to do is to give every one work, in the best possible conditions, and that later, instead of growing worse, things will improve if only people do work. He believes in work as being the great remedy for American unrest and bickering, and the experience of three centuries seems to bear him out. If they begin to work and if they really do work, employees and employers of the United States will forget to hate each other.

The real danger is not there, but in the situation of

the middle classes; between the big corporations and
the big labor unions, American professional men seem
likely to pay a heavier price than anybody else for the
N.R.A. They cannot organize and fight like workmen
or big business men: they have no lobby in Washington
and no possibility of codes; they will work harder and
earn less than the two other groups. But this is not peculiar to America; the post-war reorganization has brought
the same result all over the world: the middle classes
pay for the fight between capitalism and socialism; they
have not enough capital to defend it very efficiently,
and they have enough to be injured. They comprise too
many different types of people to organize easily, and
it is easy to strike at them. As the cost of living goes up,
they will pay more for everything, while they will not
have the compensation of smaller competitive expenses
or better organization like the big companies, or higher
wages and safer jobs like the workmen.

But if the N.R.A. succeeds, they will finally profit by
it like the rest of the nation, and in the long run they
will be better off than the European middle classes,
who suffer just as much, but do not get the same final
results, because in America money flows much more
freely than in Europe, and finally everybody, even the
under dog, has his chance. The first stage of the N.R.A.
is likely to hit the middle classes very hard; a final success of the N.R.A. would bring them back prosperity
and good fortune.

The N.R.A., like all great intellectual crusades, can
only give general good results if it is allowed to spread
and permeate the country and become an atmosphere.
Just as a little bit of religion is childish, a little bit of

Fascism is silly, a little bit of Communism is odious, a little bit of N.R.A. would be useless. It would be better to give it up entirely. It has to be a national passion and obsession, or it will achieve nothing.

Franklin Roosevelt knows this. His radio speeches, his smiles, his interviews and pictures bring the N.R.A. into every American home. His great effort is to persuade the mind of the country, and his greatest achievement is to have created an American mood that is American, cheerful and bold.

He does not trust things, institutions or even men; he trusts the mind and he tries to keep always in contact with the human mind; he had built his "Brain Trust" to make this contact closer and more intimate, but as soon as it appeared that the people at large were getting tired of the "Brain Trust", as soon as it looked like a more or less formal institution, Franklin Roosevelt allowed the "Brain Trust" to disintegrate; Mr. Moley became a magazine editor, and Mr. Berle went to Cuba. For the same reason, President Roosevelt will prefer as long as he can possibly manage it, the mental treat or dream of inflation to the hard fact of inflation and devaluation of the dollar. With the first he achieves all the results he cares for and does not take any chances; with the second he would create a situation which in the long run might become difficult to control.

Franklin Roosevelt has won over the minds of Americans and has lifted them out of depression. He has done it with a boldness, a shrewdness and a knowledge that make him the greatest living politician.

He has attacked all the problems from the political

and psychological angles; and, as far as psychology could go, he has carried it.

If the human mind rules over the things of this world, he should succeed.

So let us look at his experiment.

Let us see if *things* in America will follow American *minds* where the American *President* has led them.